The Serpent and the Spirit

The Serpent and the Spirit

Glenn Summerford's Story

Thomas Burton

The University of Tennessee Press / Knoxville

Unless otherwise noted, the photographs were taken by the author.

This book is printed on acid-free paper.

Library of Congress Cataloging-in-Publication Data

Burton, Thomas, 1935–
The serpent and the Spirit: Glenn Summerford's story /
Thomas Burton.— 1st ed.
        p. cm.
Includes bibliographical references and index.

ISBN 1-57233-246-8 (pbk.: alk. paper)

1. Summerford, Glenn—Trials, litigation, etc.
2. Trials (Attempted murder)—Alabama.
3. Snake cults (Holiness churches)—Alabama.
I. Title.

KF224.S78B87 2004
345.73'02523—dc22   2003025093

HELL IS MURKY.
—Shakespeare

Contents

Illustrations

Preface

"Of making many books there is no end"—or of contributing to them. And there have been many individuals who have assisted me in making the present one.

Because of my previous research concerning the religious ritual of serpent handling, I was alerted to the charge against Glenn Summerford soon after it was made. But at that time I did not inquire significantly into the incident. In fact, although I knew Holiness preachers who frequently attended Glenn's church, I had never visited it. When I became interested in pursuing Glenn's story, the first person I called was Carl Porter, who pastored the congregation for a period after Glenn was incarcerated. Porter put me in touch with Bobbie Sue Lynn, who in turn made arrangements for me to talk with Glenn's mother.

Donna Rizzo, with whom I had consulted relative to her creative dance presentation of serpent handling and who had previously attended services at Billy Summerford's congregation on Sand Mountain, agreed to go to Scottsboro, Alabama, with me in order to meet and talk with some of the people there who later became part of this book. She made several field trips with me and continued throughout to contribute to the work.

From the first person I called upon in 1999 to the last, there are many to whom I am indebted. For the openness and assistance of the Summerford family, I am especially grateful. To a person, they have not suggested hedging the truth. Rather, each has said that Glenn's story should be told—yet consistently adding, "He did not try to kill Darlene. If you knew Glenn, you'd know he didn't try to kill her."

Needless to say, without the family's cooperation, including Glenn's, this book would not have been possible. A number of the family generously contributed narratives, but other members also provided information, starting with Glenn's mother, Annie, then his sister Carolyn and her husband, Cecil, (who provided videos, photographs, and boxes of Glenn's documents), Glenn's sister Barbara, his brother David, son Joe, and daughter-in-law René, his son Michael and daughter-in-law Tanya, his daughter-in-law Rita, daughter Charlotte, and grandson Chris. Former members of the family assisted as well: son-in-law Kenneth Lee and Glenn's former wife Darlene, who consented to talk with me even though she was not well and was suffering from a broken foot.

Bobby Sue Lynn and her husband, Johnny, were continually helpful, not only in making contacts but also in providing stories, letters, commentary, and even fried chicken. Other friends and extended family members of the Summerfords lent their support to my research: Glenn's cousin Billy and his wife, Joyce, (his entire congregation of the Old Rock House Holiness Church have been hospitable), his cousin Boyd Smart, Donna Parton, JJ Dyal, and "sign following" serpent handlers Arnold Saylor, Rayford Dunn, Glenn Dukes, and Gene Sherbert.

There are, as well, various professionals who assisted me in a variety of ways. First, those associated with the Alabama Department of Corrections: Warden Ralph Hooks (who was most cooperative in permitting access to Glenn, including recording and photographing him); the Limestone Correctional Facility staff, in particular, Warden Secretary Diane Sisk, Receptionist Linda Tyner, and Captain Eddie Carter (all of whom contributed to the effectiveness of the prison interviews), and General Counsel Andy Redd. Second, those associated with the Jackson County legal system: Judge Loy Campbell, former District Attorney Dwight Duke, Court Reporter David Burnett, and Donna Barksdale in the Circuit Court office. Third, others in and around Jackson County: *Daily Sentinel* publisher Mike Dunlap and staff member Faye McBride, Dr. David Campbell, Dr. George Cobb, Marlin Tucker, Clyde Broadway, Jim Bailey, and Katrina Hammon. Fourth, professionals at East Tennessee State University: Chairs of the English Department Dr. Ron Giles and Dr. Judith Slagle, English office Executive Aid Deanna Byrant, Dean of Libraries Rita Scher, Director of Archives of Appalachia Norma Myers, Archives Secretary Georgia Greer, Reference Librarian Kathy Campbell, and Documents Librarian Stephen Patrick. Fifth, other professionals: surgeon Richard C. Treat, M.D., criminal lawyer Don Spurrell, Director of the Johnson City Public Library Mark Thomas, secretary to the editor of the *Huntsville Times* Gladys

Oakes, author Dennis Covington, historian of religious serpent handling in Northeast Alabama Paul Vance, and Director of David Lipscomb University Beaman Library Carolyn Wilson. Sixth, individuals who contributed substantially to the final text: Anna Lee Gibson, conducting online searches and scanning photographs; Ruth Hausman, transcribing initial tapes; Judy Parker, Dr. Jack Branscomb, and Prof. Ambrose Manning, reading the manuscript; Mick Davenport, helping obtain releases; Steve McKinney, assisting in computers; and Phyllis Olsen, RN, and Edward Kelly, consulting in medical and legal matters, respectively. Seventh, photographers Ken Elkins, former Chief Photographer of the *Anniston Star,* and Michael Mercier, Chief Photographer of the *Huntsville Times.* And finally, all those who gave taped interviews for the monologues.

To these individuals and others unnamed, I wish to express my gratitude in the making of *The Serpent and the Spirit.*

Tapes of interviews, transcriptions, legal documents, photographs, and other research materials for this book are housed in the Thomas G. Burton Collection, Archives of Appalachia at East Tennessee State University.

Holy Ghost Falling

It fell upon your preacher—let it fall on you;
Fell upon your preacher—let it fall on you;
It fell upon your preacher—let it fall on you;
Holy Ghost power, let it fall on you.

Chorus:
It's falling all 'round you—let it fall on you;
Falling all 'round—let it fall on you;
It's falling all 'round—let it fall on you;
Holy Ghost power, let it fall on you.

It fell upon your brother—let it fall on you;
Fell upon your brother—let it fall on you;
It fell upon your brother—let it fall on you;
Holy Ghost power, let it fall on you.

It fell upon your sister—let it fall on you;
Fell upon your sister—let it fall on you;
It fell upon your sister—let it fall on you;
Holy Ghost power, let it fall on you.

It'll make you speak in tongues when it falls on you;
Make you speak in tongues when it falls on you;
It'll make you speak in tongues when it falls on you;
Holy Ghost power, let it fall on you.

(Traditional lyrics courtesy
of Joyce Summerford)

The Serpent

When Glenn Summerford, a Holiness serpent-handling preacher, was accused by his wife of attempted murder by forcing her to put her hand in a box of rattlesnakes, the press and other media exploded. "Preacher tries to murder wife—with rattlesnakes!" "Preacher hubby made me plunge hand into cage of deadly snakes," "Snake bites hospitalized woman, husband arrested," "Snake-case pastor gets 99 years."

Even though the incident occurred in 1991, fascination with it has not ceased. Network television programs have sensationalized the event both directly and indirectly, and a narration springing from the case was nominated for a National Book Award. But from the first, the public and media also voiced negative responses to the sensationalism. A poignant example is an editorial of 16 February 1992 in one of the local newspapers that reported the story:

A TALE OF TWO TRIALS

Two men stood trial this week for two separate crimes.

In one Jackson County courtroom, a man stood trial for the attempted murder of his wife.

In another Jackson County courtroom, a man faced a jury on charges he beat an 18-month-old boy to death.

Hordes of print and television reporters hovered around one courtroom. Spectators filled every available seat in the courtroom.

In the other courtroom, a few reporters covered the event and the only spectators were family members.

1

It was with at first amusement, that eventually would turn to disgust, that we viewed these two separate events.

The trial of a man accused of trying to kill his wife by using deadly rattlesnakes drew media from as far away as New York. Only local reporters covered the trial of a man charged with the young boy's death.

It is a sad commentary on our society when the public is drawn to the bizarre, the unusual, and yet turns its eye from a serious and horrendous crime. And it is sad that the media is forced to pander to these desires.

Though the media is not entirely blameless it should be noted that the media can only sell what the public will buy.

If the accused husband had used a baseball bat or a knife or a gun, would there have been the same kind of interest in this story?

It became so frustrating that at one point Jackson County Sheriff Mike Wells told some television interviewers, "You're sick. The real story is in the other courtroom," pointing to where the murder trial was taking place.

But the shame of the matter is revealed by a statement made by a reporter for the New York Times who was covering the bizarre snake trial.

Asked what his interest in the story was, he answered that it was newsworthy because it fit the concept that New Yorkers have of Southerners.

Yes, indeed. It was the worst of times and it was the worst of times.

—Byron Woodfin

(Reprinted by permission of the *Daily Sentinel*)

For the most part, the story told by print, broadcast, and word of mouth has been that of the alleged victim, Darlene Summerford, the wife of the serpent-handling preacher. That was what was told at the trial, and that is what has been often repeated as undisputed fact. But the story of the accused, Glenn Summerford, the husband of the serpent-handling wife, has gone for the most part untold. How best to get at his story?

Over a hundred years ago, the poet Robert Browning was faced with a similar question. He was looking through a bookstall in Florence when he found a bound copy of documents relating to a seventeenth-century murder of a woman by her husband. For personal and aesthetic reasons, Browning

Rev. Glenn Summerford. Photograph by Ken Elkins.

was ecstatic when he read the "old yellow book" about the domestic tragedy. But how best for him to shape the conflicting facts of the case into an artistic whole? He chose to set forth a series of monologues by both the principal participants and the general public. In their several ways, all the speakers exhibit human limitation in the perception of truth. But Browning felt that through his imaginative, creative presentation of these monologues, he revealed obliquely the truth present within the "pure crude" facts of the case. He entitled his work *The Ring and the Book.*

In presenting Glenn Summerford's story, *The Serpent and the Spirit,* I follow much the same procedure. Various individuals are chosen to speak their personal views, however humanly limited. And through the framework of these monologues, and imaginative insight, the audience may be able to perceive the essential truths within the facts of the event. But truth is elusive, and even facts are difficult to determine, especially years after the incident. Memories fade, self-images must be maintained, appearances become realities. Moreover, the accumulation of facts, as Browning recognized, produces "just one fact the more"—not truth.

In the case of *The Ring and the Book,* there was no question as to the murder of the wife, only whether or not the husband was justified. In the case of *The Serpent and the Spirit,* only two people—the husband and the wife—know whether an attempted murder was perpetrated, and if it was, by whom, and beyond these questions, if there was any justification for whatever occurred.

Each of the speakers has an engaging tale to tell. And the reader should not be put off by language that might sound different, a speech less generally accepted than that heard on national television. Each of the voices presented has a beauty of its own, although no attempt is made to give precise dialectical representations. The accounts themselves have purposeful deletions, transpositions, and amalgamations—some are abstractions from legal documents. The intent, though, in all the monologues is fidelity to what each person has to tell.

The writer, as with each speaker, has his own human limitations, but he pleads in the words of the medieval poet Chaucer:

> I must beg of you for courtesy's sake that you don't charge me with villainy if I speak plainly and report accurately the words and behavior of others, for you know as well as I do that whoever shall tell another man's tale must do so as accurately as he can or he must tell it untruthfully. Christ himself spoke broadly in Holy Scripture, and you know that there's no villainy in it. And I beg you to forgive me if I have not set forth folks as they should be. You may well understand that my wit is short.

Glenda Darlene Collins Summerford

Glenn's Second Wife at the Trial

'm thirty-six, and I'm in the process of getting a divorce from Glenn after sixteen years of marriage. Most of that time we've lived in Scottsboro. We lived over on Barbee Lane, I guess, maybe six or seven years. Me and Glenn lived there with our son Marty, who's thirteen now. I was not employed anywhere during that time. I went part of the way in the seventh grade, and I had another child when I was eighteen, before I married Glenn. His name is Bobby Joe Collins. He was put in foster care. I have tried over the years to talk to Glenn about divorce; but he said if I divorced him, I wouldn't get Marty. He would be took away from me too.

I was a snake handler and handled snakes at church a lot over the past five years. I handled cottonmouths and rattlers—more than just about any woman around here. They said I was probably the best female snake handler in this area for a while. I handled copperheads too. They're not real bad deadly poisonous— I ain't never heard of nobody dying from them, getting bit by one. But one time a rattlesnake bit me because I got fear on me. It just nicked me, and it made me throw up—then my nerves made me throw up too. And at home I would help Glenn get the snakes out of the boxes and load them up.

Back early October of last year—the first week of October 1991—this incident started. Like on Monday, I guess, Glenn accused me of running around with men, going with men and stuff. He accused me of going with another preacher, Gene Sherbert. Then on Tuesday night, really late—I guess it was like one or two o'clock, something like that, you know, in the morning. Well, I was in the bed—we had been fussing and everything—and he said I was trying to kill myself, but I wasn't. The early part of the night, I had took

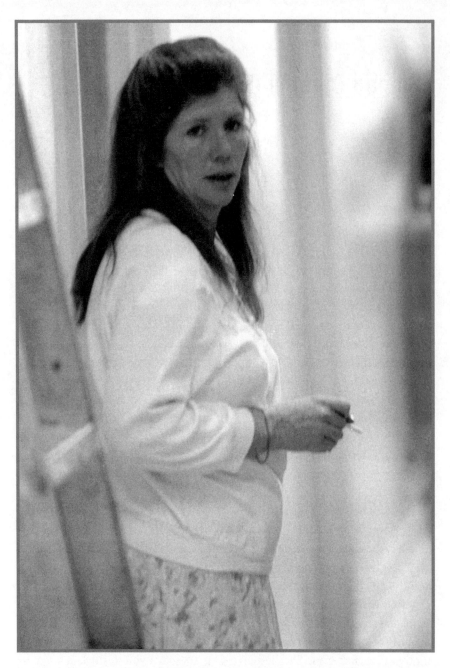

Glenn Summerford's second wife, Darlene Summerford, smokes a cigarette outside court during a break in the trial in Scottsboro, Alabama. Photographed by Michael Mercier, Feb. 12, 1992. Used with the courtesy of the *Huntsville Times*.

four sleeping pills. And he come in there where I was at, and he asked me what I was doing. And I said I was getting me some sleeping pills so I could sleep. They're them kind that you buy over the counter, Sleep-ez, or something like that. Well, he got the rest of the pills and told Marty, our son, that I was trying to commit suicide. I didn't have any intention of committing suicide. I didn't want to die. Well, he made me throw up and everything to really make Marty think that I was trying to kill myself. Then he kept on fussing on me, and I went to bed. Then about one, I guess, in the morning, the phone rung—his Mama always called me in the morning to wake me up to get Marty off to school. I jumped up to answer the phone, and Glenn was on the phone. And he said that he was talking to Gene Sherbert and said Gene Sherbert told him that I had slept with him. And I told him, I said, "There ain't nobody on the phone." And I said, "You're lying because Gene Sherbert wouldn't tell you a lie like that." I said, "You know he wouldn't." And he just started beating on me, hitting me on the body. He was pulling my hair and stuff. And when I got loose from him in the living room, I went through the bedroom, and it woke my son up. And he got up and started beggin' his Daddy to leave me alone. Well, finally, then I went back to bed. And then the next day we got up, and I sent Marty to school. And he kept fussing on me all week.

On Wednesday, Glenn made me go over to J. L. Lewis's office in Huntsville to get some money from him. And Marty went with me because Glenn never let me out of the house unless Marty was with me or unless he was with me. And J. L. gave us two or three hundred dollars. A lot of times he's given Glenn money. I told Glenn that J. L. had sent Marty out of the room to get a Coke, and J. L. got up and shut the door and kissed me. And that's all that happened. And Marty come back in the room. And Glenn just fussed and cussed on me.

On Thursday Glenn wanted to go down there and whup J. L. And we went and got there sometime in the morning between eight and dinnertime. J. L. was there and came out to the parking lot. And Glenn talked to him about the car, you know. We was checking the oil and stuff in the car, and he was talking to him about that car. Then J. L. went in, and then he come back out. And Glenn told me to talk to him, you know, to get his attention. And then Glenn come up behind him and hit him with a timing chain that he had made into a club. And then they argued, and J. L. denied kissing me and all of that. And Glenn said, we had better go, "He will call the law on us." So we left. Well, we started home. And he stopped and got him some more vodka to drink. I wasn't drinking.

On Friday evening we went over to the New Hope area to meet J. L. He said he wanted to talk with Glenn, but to leave me at home because I was just

Glenn's Second Wife at the Trial

lying. But I went with him because I wasn't lying. We went to a big oak tree down there at New Hope, but J. L. wouldn't stop because I was with Glenn.

But Glenn's sons, Junior and Bill, came. Junior is about twenty-seven, and Bill is twenty-five or something like that. Glenn and his sons talked, but I wasn't allowed by Glenn to say much. He had a gun in the car. It was a pistol that I had bought at Scottsboro Pawn and have a permit for. The gun was laying there in the car on that hump in the middle of the bucket seats.

We stayed at the big oak tree about thirty to forty-five minutes, I guess. And we started to go home. Then he said, "No," he said, "let's go over to Junior's. J. L. might be over there." So we went over there. Another one of Glenn's sons, Joe, was there, and Virginia (Junior's wife) and Rita (Bill's wife)—they was there at that time. We stayed there thirty to forty minutes, I guess.

Glenn was drinking vodka and orange juice, but I only had Coke or orange juice. We left their house and met my brother Gary and another one of Glenn's sons, Eddie. Then we went back to Junior's. We had a blowout on the way back over there. And when we got there, some of them fixed it, you know, put another tire on it because we didn't have a spare. We were there about an hour, and then left again for home.

On the way Glenn was drinking vodka and orange juice. And Glenn told me to drink some, that it would calm me down. And I took two or three swallows of his drink. He said he was going to kill me and—well, first, he was going to take me up to Woodville. There's a big old hole up there on the side of the mountain, and he said he was going to throw me in it. He said he was goin' to tell everybody that I had run away with somebody. Then he changed his mind on that, and he said that he was going to take me to the river bridge and throw me off—I can't swim. Well, he kept on fussing on me and everything. And then he calmed down, you know, he settled down. And he said, "Well, we'll just go by and get us something to eat and forget about it." We went by McDonald's and got us something to eat. Then we went home. We got home about nine o'clock, somewhere along in there. When we got home, he took the car down to the little road where nobody couldn't see it.

Nobody else was there. Marty was at Glenn's daughter Jackie because I didn't want Marty there—and Glenn said he didn't want Marty there. Earlier—before we had gone to New Hope—Glenn and me was fussing, and he was cussing me. And he said he would get up and blow my brains out. And he started through the house to get the shotgun, and I took off running up there on the hill. And I looked back, and I seen Marty had his bow and arrow drawed at Glenn. And I stopped and sat down on the ground. Then Glenn come over there and made me come back to the house. So we called Jackie to come and get Marty.

And he hid the car, he said, because he didn't want nobody bothering us. He put the car down in the woods so nobody wouldn't think that we was at home. He made me go with him because he wouldn't let me out of his sight. Then we went in the house, in the front door. Then he had to go out the side door and come around to the front door, and he locked the front door from the outside with a padlock. He come back in, and then we ate.

Then he started screaming and hollering and cussing me again and accused me of running around and all of this. Then he was telling me, he said, "I don't want you no more," he said. "I don't want to live with you no more." He said, "But I don't want nobody else to have you." And then he said that his ministry, you know—he was going to go back to ministering because we had been out of church for a week or so, I guess. And he said he was going to go back to the ministry, but he couldn't have me there. He said that I had to die because he couldn't get remarried if we got a divorce because that would be adultery for him.

Well, we was still fussing, and his brother called. They had been looking for us. Glenn told his brother on the phone that we was going to pray and handle snakes and all of that, you know. And I told him: "No, we couldn't either," I said, because we weren't in no shape to handle snakes, you know—Glenn wasn't. And then Glenn said that he was going to make me get bit and die, and said it was going to look like a suicide. He was going to tell everybody when I died that he just woke up and called the ambulance and found me dead.

He grabbed me by the hair of the head and had that gun to my head. And he pulled my hair and was pulling me by the hair of the head. And he made me go out to the snake shed—just a little piece from the house. He was telling me that I had better pray and get things fixed. And I was praying, you know—I was serious praying. He made me take the lid off of the snake box because he said he didn't want to get his fingerprints on it. And he grabbed me by the hair of the head, and he was pushing me over in the snake box. He said they was going to bite me in the face if I didn't pick them up. I have handled snakes, you know, a lot of times; and I was praying and everything. But I was scared, you know. I was scared to death. He said if I didn't reach over in there and pick that snake up that he was going to put my face in there. And he done had my head over it, you know, two or three times. He had me by the hair, and then that gun was

Glenn's Second Wife at the Trial

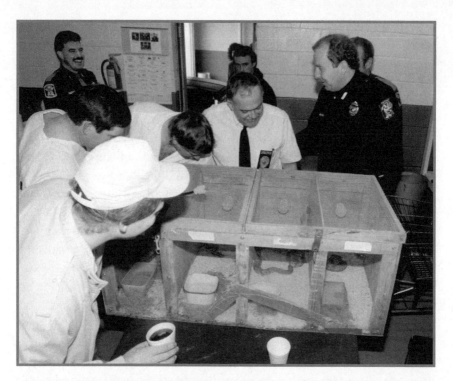

Inmates and Scottsboro police officers look over the copperhead snakes brought in as evidence against Glenn Summerford. Photographed during the trial by Michael Mercier, Feb. 12, 1992. Used with the courtesy of the *Huntsville Times*. All rights reserved. Reprinted with permission.

right here. Finally I reached in there and picked the snake up. But it bit me on the thumb, a western diamondback, one we had never took to church.

I told him that it bit me, and he said stuff about God. And I was real scared because you don't supposed to say stuff about God. And he was cussing me and saying stuff about God and everything. He told me to put the lid back on the box, and he told me, he said: "Get that other snake," you know—take the lid off this box that had two big rattlesnakes. He made me take the lid off of it. He said, "If you can handle that snake right there without it biting you," he said, "I'll let you live." Well, I was still praying and everything, and I reached in there, and I got the snake up and held it for two or three seconds, I guess, or maybe four or five. Then I put it back down in there. And he said, "Well, I'm going to let you live since the Lord let you handle that one."

Then he made me go back to the car with him because he thought that some of them was going to come up to the house looking for us. We went down

Glenda Darlene Collins Summerford

there for, I guess, an hour. I kept getting sick, and I was hurting real bad. I was crying and trying to get him to go to the house because I was real thirsty. I told him, I said, "Glenn, you don't want me to die down here." He said, "No, I don't guess I do." Finally, he took me back towards the house. And I fell on the ground. I wasn't passed out, but I just got real weak. And I fell on the ground and couldn't get up for a few minutes. He said, "Well, I'll get you up." And he used the bathroom in my face and in my hair. He said, "That will revive you."

Well, I layed there for a few more minutes, you know. I couldn't get up for a few more minutes. And then finally when I got up, we went toward the house. And when we got to the house, he was going through the front door. And he give me the key to unlock the lock, and I passed out on the porch. When I come to, he was kicking me in the side. He was kicking me real hard, but he was telling me to get up. He was saying, "Get up. God told me you was going to live." And that scared me because I knowed he didn't have nothing with God that night, you know, being drunk and being mean and saying things about God. That really scared me. Then finally when I come to myself, you know, I finally got up; and we went on in the house through the front door. Then he come back and locked it again.

He just let me lay on the couch, and he brought me some water that first night, on Friday, you know. Then he said he was going to get over there on the other couch and lay down. I must have went to sleep. I'm not sure if I went to sleep or passed out or what. But anyway, when he got up in the morning and he was cleaning up to go to the store, I thought he was goin' to leave me there. But then he told me I couldn't stay at home.

I could walk pretty good, but I was hurt. My hand was swelled, and it was hurting real bad. I didn't have use of my hand. I couldn't do nothing with it, you know. I had to hold it up because it hurt so bad. I was bit on the inside of my thumb.

We went down and got the car, and we went to Lakeside. He acted different, you know. He wasn't cussing me and stuff. Most of the time when we had been into it, he would apologize and be good to me for a couple of days. We was going to take some tapes back. They was late, and we had to take them in, you know. When we left and got to the store, he told me to take the tapes in while he went into the grocery store, but I had better not say nothing. And he said he would take me to the hospital when we got through, but he didn't.

When we got to the video store it was pretty early, and I think the woman was just opening up. I handed the tapes to her—I did not say anything to her—and I went back and got in the car. Then we went to the liquor store

Glenn's house on Barbee Lane.

down towards Goose Pond, the ABC Store. Glenn went in and got a fifth of vodka. Then we went to the Fina Mart. Glenn got cigarettes and Cokes and orange juice. I believe he got some sandwiches that you heat up in the microwave. I begged him to take me to the hospital, but he wouldn't take me. We went back home and parked the car back in the woods. It might have been ten o'clock—I wasn't thinking about the time. I was just hurting so bad. And we stayed in the house all day. Around dinner or one o'clock, his sister came over. Glenn told me to keep my mouth shut and not say a word. The door was locked on the outside. She came to the door, and she was hollering "Glenn" or something. I knowed it was his sister Charlotte. In a little while she left. I just layed around on the couch. Glenn just stayed in the house. He had drank all day.

About five o'clock in the evening, he said that I was going to die at six o'clock. He said I was going back to the snake shed. He just kept cussing me

Glenda Darlene Collins Summerford

and everything. He was telling me that I was going to have to die. Around seven or seven-thirty, he took me back to the snake shed—by the hair of my head and with his gun.

He told me that I had better pray and get things right because this time I was going to die. And he said I wouldn't pick that snake up no more, the big rattler. He got him a little pipe, water-line pipe; and he was punching the snake, you know, making it mad. He said, "You won't handle this snake no more without it biting you." The snake was real mad. He was striking and everything. Glenn grabbed me by the hair, and he was still going to make it bite me in the face if I didn't reach in there and get it. And he still had the gun. He made me take the top off. Then he made me stick my hand in there. And it bit me—the big one—right on the back of my left hand, the same hand as the other bite.

I started getting real, real sick. I couldn't hardly breathe. My thumb started tingling, and my face tingled and everything. This bite was a different sensation. Then finally, he let me go in the house. I was out there in the snake shed probably about five minutes, but I done started to get real sick. It was about seven or seven-thirty. When I got back in the house, he was still cussing me and telling me to pray. And I prayed hard. I was laying on the couch, and I was beggin' Glenn for some water because my mouth was so dry it felt like that I was choking. I was beggin' him for some water, and he wouldn't give me none. And he kept telling me that I was going to die, you know, I was going to die. He went in the kitchen; and, finally, he got me a cup of water. But the glass was real dirty and everything; but I was so thirsty, I drank it anyway. I started throwing up. And I said, "Bring me a bucket or something," so I wouldn't have to mess the floor up. Then my kidneys started moving, and he brought me a bucket at first. He had a rag on it, and he said he didn't want his fingerprints on that either. I begged him to take me to the hospital. And he said I was going to die. He took the bucket and done something with it. I guess he throwed it away or something. Then he said I would have to use the bathroom in the floor. I would just roll off of the couch and throw up, and use the bathroom in the floor. My mind was just coming and going.

Before the last snakebite he told me if I would write two notes, he would take me to the hospital. And if I didn't, he would kill me with a gun. I wrote them notes, one to my son and one was to my sister. I wrote the one to my son Marty first. Then he made me write the one to my sister that I went with her husband, David Mance, Glenn's half brother—but I hadn't.

This is the letter I wrote to Marty. Glenn told me every word to put in it:

Marty I Love Do what
daddy says daddy was
a speel I tried to fix
thatsin, but It didnt
work out ~~the~~. Dont Blame
daddy because he love
me and tryed to help
me but, I wouldnt listen
Daddy is asleep and he
dont know what I'm doing
Marty all ways remember
I love you for the
good not the bad
but love you try
to get right

You Mamer

I went out and got snake
bite Glemn is a speel And
I dont want no help
you and daddy live right
O.K   I Love you

I will read it: "Marty, I love you. I love—do what Daddy say. Daddy was asleep. I tried to fix"—I can't even hardly read it—"if everything—but I didn't work out. Don't blame Daddy because he loves me and trying to help me, but wouldn't listen . . . but I wouldn't listen. Daddy is asleep and he don't know what I'm doing. Marty, always remember I love you for the good not the bad, but love your . . . but love you, try to get right, your Mama. I went out and got

Glenda Darlene Collins Summerford

snake bit. Glenn is asleep and don't want no help . . . I don't want no help and you and Daddy live right, okay. I love you."

I didn't have any choice to write that note. He said he would take me to the hospital; and he said if I didn't, he would kill me with a gun. But he didn't take me to the hospital.

Well, he went over there and layed down. And he said if I got up and moved, that he would blow my brains out. He said that gun was cocked and he had it right under his pillow. Well, I kept talking to him, you know, trying to talk to him and begging him for water and stuff. He wouldn't get me none, and I kept talking to him. And when he wouldn't say nothing back to me, then I waited for a few minutes. And I was going to get me a drink of water, but I seen the water was there where he had unhooked the phone. The phone was sitting on the table, and I was crawling into the kitchen. So I reached and got the phone cord and drug it in the kitchen and hooked up the phone and called my sister. She called the ambulance and the police. Then I unhooked the phone and got it back like it was and went and got me a glass of water and went back to the couch. I wasn't there very long, and the dogs was barking. I thought that she must have just come straight over there or something. I went to the back door and crawled out. And I kept getting up and going. I went out to the road, you know, out to the wire gate that Glenn put up for the horses.

When I got nearly there, the ambulance was coming. And they took me to the Jackson County Hospital. I was in a awful shape. I couldn't hardly talk. And then they rushed me to Birmingham in an ambulance, to UAB Hospital. I stayed there the first time three or four days, and then I had to go back the next week for a check-up. They put me back in there and had to do surgery on me. The snakebite killed so many cells in my finger, they took the meat off the top of my finger. And they cut a big hole in it and cut it out.

I was scared of Glenn, you know. I knowed what he could do. I lived with him for sixteen years, and I ought to know what he could do.

Glenn's Second Wife at the Trial

The Court Reporter
Trial Transcripts (Abstract)

STATE OF ALABAMA VS. GLENN SUMMERFORD

Circuit Court for Jackson County, Alabama, Case Number: CC-91-564
Before Honorable W. Loy Campbell
Appearance for the Plaintiff: Dwight Duke
Appearance for the Defendant: Gary Lackey

First Day, February 10, 1992

Selection of Jury

Second Day, February 11, 1992

Morning Session (Examination of one witness for the prosecution)

(Prosecution Direct Examination by Dwight Duke; Defense Cross-examination by Gary Lackey)

Direct and Cross-examination of *Glenda Darlene Summerford* (wife of Glenn Summerford)

Afternoon Session (1. Examination of witnesses for the prosecution: re-examination of Darlene Summerford and examination of three other witnesses 2. Examination of one witness for the defense)

Redirect and Recross-examination of *Glenda Darlene Summerford*

Direct and Cross-examination of *David Kennamer* (paramedic, Jackson County Hospital in Scottsboro)

Direct and Cross-examination of *Brenda Davis* (owner of video store)

Direct and Cross-examination of *Clarence Bolte* (investigator, Scottsboro Police Dept.)

State Rests

(Defense Direct Examination by Gary Lackey; Prosecution Cross-examination by Dwight Duke)

Direct, Cross-, Redirect, Recross-examination of *Tammy Flippo*

Third Day, February 12, 1992

Morning Session (1. Examination of one witness for the defense and of one rebuttal witness for the prosecution 2. Closing arguments 3. Judge's charge to jury)

Direct and Cross-examination of *Leslie Peace* (brother-in-law of Glenn Summerford's two oldest sons)

Defense Rests

Sylvia Ingram called from court room in Rebuttal by Dwight Duke (Rule invoked by Gary Lackey overruled)

Cross-examination by Gary Lackey

State and Defense Rest

Closing Argument by Mr. Duke

Closing Argument by Mr. Lackey

Final Argument by Mr. Duke

Judge's Charge to the Jury (1. Explanation of the charges contained in the Indictment 2. Delineation of the burden of proof 3. Explanation of the possible verdicts)

Now, this case is brought to you by an indictment of the Grand Jury of this County wherein the Defendant, Glenn Summerford, is charged with the offense of attempted murder. It charges in its material part that Glenn Summerford did, with intent to commit the crime of murder, attempt to commit said offense by intentionally forcing Darlene Summerford to put her hand in a

Left: Discarded serpent cages at Glenn's house on Barbee Lane.

Below: Serpent shed at Glenn's house on Barbee Lane.

cage with live rattlesnakes where she was bitten on her hand. Now, this indict-ment also includes several lesser charges. The specific and the main charge, or the first charge, is attempted murder. Also, including in it is assault in the first degree, assault in the second degree, assault in the third degree, and the charge of harassment.

Now, I'll further explain these various charges to you just a little bit later on. This indictment is not evidence and is not to be considered by you at all as evidence in the case. It's just a means of bringing the case to trial and of informing the Defendant of the charges made against him. Now, as to all charges contained in this indictment, the Defendant enters a plea of not guilty. He says he's not guilty of any of these charges. This casts the burden upon the State to prove the Defendant's guilt beyond a reasonable doubt by competent evidence offered at the trial. The burden is never upon the Defendant to prove his innocence, but is on the State to prove the Defendant's guilt, and to prove it beyond a reasonable doubt. . . .

Ladies and gentlemen, if you have a reasonable doubt of the Defendant's guilt, growing out of the evidence, or any part of it, you must acquit him. . . .

Now, there are several possible verdicts that you might reach in this case: guilty of attempted murder, or not guilty of attempted murder, but guilty of assault in the first degree, or, not guilty of assault in the first degree, and attempted murder, but guilty of assault in the second degree, or, not guilty of assault in the second degree, but guilty of assault in the third degree, or, not guilty of assault in the third degree, but guilty of harassment, and then, a ver-dict of not guilty of any of the charges. . . .

When you have arrived at a verdict, and it's your duty at this time, to go out and reach a verdict, based upon the evidence that you have heard, and after due consideration thereof, when you have arrived at a verdict, then if you will, knock on the door, the baliff [sic] will be present to notify the Court.

End of Morning Session

Afternoon Session (1. Judge's explanation of verdict forms 2. Jury's verdict)

Judge Explanation of Verdict Forms and Jury Retires for Deliberations

Verdict of Jury: "We, the jury, find the Defendant, Glenn Summerford, guilty of attempted murder, as charged in the indictment."

Court Adjourned

Sentencing Hearing: March 3, 1992

Jackson County Courthouse, Scottsboro, Alabama
Before Honorable W. Loy Campbell

Sentence of the Court

Mr. Summerford, in keeping with the verdict of the jury, I adjudge you guilty of attempted murder, as charged in the indictment, and I find that you have had two prior felony convictions in Case 784, burglary in the second degree in Jackson County, Alabama, and Case 785 of grand larceny in Jackson County, Alabama. . . . Mr. Summerford, under the law, I have very little discretion in regard to the length of your sentence. Since I have found that you have had two prior felony convictions . . . the law provides that your sentence has got to be one of two terms, either life or ninety-nine years; and, it's the sentence of the law and I now pronounce it upon you that you be sentenced to imprisonment in the penitentiary of this State for a term of ninety-nine years.

Discussion of Motion for New Trial and Jail Term Credit

Court Adjourned

D. Kennamer, B. Davis, C. Bolte, T. Flippo, L. Peace, S. Ingram

Witnesses at the Trial

For the Prosecution

David Kennamer (Paramedic, Jackson County Hospital)

We were in the ambulance on South Broad around the Piggly Wiggly when we received the call. We were given the call that there was a snakebite victim, so we responded to what we call Code 3, without lights and our siren to begin with. We turned our lights and sirens off as we turned off of Highway 35 about Randall's Chapel, which is probably about a couple of miles from the house. As we were going down this dirt road at the end of Barbee Lane, I met this lady walking towards us. And I'd never seen her before, but she was walking out the dirt road. She was stumbling a little bit and she was unsteady on her feet, but she was able to walk by herself.

My first instinct was that she appeared to be scared. She was walking towards the ambulance, but she kept looking back towards the house as she was walking away. I walked with her to the back of the ambulance and got her into the rear of the ambulance.

She had a wound. I believe it was on her left thumb. What I made note of was some blackening. And it looked like some of the skin had died on the left thumb on the outside, and it looked like about an inch and a half to two inches long. From snakebites that I have seen in the past and what we've been taught, it appeared to be a snakebite. I also made note of an injury to the back

Road into Glenn's house on Barbee Lane.

Road from Glenn's house on Barbee Lane.

of the same hand. It also appeared to be a snakebite wound, but of a fresher nature. It looked like something that had occurred recently, where the other looked like it occurred sometime before. It had already started to turn red, and there was some swelling to it.

I took her to the emergency room and left her in one of the rooms in the emergency room with the nurses and the physicians there. They called us back to the emergency room in about an hour or a little less than that. We were requested then to transport her to the University of Alabama in Birmingham Hospital to the emergency room there.

During Cross-Examination by the Defense

No, I didn't notice any abrasions on the lady's knees. She made no complaints about her knees, so I did not check her knees. Except for the two bites, I didn't notice anything on her hands. I did not notice anything of what I would normally call someone that had been assaulted. She did not give me any information about being assaulted. Her hand was not a fresh-washed hand. It had some dirt on it, you know, but it was not . . . it had some dirt on it, but I can't say where it would have come from. Yes, the only trauma she conveyed to me were the two snakebites, and that's what I found.

Brenda Davis (Owner, Video Store Next to Lakeside Grocery)

I opened the store at eleven. I had a few things that I did when I first went in there, and then the last thing I did was turn my signs around to say that I was open. And I was up there turning my sign around when I saw Ms. Summerford walking towards the store. She had one hand up, and she had four movie boxes in one hand. And I was close to my door, and when she got to the door, it was like she was going to try to open the door with the hand that had the movie boxes in it because she didn't move the other hand. And I opened the door for her. I noticed her hand when I opened the door. It was her left hand. I didn't notice anything other than it was swollen, you know. Her fingers and the top of her hand were swollen.

When I opened the door, I thought she would come on in and put the movie boxes on the counter like she normally did, but she just kind of handed me the movie boxes. And I took them. And I think I said good morning to her or "How are you?" or, you know, something like that. But she didn't say anything back. She looked pale. And I don't know, she looked tired or upset; but,

Lakeside Grocery building, site of video store.

you know, she just looked pale. And her eyes were puffy—crying, you know, how it makes your eyes swell. As far as I can remember, she had her hair up; but it was like, you know, it was loose. You know, it didn't appear that she did it before she came to the store. You know, it was like she had some coming down. You know, it wasn't neat. She was generally neat when she came in the store. And a lot of times she was, you know, dressed very nice, you know, with her hair fixed.

She was there just long enough to hand me the movie boxes. And when I said whatever I said to her, she turned and went back over toward the way she came. Normally, when she brought movies back, she picked out more movies. She was in there a lot, and she rented a lot of movies. The movies were a day late. She had never returned her movies late before, you know. She had always been on time with her movies.

During Cross-Examination by the Defense

My husband works for the City of Scottsboro, and he has a grocery store on Highway 35, Lakeside Grocery. He's been employed by the City of Scottsboro I would say at least fifteen years. Yes, we pretty much rely on the store income

Witnesses at the Trial

and the City of Scottsboro income for our support and maintenance. Yes, at the time I had the store, I had a phone.

Ms. Summerford was only there for a few minutes; but, no, I didn't notice any smell of any urine on Ms. Summerford. No, I didn't see any marks on her. No, she did not say anything to the effect that her husband had forced her to put her hand into a cage full of rattlesnakes. No, she did not say anything like "Help, call the police—my husband is trying to kill me." No, she did not sound any type of alarm whatsoever. She did not say, "I need to go to the hospital—call an ambulance." No, none of those things. Yes, I would have called the police if somebody had come and said, "My husband is trying to kill me. He's making me stick my hand into a cage full of rattlesnakes, and I've already been bitten once."

Clarence Bolte (Investigator, Scottsboro City Police)

I first received notice of the incident at Barbee Lane Monday morning, October 7. I talked with Mr. Summerford that afternoon in my office at the police department. Mr. Summerford was at the sheriff's department, and we were notified. And we came up, and he came down with us to the police department. I advised Mr. Summerford that afternoon of his constitutional right that before I ask you any questions, you must understand your rights; you have the right to remain silent, etc. After going over this with him, he indicated that he desired to give me a statement. This is a statement that was given to me by Mr. Summerford:

> On Friday night we went to church, and I was going to give up the church because she said she had been running around on me. When we got back home, she went to the kitchen. I went in a few minutes later, and she was taking a bunch of pills. I made her drink some water and throw up. On Saturday, we rode around and went to New Hope to see my oldest boys. We stayed an hour or so and then came back home. I don't remember what time we got home. When we got home, we watched TV and ate. We had rented some tapes. We rented four or five movies. I don't know how many we watched. She was changing the tapes, so I went to sleep. When I woke up, Mama and my sister were shaking me. And they told me that Darlene had gotten snake bit, and she was at the hospital and was on her way to Birmingham. Earlier me and Darlene had been drinking some Vodka and orange juice. She had bought a fifth on Friday. We drank that,

and then I bought a pint on Saturday sometime. I went to Birmingham, and I couldn't see her. And I got arrested because a pistol was in the car in her purse.

During Cross-Examination by the Defense

Ms. Summerford contacted me on Monday morning, October 7. She told me she had been beaten on Friday and Saturday, October 4 and 5. The medical records from the Jackson County Hospital were subpoenaed, and I have not seen those records. No, I didn't take the time to find out if the medical records would verify this report of having been beaten. I couldn't get the medical records. No, I did not take the time to go to Birmingham to see if the complaining witness had marks, bruises, contusions and other physical indications consistent with the history of having been severely beaten on Friday, October 4.

The impression I was given (when I first started, you know, when I talked to her on Monday) was the first snakebite was on Saturday. And then after I talked with her, I learned that it was twice that she had been bitten—on Friday and Saturday. No, I didn't learn, until some time after I had filed the warrant in this case, anything about an earlier snakebite that she had received in church. No, I did not take the time to investigate the complaining witness's history of snake handling before I filed this case. To my knowledge she had never touched a snake before. Yes, I saw a photograph of reptiles in her purse just last weekend when we met for discovery and were going through the lady's purse at city hall. Yes, there was a video tape made of the interior of Mr. Summerford's house the day we went out there.

Yes, I talked to Ms. Summerford about her suicide attempts and her suicide note. No, she did not relate to me a history of several days of domestic squabbling. She stated that they had been fussing on Saturday. No, as far as it being a whole week long squabbling leading up to the events of the trial, she didn't relay that to me. Ms. Summerford indicated that she was tired of living with her husband like she was having to live, and she did want a divorce—but he would not give her one. No, she did not indicate that she was willing for Mr. Summerford to have custody of their boy Marty. Yes, I learned just a few days ago about her having already lost one child to the welfare authorities.

Yes, Mr. Summerford voluntarily signed a consent-to-search form to allow us to search his entire premises. Yes, Mr. Summerford voluntarily of his own free will and accord signed his rights away and told his version of what happened on these occasions. Yes, he was cooperative with me in every way. No, he didn't act like he had anything to hide.

For the Defense

Tammy Flippo (Church Member of Woods Cove Church)

I went to church one night with the side of my face black where my ex-husband had hit me, and Darlene came out and talked to me. And she told me that she wished that she could get her husband to beat her like that to where she could get away from him because she was tired of living right and she wanted to have fun like she always did.

And I called her in Birmingham on the 21st or the 22nd of October. She told me, you know, whenever I called her . . . I asked her what had happened to her, and she said that she got snakebit. And I asked her how; and she said—I said, "At church?" And, she said, "No, at home." And I asked her, I said, you know, "How or how come?" And she said, "Well," she said, "I got Glenn drunk. And I went out to get a snake, you know. I was going to put it on him and let it bite him on the neck," and then she up and said that—well, let me get this straight, you know, her exact words. She said that she was going to let it bite him on the neck, and when she stuck her hand in the box to get it, that it bit her.

During Cross-Examination by the Prosecution

When I came up to church with my ex-brother-in-law and sister-in-law, Johnny and Sylvia Ingram, I didn't want to go in. And she took my kids and went on in. I wasn't alone at first. And then the other sisters went in, and Darlene just came out and told me that it was okay to come in with them. And she was saying that she wanted Glenn to beat her up to where she could kill him, to where she could have fun, because she didn't want to live right no more. No, not kill him at that time she got beat, you know. She just said that she wanted to kill him because she didn't want to live right no more.

Yes, then I called her in October, and this was the next conversation I had with her. Before all this happened, we had talked occasionally, but just about the church and stuff. No, I didn't know at that time what she was in the hospital for. You know, she didn't never say. I asked her how come she was in the hospital. She told me she got him drunk and that he passed out on the couch. And she went out to get a snake to put it on him to where it would bite him on the neck. And whenever she stuck her hand in there, it bit her. And that's all I know. No, I didn't ask her if she had been drinking that night, and she didn't volunteer that. I don't know. No, I didn't say anything in response. I just thought that it was time for me to let her go whenever she was talking about that because that's the pastor of my church.

I am twenty-three years old. I live with my mother and daddy and brother. No, Glenn Summerford hadn't been down where I live; and no, I haven't been to his residence or been out with him.

Leslie Peace (Brother-in-Law of Glenn Summerford's Two Oldest Sons)

Glenn had been snakebitten at church about three weeks before this incident between Glenn and Darlene happened. I was at their house for family support. And he had a lot of horses and animals, and I went there to help them take care of their animals so the family could keep their mind on Glenn and what they needed to do instead of worrying about their animals.

Well, Darlene said that she was tired of living with him and she wished she could find a way out. And there was once when she got mad and come in the kitchen. Glenn was laying sick in the living room on the bed. And there was several of us sitting there, and she said, "I wished he would just go ahead and die so I could have my freedom."

During Cross-Examination by the Prosecution

Yes, Glenn had been seriously bitten, and all of the church people had gathered in there to pray for him to get well. We was there all week, you know, when he had gotten bit. Yes, Darlene would pray for him too. Everybody there would pray for him.

Rebuttal Witness for the Prosecution

(The Rule was invoked by the defense because the witness sat in the courtroom during the proceedings and heard the testimony of the witnesses, but the defense was overruled.)

Sylvia Ingram (Tammy Flippo Ingram's Sister-in-Law)

I was for two years, two-and-a half years, a member of the Woods Cove Church where Glenn Summerford was pastor.

I took Ms. Ingram—Flippo Ingram—to church, you know, my husband and I. She and her husband are not divorced at this time. I went in and got Darlene and we went back outside. And there was several of us outside, and they were discussing coming to church with bruises on your face. No, nothing was said on that occasion about Ms. Summerford wishing that her husband would beat her up like that or anything similar to that—no, it was to the contrary. No, nothing was said like that where she could kill him. I was out there the whole time, and we all went back into the church together.

Yes, I had a conversation with Ms. Flippo Ingram about four weeks ago at my trailer. She told me she had stayed at Mr. Summerford's house numerous times. She had left her husband three or four times, that I know of, and she admitted to me in there all of those times.

During Cross-Examination by the Defense

Yes, I was on TV last night—not about this case, but about Tammy Flippo. I'm testifying about her telling lies on the witness stand. Yes, I sure do understand why a woman would leave her husband if she had been beaten like that. And I can't blame her for that at all.

District Attorney Dwight Duke and Gary W. Lackey

Lawyers at the Trial

Dwight Duke (Closing Argument for the Prosecution)

This case involves some very brutal, torturous treatment to Ms. Summerford, which was done with the intention of costing her life. The case boils down to Ms. Summerford being bit on Friday night and then again on Saturday night. The first bite was to the inside of the thumb. On Saturday morning she saw one person at the video store who testified to her condition: face puffy and pale, eyes puffy as from crying, dress uneven, arm carried as if something was wrong with it. This testimony substantiates Ms. Summerford's testimony of being bitten on Friday. Ms. Summerford was hoping that her husband would take her to the hospital on that Saturday morning, but he took her home. She testified to the events that happened there that night beginning before six—the first deadline was six and the next seven, and then shortly thereafter she was forced to put her hand in with the large snake. It bit her on the back of the hand, and then she began to really get sick. The next person who saw Ms. Summerford was the ambulance driver. Ms. Summerford was wobbly walking down the road towards him, and was looking back in a scared state of mind. The next witness gave the statement that was taken from Glenn Summerford, which accuses Ms. Summerford of running around on him—the cause of making him so mad. The statement says Ms. Summerford took pills. Her testimony was that the incident happened earlier and that she took four Sominex, not a suicidal dose. The issue of the son: that she is doing everything to get a divorce and get the son. Such

Jackson County Courthouse.

a plan to fit all of these pieces together where she could get custody would be too complex for a person with her education and background. Next is the suicide note. There's a lot to be learned from the broken, scratchy handwriting, e.g., the kind of shape that this person would be in who wrote this note. Relative to Ms. Summerford's being a snake handler, she readily admits it. In church she didn't have fear. In the snake shed there was fear and the likelihood that the serpents would bite.

Gary Lackey (Closing Argument for the Defense)

The statement supposedly by Mr. Summerford is not signed, and it is nothing more than some things Clarence Bolte wrote down. There is no evidence that Mr. Summerford even knew the contents of the statement. The case was sloppily investigated. The video taken at the house shows an unkempt house, but not a place where a struggle took place. Why didn't the city video Mr. Summerford's statement? Why didn't Mr. Bolte take the time to find out about the background of these people? Where does the husband of the witness at the video store work, and where does Mr. Bolte work?—the City of Scottsboro. The case comes together if the witnesses are picked and they're all on the payroll. Why didn't Bolte find out anything about this lady: her history with serpent handling and previous snakebites, the photographs in her purse which indicate a morbid fascination with snakes, and other pertinent facts relative to the case? She has three stories, one in October (when the incident occurred), one in November (at the preliminary trial), and another in February (at the present trial). Ms. Summerford's testimony, therefore, should be disregarded. One, the beating, which she says presently started on Tuesday and went through the week conflicts with the statement to Officer Bolte, which says nothing started happening until Friday or Saturday, and with her testimony at the prelim in November that her husband had not beaten her Friday and Saturday. Next the ambulance driver. There is no evidence that she was beaten. The ambulance report indicates that everything was fine about her except that she received a couple of snakebites. She was not in acute distress. Next the opportunities to escape. Glenn went with her to three different places on that Saturday, e.g., he went in one side of a grocery, and she went in the other side, and the gun stayed in the car. Now, the movie ticket. It is not reasonable for someone to threaten to kill someone and then rent four movies on Thursday, take them home and watch them, and then return them half a day late. There was nothing to prevent her from getting that gun and defending herself, and there was nothing to prevent her from escaping. Next the sleeping issue. It is unreasonable that somebody could be forced to put their hand into a cage of snakes and then go back in and go to sleep. If she waited until he was asleep and left on Saturday night, she could have done so on Friday night. On Saturday when Glenn goes in to the liquor store, it isn't reasonable that she didn't try to make an escape, drive off, or grab the pistol. Then Glenn and Darlene Summerford go to the Fina Mart. He goes in, and she doesn't try to escape or sound any kind of alarm. Now about the New Hope episode. She was part of a conspiracy with her husband to go down to New Hope and get the attention of a man so that he could be bushwhacked from behind. Her testimony doesn't come from the kind of person to believe to convict a man of attempted murder. This is a dysfunctional family. Her parental rights have been terminated, and there is a dread fear of history repeating itself. The welfare of her son is going to be decided later in divorce court. That's where this case should have been, a divorce case. Now the evidence that she crawled out. There is no evidence that she crawled or was terrorized in the fashion that she says. She had no fear of snakes. She was fascinated by snakes. On a previous occasion in church of her being bitten, the same symptoms were experienced, nausea, vomiting—the only difference is she didn't go to the doctor. If your goal is to get rid of your husband, to use the criminal justice system as a mechanism to get rid of the husband, then you go to the doctor. The medical records don't support what she said happened. There is no way to reconcile all of the conflicting testimony between what she said in October and November and what she says to this court.

Dwight Duke (Final Argument for the Prosecution)

First, the inconsistency. I don't remember but one thing that's been inconsistent, and that's the discrepancy between days. Now, the medical records. That they don't reflect having bruises doesn't matter. They treated the injury, snakebite. The testimony of crawling: the testimony said she had dirt on her hands. The point of the witnesses' being on the payroll for the city. I don't give any credence whatsoever to that. The matter of Bolte's not checking this woman's background. A person's background isn't important as to whether or not they've been inflicted with torture. Now about reasonable people. This is not a reasonable person we're dealing with here, not by these actions. She thought it was reasonable to think her husband was going to carry her to the hospital. The Huntsville episode. She told about that. Glenn told her to; he had a pistol; he was mad, so he got his revenge there; and then he carried her home to further the revenge. Now about her as a much-troubled lady. The evidence suggests that anyone who had been subjected to what she has would be troubled. The divorce court that has been mentioned. Mr. Summerford is the one who kept this case from the divorce court and put into criminal court where it belongs. The statement that Ms. Summerford wished her husband would die. It would be stupid if this lady put all this together, to point of getting bit twice, for her to make that statement. Ms. Flippo's testimony would be damaging, but it comes out that her last name is not even Flippo. And the woman who was present that night testifies that the conversation that Ms. Flippo describes between Ms. Summerford and herself never occurred. Ms. Flippo testified that she had never been to Mr. Summerford's house, and the witness says that Ms. Flippo told her she had been to his house numerous times when she would leave her husband. Suicide note: it looks coerced. It is not a suicide note. It is an alibi note that he forced her to write. It states three times that Glenn is asleep. The only problem was she got away and lived. Now the video tape: a ransacked house, taken a couple of days after the time the incident happened. Snake handling: it was never a problem in this case. Serpent handlers have the right of protection under law. Glenn Summerford tried his best to get rid of his wife by attempting to murder her, and I would ask you to return a verdict of guilty.

Captain David Kennamer, EMT-P, and Janette Green, RN
Medical Practitioners

Captain David Kennamer (Paramedic, Jackson County Hospital)

We were dispatched out on a call to Barbee Lane and went down almost to the end where it was turning into the driveway. We met this lady who was walking toward us, and we stopped. She said she was the patient. She appeared very scared and kept looking back towards the house in the direction from which she came. We asked her what the problem was. She said she had been bitten by a snake, and she was scared that her husband might be coming after her.

She had stumbled a little bit walking, but not a lot. I put it off more to her looking back. She was on a really rough driveway—just a piece of a trail, which was rough enough to walk on in the daylight. Now, you make it at night, it's even more so. And when you're lookin' back as much as you're lookin' forward at the same time—with a gravel or anything in her way, she's goin' stumble a little bit.

She was dressed in the more conservative dress you would see among certain religious groups around here, Church of God, Holiness—hair long, no makeup. She was clean and well-kept, just no makeup or anything—an older dress, not with bright colors. I do remember about her hands that they were work hands—somebody who worked for a living. They were kind of callused, kind of weathered, a little bit rough.

Well, I went around and got her in the back of the ambulance—I got in the back with her. Bobby, my partner at the time—he's very scared of snakes—he was having to back out to the roadway because there was nowhere to turn around. And I remember that I could see him up in the front moving around and lookin' out the window. And I hollered and asked him, "What are you doin'?" He said, "I'm scared he may come out here and throw a snake on me." Bobby was trying to back up the ambulance without gettin' it off the road into the ditch and also watch out for this guy. Mrs. Summerford had told us, "We handle snakes. We raise snakes. I've been bitten. He don't want me to get help, and he doesn't know I'm out here"—so that scared Bobby. But we never did see Mr. Summerford at all. Nobody came out but her.

After I got her in the back of the ambulance, we came on to the hospital. She was doin' pretty good at the time. You could see the snakebite on the back of her hand. And you could see another one on her thumb that looked a little older—the one she said happened the night before. You could tell it had

Paramedic David Kennamer.

David Kennamer and Janette Green

been there a little while: there was more darker reddening around it. The new one had some brighter red, indicating it was a newer bite.

The older bite undoubtedly had not given her a lot of trouble if it was roughly twenty-four hours old. And since she was still doing well, there probably wasn't a lot of venom in that bite at the time. But this other bite was starting to swell up a good bit. She said it hadn't been long since she had been bitten.

At the time I did not talk with her a lot about what had happened because what I was wanting to find out was just her condition. We're not that far from the hospital—it only takes us, like, five minutes to get in—so I was very busy in the back by myself trying to get her taken care of. I knew she had one bite from the night before and another one that was already swelling up. So I needed to talk with her in a hurry and do a lot of precautionary things with her. I hooked her to a cardiac monitor, checked her blood pressure, got her on nasal oxygen, and started an IV. We want to have all this done ahead of time so we can watch her; and then, if we do need to administer some drugs, we have a line all ready for that. At that time she was stable. She was not doing bad. But she appeared to be scared—that was the biggest thing with her.

My Run Report indicates that we got the call at 21:20 (9:20 P.M.) on October 5, 1991. It was five miles there and took us six minutes to get to her from the call. She was conscious and alert. Her speech was coherent. Her skin was normal. Her color I marked as slightly pale. (Being scared could make it pale, or if her system was having trouble from the venom—that could make her very pale—or sometimes people of that religion don't get out in the sun a lot, and they're just pale looking.) The pulse was rapid, 120. (Anything over 100, we consider fast. A normal adult runs from 80 to 100. Being 120 is not life threatening by any means.) The report shows that the pulse stayed at 120 the whole time on the way to the hospital. (The rapid pulse could also be from the reaction to the venom of the snake, or just being scared.) Pupils were normal. On the cardiac monitor she was in "sinus tach." ("Sinus tach" is just a normal rhythm—all the beats are in place, no beats that should not have been there, and the rhythm is regular. The only thing about her rhythm was that it was a little fast. Everything else about it was normal.) Her blood pressure was 110 over 60. (For her that is actually a pretty good blood pressure. Whatever was going wrong with her had not affected her blood pressure.) Her respirations were at 24. (That is a little fast, but a respiration of 24 is not anything that's going to give any trouble. You're not going to pass out from that. You're not going to hyperventilate. It just means that you're a little bit scared, which she was for whatever the reason.) I started an IV in her right hand.

41

The narrative part of my report records details of what she told me about the bites. She said she was bitten the previous night around 12:00 A.M. by a diamondback rattlesnake about two feet in length. She did not get medical attention for that bite. She was bitten again on the night we picked her up around 7:30 P.M. by a canebrake rattlesnake about five feet in length. Both bites were to the left hand. She said she felt dizzy and weak. She had slight dyspnea, which is just a little shortness of breath, probably from being scared. Other than that, with us she was stable.

We took her to the emergency room and left her. About an hour after that, they called us back, and we transferred her to UAB Hospital. And as we were going on down to Birmingham, she was still doin' pretty good. Her hand was swellin' up some more, but she was awake and talking and knew what was going on. She was in some pain, but that was from the bite and from the swelling itself.

But we still didn't talk a whole lot going down through there. She didn't seem to want to talk much to us about what had happened. I think she had already spoken with the police at the emergency room before she left. Of course I had heard everything in the emergency room, and she was tellin' me a little more about all that.

It's hard to remember specifically what she said because of what I've heard at the trial and since then. But I think she kept tellin' the same story that she told the whole time—that her husband had taken her out there and pushed her hand down in there till she was bitten and that he drank a lot and that he (I believe she said) was on the couch drunk and passed out or asleep or whatever when she snuck out. If it actually happened that way, she told it good. If it didn't, she made up a good one. I don't know. Later after the trial when we were talking about it, I wondered if she had planned all this out to get rid of her husband—maybe tired of living with him and this was a way to get out.

Janette Green, RN (Former ER Nurse, Jackson County Hospital)

The night Mrs. Summerford was brought into the emergency room, I charted on the department record: "To ER per EASI"—that's the ambulance. "Status: post snakebite to left thumb at twelve midnight last night by two-foot diamondback rattler. Was again bitten to top of left hand by a five-foot canebrake rattler at 7:30 P.M. this evening. Left hand swollen. Hematoma on left thumb.

Complains of mouth dryness. Complains of nausea and vomiting. Complains of back pain. O_2 [oxygen] saturation 99%. Puncture bite marks marked with ink pen."

The doctor in ER that night was Lewis DeInnocentes—we called him "Dr. D." He was a Yankee. I knew him very well even after we quit working at the hospital and he had a practice on Laurel Street, a walk-in clinic. He died maybe two years ago.

Dr. D charted: "Thirty-five-year-old white female who was bitten by diamondback rattler last P.M. at 12 midnight. Tonight bitten by canebrake rattler five foot long at 7:30 P.M. Left arm swollen and painful. Physical: warm, dry. Thirty-five-year-old white female in no acute distress. Without cyanosis"— that's a bluish discoloration of the skin caused by deficient oxygen in the blood. "There is evidence of swelling. The left hand and left arm with ecchymosis. The left arm swollen. Area of blackness left thumb. Snakebites times two."

The record also shows that we did a complete blood count, PT and PTT—that's blood clotting. Phenergan, 50 milligrams, was given—that was for the nausea. The ambulance started the IV. I gave her the Phenergan. Her vital signs were good. Pulse was normal. Respirations were normal. Blood

Nurse Janette Green.

pressure was 106 over 66, which is kind of on the low side, but within normal limit. Rechecked it again, and it was 114 over 69. Pulse was 83 when she came in—that wasn't too fast. Later it was 114, a little elevated—that could be from pain; that could be from anxiety; it also could be from the toxins of the snake venom. But the pulse was not very elevated (60 to 100 is a normal pulse rate). Respiration was 24 (20–24 is normal for respiration). And oxygen saturation was normal, so I didn't see any problems breathing. (Blood gases from the blood work show that she was hyperventilating.) She arrived at 9:41 P.M. We discharged her at 10:30 P.M. And we transferred her to Birmingham.

Probably the biggest concern with her was her pretty severely swollen arm. Just the swelling itself could do some permanent damage. The arm was a different color than the other one. And where I marked the bites with the pen, there was ecchymosis, which looked like bruising around the snakebite. The reason I marked it was to see whether or not that area was going to expand, if the tissue was going to die at that site. I would have marked any discoloration around the puncture wound—it shouldn't grow unless the tissue was dying. Ecchymosis is not a solid blue discoloration, it looks like dots and redness. It can be red and blue, but it's a discoloration of the skin. I think the entire arm had some ecchymosis, just scattered, and could have come from the swelling.

She had a hematoma on the left thumb, which is a little different than ecchymosis—it's a collection of blood that would have been raised. I charted "hematoma" on the thumb, and Dr. D charted "area black." But if I said it was a hematoma, I bet it was hematoma—I'm notorious for arguing with doctors.

But what I charted on the emergency department record is just a little, general assessment. With the injury being an abuse-type situation, it's a wonder I didn't have some more notes. I can't believe I didn't write any more than that. I was always attachin' sheets because I would write more to legally cover myself. I've wrote pages and pages and pages of nurses notes. I was real particular when it was anything that was an abuse case or something that might go to court. You know, I'd try to be real specific and document everything and anything. I wouldn't be surprised if there weren't some more notes somewhere.

I do remember we put her in the big room, which is the room we use for trauma or heart attack or anything that might develop into something. It's where we had the crash cart and other stuff. And we didn't administer antivenin. First of all, at that time we probably didn't have any antivenin. We might have had some, but I remember talkin' to the doctor about it that they were treating snakebite differently. They weren't giving antivenin because they

David Kennamer and Janette Green

were having worse reaction out of the antivenin than the snakebite. Dr. D talked to the guy in Birmingham—his specialty was with this—and it wasn't recommended. So that's why she wasn't given any antivenin if we had it.

We transferred Mrs. Summerford to UAB by ambulance. Anytime we transferred a patient, the doctor would make contact with the doctor we were transferring to—she was transferred to Dr. Chang. And then I would make contact with the emergency room that we were transferring to. We'd give a report of what had happened, how the patient was doing, and what had been done for them.

It would have been Dr. D's decision of where to send Mrs. Summerford. Dr. Chang had some kind of specialty or had dealt more with serpent bites, and that's why she was transferred to Birmingham. And she was stable, or we wouldn't have transferred her out by ambulance—we would have flown her. If we had had any concern that somethin' would happen in the transfer, we would have called for a helicopter. Helicopters at UAB have doctors on them instead of just paramedics and nurses. We wouldn't have risked anything transferring her by ambulance.

Now, I remember some other things that night that I didn't chart because they weren't pertinent to Mrs. Summerford's physical being. I was told that there was something that happened at the church to make Mrs. Summerford's husband question or make him prove her fidelity—she had to prove that she was not unfaithful. Supposedly she did this to prove that she wasn't bein' unfaithful to her husband. I don't remember what the circumstances were—something had happened that caused him to believe that she had been unfaithful. I don't remember exactly what it was.

There were two family members—I believe her husband's family—who came with Mrs. Summerford to the hospital, a male and a female. The female I think was her husband's sister, but I didn't know any of these people before or after that night. And I don't remember if it was Mrs. Summerford that told me or if it was her sister-in-law because I talked with the people who were with Mrs. Summerford as much as with her. And you know I didn't badger her with questions if she was in pain. So I may have got a lot of information from the family members instead of her. I don't exactly remember. But I was told that all this happened to prove that Mrs. Summerford wasn't bein' unfaithful.

But I can just hear me—I can imagine I was irate and mouthing off: "A *man* made you put a snake! . . ." I can just hear me, 'cause I'm, like, "Uh, huh—if God come down and told me to put my hand in a snake box, me and him would have to sit down and have a serious discussion." I was pretty mouthy when it came to abuse cases. And I'm sure there was a lot more went on than I remember.

I wouldn't have wrote on this chart "two-foot diamondback" and "a five-foot canebrake rattler" from another source—it would have come from her. I wouldn't have done a third party thing on the chart. Now, what I'm rememberin' about the infidelity thing and all that might be third party. She may not have told me that, and then again she may have.

David Kennamer and Janette Green

Charlotte Colón Corroborated
by José Colón

Glenn's Half Sister and Brother-in-Law

O n Saturday night we received a call from Darlene's sister, Kathy—the one married to my brother David—that Darlene had been serpent bit. Darlene had called Kathy, and Kathy had called 911. Kathy then called us because she knew that we would go to Glendel's and see what was going on if we had to break the door down. She said Darlene was on the way to the hospital.

We jumped in the car and drove toward where Glendel lived on Barbee Lane. When we got to the stoplight, about where McDonald's is, we saw the ambulance coming from the direction of Glendel's house. The light changed right at that point, so we just turned and followed the ambulance to the hospital.

Since I was driving, I let Joe out of the car when we arrived at the emergency entrance. Joe was actually standing at the ramp as the rescue squad backed up and wheeled Darlene out of the ambulance. She seemed okay. Her left arm was somewhat swollen from just a little above the elbow downward. They took her into one of the small emergency rooms, and Joe followed them in while I parked the car. Then I joined them. Darlene was telling us that she had been bitten by a serpent, but nothing was said about Glendel making her do it or forcing her hand in a serpent box or anything at all except that she had been bit. She didn't say anything about how the bite occurred until after she had spoken with another sister of hers and her mother, who arrived a few minutes later. Then she said something about Glendel forcing her hand and causing her to be bitten by a serpent.

Darlene said that she felt nauseated, but she wasn't vomiting. She did not appear to be addled or dizzy or anything. She was not dirty, including her hands. Her clothes were not dirty. And there was no blood on her. When the nurse examined her, they found no evidence of Darlene's being beaten or of any injury except on the hand. Darlene did have a bruise on her leg that she said she had received horseback riding. She was not given any medication other than a shot for pain, and she was not given any antivenom. After the examination she was transported by ambulance to UAB Hospital in Birmingham ninety miles away.

The ambulance driver later reported that he had seen her staggering as she came down the road when they picked her up. But that road was in terrible condition—it's not even a paved road. It's just a dirt road leading off the paved road up to where Glendel and Darlene were living. It's full of dips and holes—and it was muddy since it had been raining a lot. You would have to weave back and forth just to keep from stepping in those muddy holes. Anybody coming down that road would have appeared to be staggering. Darlene said at the trial that she had crawled part of the way to the road. Well, if she had crawled any at all, she would have been covered in mud. Besides, there is a creek, formed by a spring, which runs across the road in front of the house, and you had to walk across some cement blocks in the creek to keep from getting wet.

It's interesting that some time later a man, who had been bit down at the church and brought up there to the hospital, was administered antivenom and airlifted out to Chattanooga. He was screaming and transported out as an emergency case, whereas Darlene chose Birmingham instead of Chattanooga (which would have been closer) and went by ambulance rather than by helicopter. And a woman who works with me, who was dating the ambulance driver, said Darlene was laughing and talking all the way to Birmingham.

One important thing to remember is that Darlene made no charges against Glendel that evening in Scottsboro. She just wanted to get away from him, she said.

Joe and I didn't go to Birmingham, but my brother David followed the ambulance to UAB Hospital. He had with him his wife Kathy, another sister of Darlene's, and her mother, Emma Collins. David said that he heard nothing on the way to Birmingham about Glendel forcing Darlene to get bitten.

When Darlene left the emergency room in Scottsboro, Joe and I drove to pick up my mother—and Glendel's—Annie Mance. From there we drove to Glendel's house. The front door was locked, not on the outside with a padlock as Darlene later said, but from the inside. We went in the other door at the front that leads into the bedroom. My mother was calling out, "Glendel, this is your mama." And we woke Glendel up. We could tell by his speech and the way he acted that he was either drunk or had been drinking heavily. We told him that Darlene was in the hospital. And he looked around and apparently didn't know she wasn't there. And he asked us, "What's the matter?" And we told him, "She's been serpent bit." He seemed completely surprised and said, "What do you mean serpent bit?"

Well, we started looking around to see what the situation was. We thought perhaps a serpent was loose in the house. The place was in an awful mess, as it usually was. Darlene certainly didn't take any prizes for keeping a clean house. But it didn't look like there had been any brawl. No furniture was turned over or drawers pulled out or things like that. Dirty clothes were scattered here and there—it was just in terrible shape. There was a vodka bottle on the floor, and there were several glasses around where they had obviously been drinking. One glass on the table still contained several inches of orange juice and vodka that smelled really strong. When I asked Darlene at the hospital about their drinking, she said, "Yes, but I just had a sup or two."

We didn't find any serpents loose. Darlene's purse was on or near one of the couches, and Glendel picked it up and looked through it. He didn't find anything unusual, put anything in it, or take anything out. He asked me to keep the purse for Darlene. But knowing her, I didn't want to be accused if something happened to be missing.

Then Joe and Glendel went out to the shed to check on the serpents and see if the boxes were open or whatever. Mother and I stayed inside. Nothing in the shed was out of order or looked disturbed—all the serpent cages were closed and padlocked. After checking everything, Joe and Glendel came back, and we continued to look around the house. Glendel found a note in the kitchen on top of the microwave. "What do you make of this?" he said, and that sort of thing. He didn't know what it was all about—and neither did we.

After we had been there all told about forty-five minutes, we got ready to leave and went outside. Glendel was standing there at the door as we drove off.

We took my mother to her house and went on home. Glendel, I think, went to get something to drink. Then he went to Mother's house and called over to Jackie's—Jackie is one of Glendel's daughters by his first wife and, at that time, was married to Kenneth Lee. Marty (Glendel and Darlene's son) was at Jackie's. I think what Glendel wanted to do was to get Marty, take him to the hospital, pick up Darlene, and go home. Jackie and Kenneth didn't want

Marty to leave; but Glendel got Marty, and I think he went by the Jackson County Hospital before driving on to Birmingham.

Anyway, Glendel drove to Birmingham hospital, and the police were waiting to pick him up. They arrested him for assault and took him to jail in Birmingham. Barbara (Glendel's and my sister) went to the jail and bailed him out. One of Darlene's sisters called us and asked if Glendel would try to return to the hospital again. We told her that he had gone on to bed and was asleep at his mother's house.

Joe and I didn't go to Birmingham. My brother David, however, was there at the emergency room at UAB Hospital when Darlene was admitted. He says that Darlene was bit only one time by only one serpent, and that was on the thumb. She told the doctor she'd been bitten by two different serpents, but the doctor brought out x-rays that showed the puncture of only one serpent bite. And the doctor told her that he could remove a little tissue around the bite to keep it from turning black, put in a couple of stitches; and soon she'd not be able to tell she'd been bitten. So that's what they did. And David said the surgery on her thumb was about an inch long. We called her several times while she was in the hospital; and on one of our calls, her sister told us that Darlene was in the whirlpool because she had had a reaction to the antivenom shot. When Darlene was released, her family told it that she was being protected in a place for abused women, but she went home with her mother. And later she stayed with her older brother and his wife in Rainsville.

At the trial we didn't hear the proceedings because we were in the witness room—but we were never called! We were the first ones after the emergency squad to see Darlene. We were also the first ones to see Glendel. We are responsible citizens with good jobs and reputation in the community—Joe is well known through various activities, like coaching kids' baseball teams. But neither of us was called to testify. Neither were his sons—almost no witnesses were called in his defense.

We didn't know at that time who all were called, because we were separated from the courtroom. But during one recess, we did speak to Gary Lackey at the water fountain. He told us that he wasn't going to call Glendel on the witness stand because Glendel couldn't get the days straight of when things happened, and he was afraid that the district attorney would turn all that around and make Glendel look like he was lying about everything. Glendel, however, had told Lackey, as well as us, that he wanted others to testify first and then he would go last. But Lackey didn't put Glendel on the stand, and he didn't call us.

We believe they had it in for Glendel. Even Lackey said so at first. When we went to his office and asked him if he would take the case, he picked up a newspaper on his desk and said, "I'll be glad to represent him. They're trying to railroad him. What they're saying right here in this newspaper shows that they're trying to railroad him." And they did.

Besides all that, Glendel could have plea bargained and been out of prison by now. We were outside Lackey's office before the trial was held—Glendel was with us—and Lackey said that if Glendel would plead guilty, he would get ten years but serve only three. He also told us that Glendel didn't have anything to worry about in winning the case. But Glendel said he wouldn't plea bargain because he wasn't guilty.

David Brewer and William Bynum

Newsmen

David Brewer (Chief, Jackson County Bureau, Huntsville Times)

There are actually two sides about this story, you know. People wondered about how much it was Glenn and how much it was Darlene. Some felt it was just as much her doing as Glenn's.

The women—like in the circuit court's office that I talked to regularly—they'd say, "He deserves what he got." You know, most people have a fear of snakes. And to them, the idea of forcing somebody to be bitten by a snake would be a traumatic and brutal thing to do to anybody. That probably prejudiced a lot of people right there.

My impression is that people for the most part seemed to be really embarrassed with all the publicity, the image of being just a bunch of barefoot Southerners with no plumbing, and that kind of thing.

And there was some concern about getting serpent handling out of Scottsboro. But it wasn't a wide-spread or major effort to get it out. The serpent handling was not that visible anyway. There was the place on Woods Cove Road; however, most of this activity was up around Macedonia or Powell Crossroads near Rainsville. I think it would be frowned upon around here—I can understand that. But I believe the people who feel that way are prejudiced to a large degree. They look down in a condescending manner, "Well, they're just poor. They're ignorant. They read everything verbatim. They take everything literally." I guess I was guilty of that myself, sort of inwardly at first.

53

And maybe there wasn't anything outward that you could see that was being done to move people out—just that attitude. If a situation came up like that again—I try to be sensitive about things like that anyway—but probably I would try to be even more sensitive.

Now, about Glenn's lawyer, Gary Lackey—he is kind of a political person. He is the county attorney. He represents the Jackson County Health Care Authority. I think he still represents the Cumberland Mountain Water Board. He is one that likes to get in and tackle issues. There's a lot of a sense of pride in Gary. He sort of pulled himself up by the bootstraps, worked himself up through college. And he's always been the common man's lawyer. He's against the old establishment here in town. It used to be the Word family: the Word Lumber Company, the old Word Theater up here in Hollywood—I don't know if the screen is still up—the Word Sawmill, Word Chevrolet. Of course it's all cut up now with family members, brothers and their descendants, dividing it all up. But that used to be the ruling power here in town. And Gary didn't go with that stream or that class of people. He's been trying to make a name for himself. That's what I mean about the political part. Gary's very political. He may say that he's not, but he is.

And after Gary defended Glenn, he was upset. He appealed the case, and he was kindly hurt by it. You know, Gary is very competitive. And like most lawyers, but Gary to an extreme, he does not like to lose—especially a case that had this much publicity. I mean, for Glenn to get a sentence like that . . .

I remember the first day that this story came up. There was a police officer I used to know, and he came in when all this began. He said, "Look, I got a story for you. You'll want to go up to the city dog pound and get a picture. I think you'll be interested in it." Then he proceeded to go on about what happened. And I said, "Ah, I guess so." (Of course the *Times* would be interested— I don't know what it was I had that night.) He said, "The police chief is still up there. And if you're lucky, you'll get up there and get a shot of him and that snake." Well, I got up there in about fifteen minutes. And, sure enough, I asked the police chief, Keith Smith, "Would you mind to hold this snake up?" And he held it up, and I took a picture of it—just a quick shot and I was on my way.

Then I guess that photo went everywhere around the world. We had somebody from the Economic Development Authority or somebody with the Industrial Development Board that happened to be visiting over in Hong Kong, trying to recruit some industry. And, lo and behold—I guess it was the next day—there was a laser AP photo of the police chief holding that snake up.

And I was the one who took the photo. "Golly," I was telling people, "I almost didn't go up there to take this shot."

And the interest that the story generated—I mean that's all people could talk about, was this snake and how this preacher forced his wife to get bit. I mean it was the talk of the town for a long time. And when Darlene went on *Sally Jessy Raphael*—the way she acted on the show—people probably found that more embarrassing than the original situation. It really made everybody come across as a bunch of hicks. That was the image being presented to the world.

You know we already had one situation, the Scottsboro Boys—it still continues. People have not let the town live that down at all. And I mean it drives the Economic Development director nuts whenever I write about something like this. He'll call me up and say, "You're not doing another story on this are you? You know we don't need that. We're trying to recruit some industry, and we don't need that. They're goin' to think everybody's like that." It just gets on his nerves.

William Bynum (Former Reporter/Managing Editor, Daily Sentinel, *Scottsboro)*

I was fairly well convinced that Glenn to some degree did what he was accused of doing. Maybe he didn't set out to kill Darlene. Maybe he just set out to put a good scare of God into her. But whether or not he was guilty is not the same question as whether or not justice was meted out. And I firmly believe that justice was not served with that trial. But from my experience it is a rare trial in Jackson County that sees justice done. There is such a good-old-boy system. The judge in this case is the "baddest" of the good old boys. He ruled the roost in the courthouse.

For one thing, Glenn obviously had a checkered past. And I know that the judge said that he sentenced him the only way he could according to the Habitual Offender Act, but that act was passed after Glenn's previous crimes. And I think the judge had a lot of leeway, and he chose to be excessive for whatever reason. I don't know why things happened as they did. But there was such a tight-knit relationship between the DA's office, the sheriff's department, the city police department, and the court system—and there has to be, in a way—but the court system needs to be separated to some extent from that whole process. I don't think the DA, the judge, and the sheriff or the chief investigator need to be having closed-door meetings before the trial takes place to decide how things are going to go. At the time of Glenn's trial, the court system down there just reeked of conspiracy, of working in tandem to achieve a common goal.

Now, why they would have wanted to nail Glenn Summerford, I don't know. Maybe he had done something to offend somebody in the circle of friends in the courthouse. It doesn't take much to get these people turned against you. Why pick on Glenn? I don't know. But I believe that it was an orchestrated attempt to do away with the man. It's almost like someone put a hit out on him because putting him in jail for ninety-nine years is the same as killing the man—he's out of the system, he's out of circulation, he's out of somebody's hair.

I'm not saying Glenn was an angel or saint or anything because obviously he had some problems, and maybe Darlene did too. But by the same token, I don't think anybody should have the power to decide: "Well, this guy needs to be done away with, needs to be put away somewhere"—and then orchestrate an attempt to do precisely that. I just don't think it's right. But as a reporter in Scottsboro for eight years, observing the Jackson County court system and the law enforcement (particularly the sheriff's department)—and then as a managing editor of that local paper for three years—I found the political system, the court system, and to a lesser degree the law enforcement system to be that corrupted.

When you get to Jackson County, Alabama, you might as well be stepping back fifty years in a time machine. You're stepping back into a time and place in which only a few people run the county. There's no real democracy. There are no real elections. There's no real court system. The elections and the courts are controlled by certain people empowered there.

Now, over the years since the Summerford trial, things have changed to some extent; for example, in the DA's office. But I don't think that the corruption there has been completely weeded out because you still have some of the key players that were in that office under Dwight Duke. They're still playing the good-old-boy game, the favor game. There's been change in the sheriff's department too, in part simply by being shoved into a different climate by force of the twentieth century. And the Scottsboro City Police Department adds a lot of credibility to the system. The city police are straightforward guys. They've been trained properly, and Keith Smith—I think he's still chief—is a good guy. He has managed to steer clear of becoming embroiled in that political system.

56

A lot of the power down there has shifted out of the good-old-boys' hands into those of more progressive-thinking people. It's a completely different system down there, I think, than it was when Glenn was being tarred and feathered. It's not completely 100 percent better—it's not well—but its health is improving.

But when you get into the courthouse, particularly during the time when Glenn was being tried, that's another matter. For example, the circuit clerk was involved up to his neck in wrongdoing. We uncovered and reported on a broad case of ticket fixing. Say, if a ticket was written for a $100 fine—well, whoever received the ticket could pay under the table the circuit clerk or one of his assistants a quarter of that amount, and the ticket would be done away with. That kind of stuff is still rampant down there. There are things that you just don't think of happening anymore in a modern age, but they are.

I would never live in Jackson County again, never. It's kind of scary living there because you just never know—anybody can come up and arrest you for anything, anytime, and you're gone. If they want you, they got you. Personally, I never had any trouble except I did received a couple of threatening notes—from whom I don't know—under my windshield wipers on a couple of different occasions. Once was covering the hospital board fiasco, and once was covering the county commission deal that was going on at the time.

Scottsboro was not a place for a serious reporter to be because even the publisher of the paper at the time didn't want us to be doing investigative reporting. He wanted the front page to be "the Chamber of Commerce bragging rights"—we're talking about what the Chamber of Commerce has done and how great tourism is growing and Goose Pond is doing. It was a constant fight to get any real editorial content into the paper. More and more, unless you're at a big city paper—which doesn't appeal to me—you're not allowed to be a real journalist. You're basically a PR person for the community.

Now, about Gary Lackey—he's a friend of mine, although he's probably not the most honest person I've ever met. But there's never any doubt where he's coming from. And he doesn't try to fool anybody into thinking that he's the most honest man in the world. He is what he is. He's a scrapper. He'll fight for his client to the very last. And I've seen him walk the line between right and wrong.

But in the Summerford case, I think he did the best job he could to defend Glenn. I think it was an untenable situation. I think it was an unwinnable case, and Gary knew that. He knew the deck was stacked against him, and I don't think he was willing to put his career on the line for that case. I don't think Gary was involved in a "conspiracy"—I think Gary was just a victim of the "conspiracy." I think it was made clear to him what the outcome of the trial was going to be—guilty. And the hammer was going to fall on Glenn.

I may be dramatizing it too much, but Gary made a vicious stand in a situation years later that I was fortunate to cover for the paper. He was voted in by a rebellious, slim majority of the Jackson County Hospital Board as their attorney. And they made a stand to prevent another faction of the board from selling the county hospital to a huge national conglomerate owned by Senator Frist. The faction of the board that wanted to sell the hospital attempted to deceive the public by hiding their intentions. And the other faction (that barely had a majority on the board by one person) fired the existing attorney, who was trying to make the sale all come together. Well, this caused a turmoil, a public outcry—it was a bitter battle. And they hired Gary Lackey, and Gary and these guys fought the establishment crew and saved the hospital.

Gary at one point was questioned as to why he was taking all the heat. I think a reporter for the Huntsville newspaper asked him why in the world he would put himself in the line of fire for a cause like that. I can't quote him exactly, but Gary said something to the effect that in the past he'd always taken the easy way out and done things the way the establishment wanted because he knew that he could make a career for himself if he did. And he said, "Well, it comes a time when you just have to stand up for what you believe in and fight." I couldn't help but think, Well, he's making up for the Glenn Summerford thing—trying to. I'm not sure it would balance out in the long run because there was not a life involved in the hospital dispute: it was a political entity that didn't want to go away. But he was standing up and fighting for what he really believed in, and he fought hard and long. And they won eventually. I was pretty proud of Gary there.

But in the Summerford case I think, like I said, he was just in an untenable situation. He didn't do a good job. He folded in. And I can't excuse him for it, but I can understand. At that time, you didn't fight Judge Campbell; you didn't fight Dwight Duke. If they told him what was going to happen, and they needed to write it out—at that point in his career and in that point in time—he probably didn't think he had a choice. The political system at the time was rough. If you were an attorney, a doctor, or even a professional man, you didn't cross these people because they would ruin you—they would destroy your career.

Our situation at the paper was that we were forced by the publisher just to cover the trial. We never did any investigative reporting on that particular

David Brewer and William Bynum

case, never did any background work. We did the story after the bite happened, and I don't think our paper did another story on that case until the trial started—which I hated because it was building up all the way toward the trial. Any paper worth its salt would have had deep background stories on all the key players, including the attorneys and the DA, looking at all the background. And we might have uncovered connections.

Now, as far as the relevance of serpent handling to Glenn's conviction—I never had the impression that serpent handling was a big deal to the people in Scottsboro. It was an oddity. It was something different. The community took it in stride for what it was—a small, cultist sort of religious practice. They didn't particularly like the fact that it was in Scottsboro, but they didn't have anything against the people. For the most part, the folks taking part in this activity were nice people—they worked, they shopped. It may possibly have played a small part in affecting the jury. But there was never any reason given to the jury to find Mr. Summerford innocent. It was all about *his* guilt. And one of the few defense witnesses, the Flippo woman, was not taken seriously by anybody. It was obviously a last-ditch attempt to create some reasonable doubt. The gallery knew it. The jury knew it. She was never taken seriously. If the jury would have been given any room for reasonable doubt, I don't think the serpent-handling thing would have outweighed it. If they were given any other scenario, any other possible explanation for the incident, I think they could have come to a different decision. I don't think the serpent handling precluded an innocent verdict or acquittal.

As a matter of fact, Jackson County has a lot of different religious groups, and it's pretty open-minded as far as religion goes—Protestants and Catholics work together. Serpent handling is a little odder practice than most, but there are the people at Skyline who still wear their hair in a bun. They look like they're nineteenth century too, and they're not ridiculed. People are not prejudiced against them. They're all a part of the same community.

Serpent handling just wasn't that big a factor except that it created all the media frenzy. We covered the story because it was a local case, and it was pretty interesting. I still don't understand why the *New York Times* covered it. Except it gave them a chance to ridicule the South a little bit with some flamboyant prose about the snakes and the people who pick them up and worship. The snake-handling trial was an interesting case, and it was an odd trial. But it wasn't big news in Jackson County. It made our front page, but it wasn't the sensational event that you would have thought it was—the Manson murders or the Son-of-Sam thing all over again. I mean, the woman was snakebit. It just blew my mind that it became such a big national story and that it's still generating all this interest—for example, the A&E program. That story was not worthy of a *City Confidential* episode. You could tell because they had to pad it with so much history of Scottsboro. The other trial that was going on at the time—of the murdered child—created more turmoil in the community than the snake handlers did. Everyone was just appalled about that case.

But as far as Glenn is concerned, he was a victim of the system. And I feel he was not important enough, not interesting enough, to really draw the attention that he drew and the level of justice, if you will, that was aimed at him. There's something there. I would love to know—why him, why go to all that trouble to get rid of him? There's no telling what the connection was. Who dropped the dime and said, "Look, this guy needs to be put away"? It just happened.

Another interesting fact is the length of time between Glenn's arrest and trial. I think the typical time in Jackson Country for a major offense is nine to twelve months. This trial took place in February after the arrest in October—justice doesn't move that fast in Jackson County. That in itself is telling. For a court case to go to trial that quickly after the event—somebody was moving it on through the court system, taking it, and personally pushing it through. That just reeks. Murder trials even didn't get to trial that quickly in Jackson County. That's unreal.

And then there's the short duration of the trial itself—when the conclusion is preordained, why drag it out? And at this point, they didn't even care about *image*. They didn't say, "Let's stretch it out two weeks to make it look good." They didn't care if it looked good or not. The attention of the media might have scared them a little bit, but this case didn't get the media attention that would scare "conspirators." The press was there for the entertainment value, not the investigative.

I know that Summerford, if not framed, was at least railroaded. And I've always wondered why.

David Brewer and William Bynum

Glendel B. Summerford

In Earlier Years

I don't want anyone be offended by what I say. I used to have a sign in church:

> If you meet me and forget me, you've lost nothin'.
> If you meet Jesus and forget him, you've lost everything.

I feel that a-way. In my lifetime, there's a lot of people that I met that I forgot. I put all the past out of my mind when I got the Holy Ghost. When I really got right with God, I tried to put all my past out of my mind. So whatever I tell will be some things that probably I can't even prove. It might sound like a fairy tale, but I've did a lot of things.

I was born in Jackson County. My name on my birth certificate is "Glendel B. Summerford"—"B" is for Buford. On my Social Security card, it's "Glendon B." Most people if they use my first name, I guess, call me "Glenn."

My mother and my daddy's separated. My mother, she'd been married once before. She had a daughter, and her first husband had took her. I didn't see her until we both was grown—or she was grown. She was older than me. I didn't ever see my daddy till I was fifteen years old. I didn't know who I was, you know. I got twelve brothers and sisters on my daddy's side, six brothers and six sisters. I got one brother and four sisters on my mother's side. My oldest sister on my mother's side, she got killed out in Texas.

Anyway, I growed up thinkin' nobody didn't care nothin' about me. My mother, bless her soul, she's real good mother now. And I love her, you know, more than anything—I always did love her—but when her and my daddy

If you meet me, and forget me, you've lost nothing, but if you meet Jesus and forget Him you've lost everything
by: Bro Glenn
Sis. Darlene

Sign in Glenn's church. Photograph by Ken Elkins.

separated, well, she didn't want to lose me because she'd already lost her first daughter. She'd go from place to place and keep me hid out, keep my daddy from findin' me. Of course, I didn't know why I was goin' so many places as I was growin' up, you know; but I learned it later. And she give me away two or three times. She really wadn't givin' me away, she's just placin' me somewhere so he couldn't find me. But to me, she was givin' me away.

So I growed up rough. And when you grow up like that, you have to take a backseat to ever'thing, you know. At Christmas, you take the back seat. You take the hand-me-downs to everything. So I never did want any of my kids to grow up like 'at.

I'm Native American, you know. I'm probably three quarters Indian. My daddy was Indian. My mother—her mother was full Cherokee, and her daddy was like probably half. My mother used to be real high tempered. If she got mad at you, she'd hit you with anything she had in her hand, you know. But I was always quiet. I stayed by myself all the time. And other kids would want to pick on me 'cause I was quiet.

Glendel B. Summerford

But anyway, my mother got married again to my stepdaddy. Soon—I was just small—he seen that everybody picked on me. I'd have to fight a lot, but I didn't know how to fight. I had cousins that worked me over pretty good. And other kids would work me over pretty good, but I'd still tough it with them, you know.

My stepdaddy—he just come in out of the war—he asked me did I want to live with him? And I said, "Yeah." So I's happy. I told ever'body I had a daddy then. To me, he was closer to me than he was to his real children. My stepdaddy stayed overseas thirty-six months, and he was in Special Forces. He's a war hero, but nobody didn't know it but me until he died. And then they found out that he'd been wounded several times.

But since he was in Special Forces, he knew special arts in fightin'—how to fight, how to kill with just his hands. And he told me, said, "Son, when you get a little bit older," he said, "I'll learn you how to fight. I'll learn you how to win." And he said, "But if you ever fight any of your family," he said, "you'll answer to me." So I looked forward for him to learn me how to fight.

I guess I's probably eight, nine, or ten years old when he said, "Son, you want to go huntin' with me?" He was about half Cherokee Indian too. I said, "Yeah." So we went huntin'. He carried me down to the woods where this log crossed the creek. And he told me to go ahead. And when I went out on it—it was an old saplin' pole, you know; it was limber—he kind of bumped it a few times. I looked back and dropped down on it. He went to laughin': "I see the first thing I got to do is learn you how to hold your balance."

Then he said, "You ready to start learnin' how protect yourself?" I said, "Yes." So he started learnin' me how to have my balance and how to swim. Me and him swim ever' day; and when he wasn't workin', we be swimmin'. And we'd cut poles, and he learn me to throw poles 'cause we didn't have any weights or anything, you know. He'd gettin' me build up. Then he started to learn me how to fight. He'd be like a sparrin' partner with me.

So he told me, said, "We goin' go out to you cousins." He said, "You goin' whup all three of 'em." He said, "You not goin' to start nothin'. If you start anything, I'm goin' whup you." But he said, "When they get on you this time," he said, "you goin' whup 'em." He said, "You ain't quittin'. If you quit, I'm not goin' he'p you—I'm not goin' train you no more. I'll be finished if you quit. But you goin' whup 'em. I know you are."

They was three of them, but they was two of them that I'd fight with all the time. But one of them was a whole lot older. When I first got there, we played around—we's happy to see one another. And after while the fight started. So I whupped one of them. But when the second one of them seen that that one was whupped, he was kind of puzzled. He didn't know what happened 'cause instead of tryin' to wrestle, I was goin' at him, you know. Then the biggest one, the third one, he run in and was goin' he'p 'em. And he pushed me down—I wasn't no size no way. So I just grabbed him around the leg, sunk them teeth in his leg. And he went to hollerin' fer "Daddy," you know. Anyway, they respected me then.

So as I growed up with my stepdaddy, he was more than a daddy to me. He was my best friend, 'cause I didn't have any friends hardly. I'd stay with him ever'where he went, except when he went to work. Then when he'd let me, I'd go to work with him. He'd take me fishin', huntin' all the time. And he learned me how to take care of myself in any way.

When I started to school, why, I didn't know my name. But I went to school in his name—Mance—what little I went in school. Mama, she'd always want to move. Ever'time we'd be settle' down, she'd want to move. She had it in her to move, so we moved from one place to the other'n. I didn't get much schoolin'. I's fightin' boys growin' up, and I guess I just kinda took it out all my life, all the way up. And I got into boxin' and tried that for a while. And I learn I could make a little money by sparrin' out, you know.

So I left home when I was fifteen years old. And I was in Chicago. I met different people that was into fightin' and all. Some of them took a likin' to me, some of them didn't. But anyway, I had a cousin who was into all kind of stuff back in them days with the syndicate and all that, gangsters. They'd have fights in warehouses and in different places. I's just young, so I thought I'd get in on that. I'd fight a grown man, you know, as long as he wasn't too big. We'd fight with the small gloves. And I got pretty good.

At fifteen years old, I's a pretty good man. I was big and husky and stout too 'cause I worked hard all my life. I wanted to win the Golden Gloves, and I had several fights towards the Golden Gloves. I wanted to go on and be a professional. But, you know, it takes a lot of money and a lot of backin'.

When I met my real daddy, I didn't know what I's goin' to say to him. He was on the mountain, and my aunt had told me about him. She called him and had him to come and meet me. He was really excited 'bout meetin' me, and he wadn't like what I'd heared. He wanted to take me and introduce me to all my brothers and sisters. And he'd carry me around, introduce me to ever'body.

So when I got ready to leave, he didn't want me to. He asked why I was wantin' to leave. And I told him, I said, "Well, I'm gettin' in the fightin' business.

64

Left: Annie Mance, Glenn's mother.

Below: Carolyn Esslinger, one of Glenn's half sisters.

I'm fightin' with gloves, and I make a little money that way." He asked where I wanted to go, and I told him. He said, "What does a bus ticket cost?" I told him sixteen dollars—I won't never forget it. And he said, "Well, if you goin' live that kind of life," he said, "you'll learn what you'll want to do later on. I'm not goin' try to stop you." So he give me sixteen dollars, counted me out sixteen dollars. He said, "I want to pay your way, if that's what you want to do." Then he told me he put money in the bank for me and all. But I never did go back for it. I made my livin' on my own. I thought about that many a time.

Later I moved from Chicago back to Florida with my stepdaddy and then back to Alabama—moving back and forth. And I didn't see my real father no more for a long time. But anyway, I'd been trainin' hard and workin' out real hard. And I'd already had a lot of fights in Florida, Alabama, and Tennessee. So I made connections, and I went back to Chicago and had a lot of fights up there. Then I come back to Alabama. I'd won a new car fightin' in Chicago. I's the only young man, I guess, at that time that was driving a new car. I won a beautiful '56 Ford. And I drove it back to Alabama.

I stayed, I guess, a couple months with my stepdaddy again. He'd work out with me. One night my uncle was there, my mother's brother. I was never bad to drink—I'd take care of myself and all. But my uncle had made him some homebrew, and he told me he had some over there in the woods. So I said, "Let me take you over there." And we went over there. I got to sippin', and I got pretty drunk too.

Then we come in where my mama and my stepdaddy lived. They lived up on the hill, and the house was agin the side of a mountain. You'd drive up to the house, get out, and you just walk in the back door into the kitchen. And then you go to the left, you was in a livin'room—then on through and you was in one bedroom. You come back out and went to another door, you's in another bedroom.

We'd stopped in the kitchen. We's talking pretty loud, you know, and my stepdaddy said, "You-all boys, quieten it down in there a little bit." So we just got louder. And he come into the livin' room, and I went from the kitchen into the livin' room where he was.

On the front of the house it's high off the ground. You could just walk under it. In the livin' room there was a winder, and it was way down there to the ground—ten/fifteen foot, I guess. Well, when I walked into the living room, he said: "You and Sam, go ahead in there and go to bed." My uncle, he mouthed off too. And he's pretty rough, my uncle was.

Glendel B. Summerford

I told my stepdad, I said, "I believe I'll just whup you. Now, I ain't never whupped you." And he laughed, and he said, "Why don't you just try." So I cut down at him, cut down at him pretty hard. And he caught me by the wrist and under the arm and throwed me through the winder. And I hit the ground with the flat of my back, and it knocked all the breath out of me. Hit so hard, it made me sick at my stomach—been drinkin' that old homebrew. So I crawed up under the floor there. And I hadn't much more got under the floor, and I hear my uncle in there. He was tellin' him, "You ought not a-done that boy that way." Then directly he come through the winder.

So next morning pretty early, why, my stepdaddy was out there kickin' me on the foot. "Get up from there, boy. Let's cut some pulpwood. I need you to help me today." And I said, "Have I got to?" He said, "Yeah, come on out." He knew he didn't hurt me, you know. And he knew I couldn't whup him. Anyway, we'd play like that a lot. We'd have a lot of tussles.

I come out from that floor, and I was sick. My uncle was sick. And my stepdaddy, he carried us over there where he had some pulpwood to cut. And it had been burnt, you know, old black ashes and stuff. We worked with him all that week. Then after that week was up, I told him, I said, "Why, I gotta go. I'm a-go to Florida."

So I went to Florida. Brother Uly had went to Florida, and he was one of my best friends. So I got down there and got in connection with Brother Uly. Then I went on down to Immokalee. I was wantin' to make some connections down there to have some fights in warehouses 'cause I could make me a hundred fifty, two/three hundred dollars, you know, if I won.

But I couldn't never make any connections, so finally I just got me a job in a warehouse. I was stackin' produce in a box car. A lot of Mexicans worked there. So the talk got out, you know, and we had a fight lined out for when we got off. I won the fight, but I got a broke rib. I got pretty sick, but I didn't tell Brother Uly I had a broke rib. I wasn't able to go to work next day. But I had me about five hundred dollars in my pocket, plus I had money comin' from my pay day. So Brother Uly—he was tryin' to live right—he prayed fer me, him and his wife did. Then I got to feeling pretty good, good enough I could travel. So I eased over there and collected my money. I come back and told them it was time for me to go again. I told them I's going to Alabama.

But I went back to Illinois when I left there and got in connection with my cousin. One of the trainers that I met was really from Alabama. He knew me when I was grownin' up, Sammy Baker. He was a good fighter, and he give me a lot of help. I guess at one time he would have been world champion. He made connection with me, and I went from Chicago to New York, to a place called Glassie or Glasgow, down in the Bronx.

I met Joe Louis over 'ere, and he gave me a few pointers. I was tryin', you know, to get where I could get it with the big boys. I's done gettin' a little more age on me. I had a few fights, and I was doin' pretty good. And I met another old fighter, Archie Moore. He give me a few pointers. So I was really comin' on strong. By then I'd probably had twenty-five to thirty fight under my belt. I's probably close to eighteen. And I was gettin' old enough where that I didn't have to have nobody forgin' names, to sign fer me and stuff.

We had a fight in Chicago, and we was down there about 101st or somewhere. Back off over there, they had some warehouses, and we had a fight there. Well, really, I think we had three fights that night. But it was winner take all, and I won the whole jackpot. And they had a big gang fight outside. And I got my skull busted and went to the hospital.

As I got out of the hospital, the doctor told me that I couldn't fight no more. My fightin' was over. Said if I got knocked out, well, I wouldn't never gain conscious. It brought the memory back in my mind where I had been knocked unconscious when I was small. And doctor said I was goin' die; but when I come to, I had an uncle that was prayin' for me.

I was goin' go after the belt, but now I was out of the fightin', professional. Course I really didn't get out of all the fightin', but I got my mind off of being a professional 'cause what the doctor told me. So I come back to Alabama and started cuttin' pulpwood and live with my stepdaddy. I wouldn't tell nobody but him what had happened to me. And he told me that I didn't need to be fightin' with gloves 'cause the gloves give you more of a jar. He said I'd probably be okay, but I's gettin' old enough to settle down, you know, and didn't need to be fightin' like that.

But I had another friend here in Alabama—his name was Joe Whitmore—and me and him got to linin' up some fights back there on the mountain. See, there'd be a lot of Mexicans come in. He would line up the fights, and then he would bring me in. They would put up fifty dollars or hundred dollars or whatever—and winner take all. They's couple places out there, some old schools and stuff where Mexicans would move in—big bunches of them whenever they would be pickin' up taters or doin' farm work out there, on times of year they'd go through. So I won several fights like that. I went, like, Florida, Alabama, and Georgia, Tennessee, Texas, Louisiana, St. Louis (Missouri). I fought all over them places.

Glendel B. Summerford

Doris Summerford and Glenn's and her sons Bill, Michael, and Joe.

But I come back then to Alabama, and I settled down. I met Doris and got married, my first wife. I was about nineteen, I think. It was at Scottsboro where we got married. So we lived in Scottsboro for a while, and that old part of me's still wantin' to fight, you know. I set me up a ring, and we sparred out a lot. I had good friends, you know, and we'd fight. But no money passin' hands or nothin'. So I decided to go back to Florida and make connections down there. It was all illegal anyway.

I was workin' at this dairy farm, and they had a fight set up out there on the riverside in a warehouse. I'd got another guy to work in my place, and I went over 'ere. Well, I got through that fight, but I got another rib broke. It punctured a lung. And when I come in, why, I told my wife I'd got kicked by a cow. I didn't want her to know what was goin' on. The money that I had, they thought it was a bonus.

And I got to the point of death. I laid on the couch, and my aunt and them come over to pray fer me. But I wouldn't let nobody pray fer me 'cause I didn't live right, you know. So I laid there about two weeks, and I had to go in hospital intensive care. I got to the point where they give me up to die. And I couldn't eat nothin'; I couldn't drink anything. It was like floatin' in water on the inside. One of my lungs was full of blood, and the other'n was fillin' up with blood. And they couldn't operate on me. They was goin' take one lung out or somethin', but then the other'n startin' fillin' up with blood, so they couldn't do nothin' about it. The doctor called 'em in and said, "This man's goin' home. There ain't nothin' I can do." Said, "You'll goin' have to sign ever'thing. He's got three days to live." And he said, "I done had all the specialists to check him and ever'thing."

So they checked me out, and I went home. Mama called Alabama and got these prayin' people to pray fer me. And God healed me. I went back to the doctor 'cause they wouldn't let me go back to work till I went back to the doctor. And he called me in there. He said, "You can't be the same man." And I say, "Well, I am." They x-ray me and ever'thing. He called them in there and showed 'em the X rays before, when my lungs was fillin' up with blood. Then he showed us the X rays then, how white and clear they was. He said, somethin' happened to me—he didn't know what, but keep doin' it. And he let me go. And that was before I ever started living right.

Then I went down to Immokalee near the Everglades—course I lived all in there with the Seminoles. Me and the Seminole chief, Francisco Osceola, was blood brothers, you know. And like I say, I's raised all in there, in Alabama, and ever'where else. So I wanted to go back down there and take my wife. I wanted her to meet my Indian people, you know, like family to me. I really never had a family, tell the truth, except my stepdad. So when I got down there, I met with 'em. But they didn't want to meet her. And that hurt me real bad. So I never seen Francis for years after that until I got married again and went back.

But me and Doris stayed in Florida awhile, and my friend Sammy Rollins was with me. He went ever'where I went. He was always by my side. Anyway, we was goin' get a fight set up. But we couldn't never make connections. They done changed some things, so I didn't do any fightin'.

We couldn't get no work to do much, and we got in such bad shape, we had to call my wife's daddy and borrow money to come home. So I didn't go on a wild thing like that no more. We settled down. We had our family and raised them up. Different times I'd meet people would know me, but I was always fightin' under different names 'cause I didn't never want to bring it into my family after I got married.

I went up to Jackson County, and me and my cousin and another boy got arrested. These women lived in this house, and they'd have gamblin' and all ever' weekend. So we was goin' over there to have a fight. When we got over there, there wadn't nobody there, the gamblers and all. So the other boys walked in and looked around, and we leave. Somebody sees my car leave—I had a red-and-white Crown Victoria Ford, and it stood out, you know. And somebody who knew the car knew me. They was couple stores up there, and we'd stopped at one of the stores and bought somethin' on the way out. So that's how they knew who it was. And the next thing I know, somebody had a warrant for me for second-degree burglary.

So I got sent to prison for eighteen months. When I was at prison down there at Draper, well, I met some guys that I'd met in different states. And they knew I could fight. Now, I'm five-eight and weigh about 170, but I used to weigh about 225. They had a couple of bullies down there was good fighters. And they's gettin' a carton cigarettes a week, the winner was. I didn't know what the deal was—ever' week I was takin' the cigarettes, and then the guys was gamblin' on the side. Back then they had money. That's one thing I never did do was gamble, but they would gamble for me, you know. So I'd get the carton of cigarettes, plus I'd get me ten or fifteen dollar. That'd hold me over pretty good. I fought for about five or six weeks.

Then the warden stopped me. He wouldn't let me fight no more. He called me up to his office—had a officer come and bring me up there. I thought there might have been a problem at home 'cause I didn't ever see none of my family—they wadn't able to come see me. When I got up there, well, I walked in. And I won't never forget him. He was a big warden. He got me by the arm, and he said, "Well, Glenn, your fightin' is over." I think, What you goin' do with me . . . put me in lockup? And he had some papers layin' on his desk, and he walked on around, and then he's sittin' there behind his desk. He said—he pointed his pencil at me—he said, "I found out all about you. You can't fight no more here." He said, "If you want to help some of the guys train, you can train. But you can't get back in the ring—not to fight." And I said, "Why?" And he said, "Don't even ask. You through." He said, "If a officer finds you in the ring with gloves on," said, "you goin' to the dog house." I said, "Okay." So I didn't fight no more.

Next thing I knew, they give me custody and sent me to Ft. Payne Road Camp. But I had knocked out about five straight. I got one tooth knocked out, you know, jaw tooth. I've had my jaw broke. I've had my nose broke. I've had these bones above my eyes broke, broke down—I had 'em fall all way down. And I've had my hands all broke up. Of course my hands used to be real big. I used to have more scars on my knuckles and hands than most people have. But when I went to Ft. Payne Road Camp, my fightin' was over, and my family could come see me there.

That was the first time I'd seen Jackie, my first little girl. She was six months old, you know, pretty as a picture. I had a good wife. She'd stay home and take care of the kids. My stepdaddy, he was probably one of the best men that I ever knew in my life. He'd take care of my family while I was in prison. He was just that kind of man. And him and my mother, they'd take care of 'em.

Anyway, I got out of prison, and I had statewide custody. I'd go anywhere in the state of Alabama, hauling tile and stuff, buildin' bridges, and first one thing and the other. I worked real hard, and the warden, he liked me real well. So I went up for parole, and I made parole. So I started work for Word's sawmill down there. I worked at Word's for pretty good while. I still had that fightin' in my blood, but I was keepin' it hid. So I decided that I wanted to do some coon huntin' and try to get fightin' out of my blood. I got me some coon dogs, and I started trainin' dogs and working at Word's. I was wantin' to start me a business on my own, but I didn't have the money.

I was just barely makin' ends meet, so I finally got me a fight set up. I made me four/five hundred dollars. And I changed my job. So I was comin' up pretty good. They had a school house up there near Fackler, back up in some old roads back there. A lot of young guys and older guys, too, go up 'ere and train, fight. I decide I wanted to look it over, you know. So I checked it out. I had me one fight up there and made me a couple hundred dollars. I'd still be workin', too, and savin' my money up.

Then my cousin wanted me to move to Paint Rock. So I'd got me another job at the rock crusher down there. And Sammy, he's still with me, you know. He's like a friend that's so close to you, where you go, he's always there. So he's workin' for the rock crusher, too, and he helps me line these fights up, sometime. But my cousin, Bill Busby, had a little house there, pretty-nice little house, so I moved in.

By this time, years is goin' by, you know. We had another little girl, I think she was eighteen months old then, close to it. We'd had a couple of fights set up in a big garage, and I won both of them. Sometimes the fight was in a ring, sometimes it was just ever'body standing around in a circle. I had another fight set up over at Gurley. He was a pretty big fight, big bully, you know; and he done whupped ever'body, just about it. I took that fight. And then after that, I made a lot of enemies 'cause this guy that I whupped, he had a lot of friends all around there—made a lot of enemies.

Somethin' came up about this guy's having a friend at New Hope, couldn't be whupped. So Sammy put a little money on it. Him and I had another friend, Kenneth Smith—he died since I've been in prison—he would put a little money on it too, you know. Anyway, they had it set up, and I won it. After I won it, well, then I was makin' more enemies than I wanted. Know

Glendel B. Summerford

what I mean? It was kind of catchin' up to me. My wife knew I fought a lot, but she didn't know really a lot of this stuff I was doin'.

One night I come in from work. It was in wintertime, and it was pretty late when I come in. My wife fix me somethin' to eat. And my little girl, she sit down there with me, you know. She was just a daddy's girl for real. She'd had asthma, and I'd sit up with her a lot at night. My wife, she would too. But no matter what time of night I come in, my little girl would sit up with me.

My house caught afire. I knew that one of my enemies set it afire. I was layin' on the floor asleep in the room where the boys was. Junior, my oldest son, he woke me up. At this point, I'm lookin' up, and flames's all in the house. I jump up and grab a TV and throw it through the winder. Couldn't get to no other door. I come into the bedroom waking their mother up—the two room's real close together. And I'd been doin' mechanic work that night at the garage, and I have on two sets of clothes—if it hadn't of been, I wouldn't never got as many as I got out alive.

My wife jumped up, and she was handin' the kids to me, and I'm trying to set 'em out the winder the best I can. As I could grab one, I'd throw 'em out. I didn't have no other choice. I don't know who I set out first or last, but I'm gettin' 'em out 'cause the house is fallin' in already.

My wife had a kind of a nylon nightgown or like a negligee, but it was long. I grabbed my wife, and she was on fire. Her clothes just melted and stuck to her. I had to, like, tear part of her clothes off. I mean it was stickin' to her. I couldn't even tear 'em off. I thought she'd handed all the kids to me, and I'd put 'em all out, and she was the last one. I just grabbed her and throwed her through the winder. And when I throwed her out, she, like, hung on to my hand. And as she went out, I just fell out with her. I hit the ground, the flat of my back—Oh, man, what a cool feelin' this is—my clothes, you could just pull off pieces.

My wife couldn't say nothin'—she was like burn all over. She was a real pretty woman, you know. I put her in the car, and she looked awful. I'm countin' the kids. I'm missin' one. I make a dive for the winder. And just as I run for the winder and I start up, well, my cousin Bill Busby was there—he'd weigh about 300 pound—he helt me, wouldn't let me get in. And the house fell in.

I had a '56 Ford then with a four-speed transmission, three carburetors on it—I put money in cars when I had it. Anyway I didn't have no keys. My little girl that was burnt was playin' with the keys the last time I'd seen 'em. A lot of people come around, but like no one was noticin' us. Ever'body was lookin' at the fire.

And I grabbed . . . my car had speakers in the back and in the doors . . . and for some reason or 'nother . . . I don't know why I even thought of it . . . I just grabbed one of those speaker wires and just jerked it. I peeled it with my teeth—I had pretty good teeth—and I tied it on the battery and hooked it on the coil. I kicked the car out of gear and pushed it off by myself. And when it cranked, why, I had pushed it half a block, just about it. So you could tell about what kind of man I was. I had all the rest of my kids in there. I'm in like a daze, too, with what I'm goin' through 'cause I know what I'm leavin', you know—it's nothin' I can do.

So I headed to the hospital. They had already called the ambulance and fire truck before I'd ever left there. And I was already through Paint Rock, done went through Lim Rock, and was on that long stretch for Scottsboro when I passed the ambulance and the fire truck. The police car—they said I was goin' so fast when I went by till he turned around and couldn't catch me. He never did get in sight, or I never did see him.

I went on and pulled down in the hospital. We's all full of smoke. I know God had his hands over me all my life, you know, *now*. But I didn't know it *then*. So they put my wife in the hospital and checked all my other kids. Jackie and Charlotte, they had a little burnt places on 'em. I didn't have nowhere to go 'cept to my stepdaddy's. And I knew it would be fine with him. So I took my kids up there, and Doris stayed in the hospital.

There is some stuff I need to tell that connects with this, so I'll stop right there and then come back to that part. I got to my stepdaddy's house . . . and, see, my mother's daughter, she'd just got killed a few days before then in Texas. And my wife's grandmother—that thought so much of me and my wife too, and that we was so close to (she's a real old Indian woman, you know, just a real good old granny mother; we thought wadn't nothin' like her)—she just had died. And we just had buried her, like, three days before this had happened.

Then I'm there with my stepdaddy and my mother. Friends and families come in from everywhere, you know. And it's puttin' a lot of pressure on my stepdaddy, and I know there's nothin' I can do. He went down to my house that burnt. I had a couple of hounds down there, and he brought 'em back. Ever'-thing else burnt up. I knew he was hurt worst than I ever seen him. People's callin' and wantin' to give us stuff and help us. But my stepdaddy, he used to keep my money fer me—like the money in these fights and all, I'd get it to him, and he'd keep it no matter what. So I had a little bit. And we had to have the funeral for my little girl.

Glendel B. Summerford

Anyway, my stepdaddy told me, "Let's take the pickup. Don't you go back up to the hospital right now." Said, "Go with me. I want to go over there and get you a deepfreeze. I done got you a house up here." Then we went and put me some stuff in the house. Right after that, my stepdaddy said, "You go on to the hospital now," and said, "I believe ever'thing's goin' be all right." Said, "You take care of ever'thing. I know what you goin' do. And you're man enough to do it." But he said, "Not but one thing you can't give back anybody, and that's their life—you can't give it back to 'em." He said, "I taught you how to be a man, and I've taught you how to whup any man alive, just about. I've taught you ever'thing I know. You go on and do what you've got to do. But always remember, you can't give life back if you take it." He knew what was in my mind about my house.

So I went on to the hospital. And in my mind I was never goin' to fight no more. I was through with that prize fightin'. I was makin' money; but, you know, it just wasn't the right kind of money. But I go in the hospital, and they had my wife covered with this thing—you couldn't touch her, you know. They just let me stay a few minutes at a time. So I's waiting for 'em to tell me, she was goin' to live or die. My brother-in-law, his name is Junior too. He come to the hospital and got me and said, "Glenn, I need you to come and go with me." I stepped outside, and my daddy-in-law, Doc—I had a real good daddy-in-law and a good mother-in-law—he said, "Glenn, your stepdaddy just died."

It's just like ever'thing that was set up in my life, you know—just like when things start goin' right, it would just crumble. Look like I lost ever'thing that mattered. I had my other kids, and that's all that kept me goin'. So after that—me and Doris—things just wadn't ever the same. We didn't never fuss and fight hardly after that. We'd have a few short words, but we never did blame one another. I felt it just wadn't the same. I know she probably still loves me, and I still love her like a sister. And we even had some more kids, you know.

We lived together there for a while longer. Then she told me one day, she said, "Glenn," she said, "I'm go stay with my mother. She's in bad shape." Then she would go stay like a few weeks at a time. So me and her, we separated under good conditions—I could see or be with the kids or get 'em at any time, and I's gonna help raise them.

When me and my wife separated, I just got tired. My life was just—I don't know—just run-down like. I worked, and I couldn't make ends meet. I never took dope in my life or nothin', but it was just like nothin' didn't matter, you know. I loved my kids, and I'd keep workin', tryin' to make ends meet.

Anyway, I started runnin' around with different women. It wadn't Darlene, not at this time—I just started runnin' around with different women.

My wife, she knew that I was runnin' around. I knew it hurt her, but she wasn't the type to give me no hard time. She was a good woman. She wanted to go stay with her mother and daddy. So that give me a good excuse to, you know, split off. And that's one of the bad decisions in my life I made. I let her go. She wanted to come back, and I wouldn't let her. And I was runnin' around with—I don't know—I went with four or five, six, eight or ten. You know, I went with a lot of different women. And I done started back fightin' again.

I told Doris one night that this lady was goin' take me to Atlanta and that I had a friend over 'ere I's goin' to borrow some money from. And I'd be back the next day. So she knew that I was up to somethin', but she wasn't questionin' me. She knew that I wadn't goin' off stealin' or robbin' or nothin'. So the lady come and picked me up 'cause that was my ride to take me over there to a fight. So I went over there, and I fought, and I come back with seven or eight hundred dollars. And I was goin' start a new type of business, you know. I was goin' start fishin', commercial fishin', or somethin'. Maybe I bought a boat— didn't nothin' ever work out, though.

Then I'd go fight again. I decided I'd just let my family live with my daddy-in-law, 'cause I knew they was good people. I knew they would be well took care of. I figured it: I'll run around a little bit, and I'll skip the country. I'll get out and pick me up some good fights, make me some good money. And I'll be he'pin' 'em, you know. But I didn't.

I got with Darlene. I went a lot of places with her, and I had a lot of fights—but wadn't no money involved! I got a divorce from Doris later. But when I first met Darlene, me and her got married before I ever got a divorce. And my wife was good enough not to try to get no charges passed agin me or nothin'. Me and Darlene got remarried again later.

Right after me and Darlene first got married, I'd talk to my first wife, and Darlene didn't know about it, you know. I was goin' to see her and see the kids, and I told Darlene I was just goin' to see the kids. And Darlene said, "Okay." She'd want to go see her mother. So she went to see her mother, and I went to see Doris and my kids.

I got over there one time, and my sons told me—Junior and Bill—they told me, "Daddy, Mama's got a boyfriend." Said, "We scared of him. We want you to run him off." So this is how I got one of them assault cases, you know, way back a long time ago.

Glendel B. Summerford

Well, the guy, he come up, and she told him, she said, "I told you I didn't want to go with you when you come yesterday." He was just tryin' to push his way to go with her, you know. Me and the boys was in the kitchen, and she's in the livin' room. But he's on the porch. He ain't made it in the livin' room. She's tellin' him to leave, that she don't want to have nothin' to do with him. He says, "Well, I told you yesterday, I'd come back today, that I wanted to talk with you." She said, "I told you to leave." She said, "My husband's here." Said, "He's here to see the kids. I don't want to talk to you—I want you to leave." And he said, "I ain't leavin'. I got as much right to be here as he have."

So I looked at Junior and Bill, and they just good-size boys you know. And they said, "Whup him, Daddy." And I said, "I don't want to whup him." I said, "She's gettin' rid of him."

This man's gettin' pretty loud. And I ain't looked in there and seen the man or nothin'. But I see that he ain't gonna leave, so I get up and told the boys, I say, "Well, boys, I'm a-go. I'll see you-all. I'll come back and see you-all boys later." So I step in the livin' room to go out the front door. And when I did, well, he's in there. And I'm havin' to look up at him—he about six-nine or somethin', look like. Big, tall, *biggg* guy. And I think, I seen him somewhere before, but I can't remember. And I'm studyin', runnin' it through my mind. It's like I'm seein' somebody, but I can't remember who. He knew me, but I didn't know him. And he said to my wife, "I told you that I was comin', and if anybody leave, he's leavin'." And when he said that, then—I was already there—I said, "Naw, you leavin'. I'm goin' leave, but you leavin' too." I said, "Kids are in here, so just come on out 'ere."

We step out the door, you know, and we get in a fight on the porch. And I knock him down 'bout twice on the porch—and sound like I tore the porch down, you know. The boys, they's wantin' to see it. They's watchin'. So I knock him plumb off the porch, out in the yard. Ever'time he get up, I'm knock him down. I'm not goin' play with him, you know. I'm knock him down ever'time he gets up. And I beat the man real bad. I beat his eyes plumb out of his head. I hit him in the side of the head and knock his eyeball plumb out on his nose. He would try to get up, and I'd wait. I'd get braced and ready for him to get up. He tried to get up, and he just didn't have enough. I done knocked ever'thin' out of him, and I just keep hittin' him. And I beat him unmerciful. I shouldn't have did it, you know, but I did.

So a man came up that was a police officer, but he wadn't on duty. I knew him, and I said, "Hey, James, look here. I'm fixin' to leave." I said, "What about callin' ambulance to get this man?" And he said, "I will." He said, "You need to get out from here." So I left.

In Earlier Years

I stayed gone then a long time. When I seen he wadn't goin' die, I called my cousin Bill Busby, that was K-9, special-duty police officer, at Huntsville. So he picked me up and brought me to Jackson County, and they arrest me. And he turned around and signed my bond, took me back. 'Cause he knew what they'd do to me if they ever kept me up there, you know—they figured they'd hang me or somethin'. 'Cause they always had it in for me up 'ere.

My boys seen that, and I did it for them 'cause they asked me to. But God was just merciful to me that the man didn't die. I thank God he didn't die. He stayed in the hospital a *long* time. And I had to stay gone long time to find out if he's goin' live. He wouldn't press charges. He knew he was in the wrong anyway, 'cause I'd met him once before in a fight. But I think he was a friend of somebody I'd fought in a prize fight. I think he was really huntin' me is why he was there. So I stayed gone a long time. See, that kind of stuff is how come my house got burnt.

Then I started back into business. I got me some money, and I started roofin' again. At one time, I owned a business roofin'. I owned two or three garages and done mechanic work. I could do 'bout any kind of work when I wanted to. So I started back roofin'. Me and Darlene, we did real good, was makin' good. And me and her, you know—I just fell deeper and deeper in love with her.

I had me another home, and I still had my kids to take care of. But Darlene was always jealous about my kids—she was always jealous of me and my kids. Then I moved to New Hope and stay over there awhile. I started havin' a few fights over there. And I whupped about ever'thing around New Hope. People would even hire me to whup somebody.

Then a buddy of mine over there, James Burrows, he had some guys was takin' his wife away from him. They done beat him up real bad. So he sent me word to come to his house. He wadn't able to do anything—they done beat him up bad. So I say, "Okay, I'll be over 'ere." I got over 'ere. And about time I got there, this other guy had called James' wife on the phone and said, "Tell him I'm comin' over 'ere and whup him again if he don't leave or somethin'." She turned around there and said, "You can't come over here now." Said, "Glenn's over here with him." And he said, "I'm goin' whup him when I get over 'ere." I said to James's wife, "You tell him, bring his buddy and come on over here. I've been whuppin' ever'thin' here. But," I said, "I'm not goin' whup him—I'm goin' shoot him. Tell him come on over here. You tell him, I'm goin' shoot him." She told him. And I said, "I'll be waitin' on you."

So they come up—tires on the car squallin', you know. I'm standin' out there beside my car, and they come runnin' up. One of 'em had a big chain tied around his arm. He knew he wadn't goin' fight me, you know. He didn't believe I's goin' shoot him neither. And that other one, he jumped out and opened the trunk and got a pick handle.

The one with the log chain started up in the yard, and old James—he's a little, bitty feller, and he's done beat to death, and he can't do nothin' hardly. This guy, he steps up, and I said, "I told you I's goin' shoot you if you come over here. I'll whup you if you want to be whupped, but today I'm goin' shoot you. I'm not goin' bruise my hands up on you today." I said, "I need to give you what you give this man layin' in there in this bed. But I'm not—I'm goin' shoot you. I'm goin' give you somethin' to remember."

He had that big chain tied on with a grass rope, and he started to takin' it off. "It ain't no need to take it off," I said. "You know that I can whup you, but," I said, "I'm goin' shoot you. And I'm goin' shoot you where that you goin' always remember it." And I said, "Then later on, if you want me to whup you, I'll whup you. But today, I'm goin' to shoot you, 'cause I told you I would." And I pointed the gun at him . . . He went to beggin'. And I let the gun down to his knee, and I said, "When this gun goes off, you goin' feel this bullet go through your leg. I'm goin' hit you right in that kneecap." He said, "Please don't." And he went to tryin' to get that chain off. And he has a big roll of marijuana in his pocket—he's takin' that marijuana out, and he throwed it down. I said, "Well, here goes. I'm goin' shoot you." Pow! . . . Shot him right through the leg.

This other boy, he was running up and down the road there. And I never did aim the gun at him because if I had, I had a-shot him. But I told him, "If you want to get shot, get in the yard. If you want to get whupped," I said, "you wait till I leave this man's house here, and I'll whup you down the road." I said, "Well, I already shot your buddy."

The guy I shot in the leg was Willie Southard. He became one of the best brothers in church there is, and he really thinks the world of me. He's one of the ones I later went and talked to about Darlene, you know. He said that they did call one another all the time, but that was it.

Anyway, some time went by, and I had a bunch more fights. I's so crazed up, I whup some polices over there—they was from Jackson County. And I whupped them at New Hope. These polices—one of 'em, he hated me. He wanted to whup me, and he's always scared to. I knew his voice from the CB 'cause I had a CB in my car. And I heared him on the radio one day, talkin' to a call-and-tell program, wantin' to buy a bass boat. So I said, "Okay, he's wantin' to buy a bass boat—I'm goin' set him up a deal with a bass boat."

So I come to New Hope. A friend of mine over 'ere, he had a nice bass boat. And I said, "Look, I want you to call this man. I got his number, and I want you to sell him your boat, make a deal to sell it to him to get him come down here. I want to whup him." He said, "Okay." So he called, and they told him, they'd be there Saturday. So I'm waiting till Saturday comes, you know.

Well, Big Jim Morgan, he weighed about 300 pound, and Sam Vance, he weighed about 230, I guess—and he's about six-foot-somethin' tall. (Sam, he married Darlene's sister.) Anyway, they come on down there to buy that boat. And I come scootin' up in my car and blocked 'em in. He couldn't get to his car. I run around there, and big Jim Morgan, he just backed up 'cause he knew what was goin' take place. I fired Sam up and whupped him—give him a good whuppin'. And he had to go to the hospital.

Sam got an assault charge agin me or somethin', but the judge throwed it out. Told him, stay in Jackson County. But it cost me forty dollars. I told the judge I had forty more if he'd let me go outside first—I was goin' to whup Sam again on account of some things he said in court. And the judge told me he's goin' get me with contempt of court if I didn't be quiet. But that's the kind of life I lived, you know. Anyway, he had to pay his own hospital bill.

Then not too long after that, I'd had a couple more fights. And some of these other fights, I was gettin' some money out of. And I was travelin' all over. See, me and Darlene when we first got married, we loved one another. But seem like our love growed more for one another as time went by. I loved Darlene too much to even think about another woman. I loved her more or as much as any man could love their wife, and I loved her more than I did my own self. I wanted to provide for her if I didn't have nothin'. I was probably the only help she ever really had. In her lifetime growin' up, she had a hard life, and I knew it. And I stuck with her, just the very best I could—give her ever'thing that she ever wanted. We partied and drank and fought (not with each other)—but we had a lot of fightin' and stuff (not for money), just fightin', you know, just drinkin' and them dance halls and stuff like 'at.

We went just ever'where to all the dances. We enjoyed dancin'. We could pretty well hold our own with anybody dancin'. She was just a play-purty, you know, like to me. I never had nobody go with me and stick with me, and Darlene would stick with me. And I'd stick with her. We'd go to them dances, and lot of times go where they'd stay 'bout all night dancin'—have live bands and stuff. We'd go to Holiday Inns—Florida. And just ever'where we's at, we'd live it up. We'd work hard, but we'd live it up during the time we weren't livin' right.

80

But it's just like the Lord was dealin' with me, you know, to straighten my life up. And I'd never had that kind of feelin' before. The Lord was dealin' with Darlene too. And we got right with God. And the time when I really started tryin' live right, why, I made it.

I'd tried to live right two or three times before I really got right, you know. One time when I was tryin', I'd got into it with a preacher's son where we was goin' to church. And I was even tryin' to fast. He'd come over, and he was kind of a loud mouth. He was a grown man, probably about thirty, thirty-one, thirty-two at that time. He'd weigh about three-hundred-and-somethin' pound. He kept comin' over, cussin' Darlene out when I'd be at work.

One day I was there. And he come in, and he was goin' cuss her out. I was out back, and she said, "Well, he's around the back. Go cuss him out." So he started around there and went to cussin' on me. He's a big old bully, but that's all there was to him. So I'm over in the brush pile cuttin' big limbs that fell in the yard, a big pile of it. I was over in the middle of it, runnin' a chain saw. He come up runnin' his mouth, and I's runnin' that thing wide open. I'm not goin' listen to him 'cause I'm really tryin' to live right. But I ain't *really,* you know— I'm tryin', but that's all. I could hear him above that saw. So finally, I's just tired and just throwed the saw out of the way and climbed over and fired him up. When he got to where he could get back in the car, he didn't come back. So I didn't go back to church.

The first time I tried to live right was when Darlene was pregnant with Marty, or along the time she was pregnant. I got her out of jail at Ft. Payne and moved to Madison County. We was tryin' to go to church, tryin' to do right and all. She was in jail on the same thing her mama was, on shop liftin', prostitu-tion, and all this kind of stuff. Her mother had been given thirty years, I think, and they give Darlene ten years. I hired her a lawyer over 'ere is the only reason kept Darlene from goin' to prison. See, when me and her got married, she'd already had that case, but she'd been on bond. And they'd picked her up. I went to get her out, and I couldn't 'cause she had to go to court on it. So I went and hired her a lawyer and got her out. But when Marty was born, I'd quit livin' right. And he was three years old when I really started livin' right. And I never did backslide after then. But up until then there were a couple of times, a week or two or a month or two—but it didn't work out. I didn't live right, and so we partied some more.

Then a few years went by, and one day just before we started livin' right, my cousin Jamie Summerford come down to the house. I lived down there at New Hope. Well, he come down and want me to go out to his house with him to get a dog. And he was goin' come back and go coon hunt with me that night. So I got out there, and Jimmy Brown had been whuppin' his wife 'round and talkin' to Jamie's mother real bad. His mother was tellin' us about it, and we's sittin' 'ere on back of the truck. Jamie said, "I would whup him, but I ain't got but one leg. I don't think I can handle him. I'd have to shoot him or somethin' 'cause he's a big feller, you know." And I say, "Well, where's he at? I'll whup him fer you."

So we sittin' there talking, and a'ter while, he said, "Well, yonder he comes now." They just pulled up, and Jimmy Brown got out, and he was cussin' his old lady all way to the house. And they was walking through there, so I just walked off there and met him—you know, I whupped him. And he got a warrant fer me, but he dropped it.

And they still had his mouth wired up when he started trying to live right. Him and Kenneth Smith got together, and they was prayin' over on the bluff. So they come over and told me they want to get me to pray with them. Said, God had told 'em that he'd sent them over there to get me to pray. And I said, "I don't know about Jimmy." I said, "I had that problem with him." And Jimmy went to cryin', and he says, "I'm livin' right, now. I don't want to have no more problem." And he said, "I know the Lord sent me wantin' me to come get you to pray." So they argued around there for a while, and Darlene told me, she said, "Glenn, I been feelin' like I need to pray too and do right, change my life."

So I knowed God was dealin' with me, you know. I knew it 'cause God had done spoke to me and said he was goin' send somebody and for me to hear 'em and pray with 'em. But I didn't know who it was goin' be. So it was them two brothers.

I prayed through to the Holy Ghost that day, and she did too. And I don't remember what day it was, but we never did backslide no more till plumb on up until, I guess, '89 or somethin'—they wadn't no backslidin'. But that's whenever this lady confronted Darlene and told her she knew Darlene was goin' with her husband, or first one thing and 'nother. That was when Darlene started havin' boyfriends, you know. But I wouldn't really call it boyfriends—like runnin' a'ter men, you know. But she was always that-a-way, and it wadn't nothin' new, you know. But she'd quit it in the time she was doin' right, and then the same thing again. Then straightened up until '91—same thing again. She's just lookin' back, you know. And she done got out of my reach.

But there for a long time, once we started—me and Darlene, we had went to church ever' night. We wouldn't miss church night. We was in church all the time, constantly ever' night. She just got tired of goin', you know, is all I can think of.

Doris Holcomb Summerford

Glenn's First Wife

Glenn and I started dating on May 11, 1963, at Rich Theater in Scottsboro. I had went with my cousins—a carload of us went up there to see a movie. My mom and dad didn't let me go very much. My brother Alvin came with Glenn, and I was sitting up there with the rest of them. They all had dates but me. I was the oddball hang-along, I guess. Alvin came up there and asked me if Glenn could sit with me, and that's where it started. We went together till September, and we got married on Saturday morning, September 11, about ten o'clock. I didn't know at the time, but he was running moonshine when we were dating.

He had lived up north in Chicago with his uncle J. B. Smith. He told me about prize fighting. And he was also in gangs up there—that's how he went into prize fighting. But he got into it with somebody and came back down here. And that would probably be the last of '62 or first of '63 that he came back from up north. He was eighteen when he and me started dating, and he hadn't been back down here that long.

I went to school with him, but I didn't like him—point blank, I didn't like him. But, as he says, he told me in the first grade that he was goin' to marry me. I told him he was crazy. I liked the little red-headed, freckled-face boy 'cause I'd never seen one. That changed, definitely. Glenn went to school there a little while, and they moved off to Florida. They moved from Alabama to Florida a lot when he was growin' up. And he spent a lot of time with his uncle J. B. in Chicago and Florida (J. B. lived in both places).

He had a rough childhood. But I grew up on a farm. I had a mom, a dad, and a bunch of brothers and sisters. We weren't rich in what you would call

Doris Summerford at work.

financially. We were always poor, but we never went hungry. If we done wrong, we got a whuppin' for it—that's just the way it was. But we weren't cussed, and things weren't throwed at us. We got a whuppin'—it was with a switch or a belt. The way Glenn was brought up, you'd get knocked, slapped, and whupped with whatever was handy.

I was born and raised on what is now Revere, which was called Goose Pond Island. I was sixteen, almost seventeen, when we got married. Glenn lived on the island at that time. He worked with his stepdad for William Allen, a pulpwood logger. About October we went to Florida with a friend. We were going to work on the vegetables; but the day after we got there, there came a freeze. So we didn't stay too long. My dad sent us the money, and we came back up to Alabama. We stayed with Glenn's mom and stepdad over on the island until we all moved back to Florida in '65. Junior was born in March of '65, and we left here about May for Jacksonville. Glenn worked at a dairy with his stepdad for another man. And we live there until '67.

That's when he came up here with a couple of other guys and got into trouble—they came up here on a fishing trip. They got with another friend who lived up here—Glenn always said they went to this house to buy some whiskey because the woman was a bootlegger. Anyhow, she wasn't there, and they broke into the house. They got whiskey and some other stuff—something

Doris Holcomb Summerford

about a shotgun. And they were put in jail—she didn't report the whiskey! Burglary and grand larceny—whatever they took was valued at more than 250 bucks because that was the law back then—and that's what they were charged with. Glenn's mom and the mother of one of the other guys came up here and got him out of jail. My mom and dad came down there to Florida and got me, and I came up here and stayed with them awhile until my son was born, which is Eddie Ray. He was born in September.

Glenn had had his trial in August. Andy Hamlet was his lawyer, and Andy told him if he would plead guilty to those charges that he could get him off on probation. So Glenn listened to Andy. And they were doing a check on everything for him to get probation when Mr. Bill, Glenn's stepdad, had a heart attack. It was a light one, but we all took off down there. Well, Glenn talked with Andy—of course Andy's dead now, so he can't verify anything—but he told Glenn that it would be okay, that they could run the probation through Jacksonville. Glenn gave him the address and everything where he was going to; but, anyway, Glenn never did hear.

And we came back up here in '68, and me and him lived at Geraldine (Hog Jaw)—it's out on Sand Mountain. We lived down there, and he went to work for a man loggin'. Then his mom and stepdad and Glenn worked in the chicken house up there. And we lived there until January.

Then the county picked him up, brought him over here, and put him in jail. In March they sent him to prison. They denied his probation or whatever, so they just sent him off to prison. He went through Kilby two or three weeks and transferred to Draper. He stayed there for a few months, and then he was sent to Ft. Payne. They had a road camp that they carried him to out there, and he worked on the road. His mom, his stepdad, me, and the boys went out there to see him. Then in November, I believe, he was paroled out. He had received a sentence of eighteen months. He stayed in prison and road camp about nine months, and the other nine were paroled.

We lived over here in Scottsboro for a while. Then we moved back to Geraldine, and he went to work again for the logging company out there. Then in '70 we moved to Paint Rock. In '72 the house burned.

The memory of the house burning, I don't have. All I can tell is what was told to me. I was burnt. Of course we lost our daughter Sarah, who was one year and eight months and twenty-five days old at the time. Glenn Junior was the one who woke us up—4:30/5 o'clock in the morning. And the house was on fire. We could not get out a door, so we broke a window out by the side of the bed. And Glenn threw all the kids out. I was reaching for the little girl that didn't get out when I caught on fire. According to Glenn, he seen my hair blaze up, and he was trying to put it out. He said I was fighting him, and it knocked both of us out the window. And he told me, you know, later that he rolled me in a mud hole out there to put me out. He said I kept running to the window hollerin', "My baby." And Glenn grabbed up Charlotte to show me that he had the baby out. Then he realized which one was not out. And he tried to get back in. But by that time, the people that lived there by us had got over there, and they wouldn't let him back in—he couldn't get back in anyway. (Charlotte was the baby at the time, eight months old—I had three boys, Glenn Junior, Bill, and Eddie—and then Jackie, Sarah, and Charlotte.) Sarah's birthday was August the first. Charlotte's was August the third, one year difference.

I always said, "God made me an instant baby machine." I had nine all together—Glenn Junior, born March 29, 1965; Bill Lee, April 28, 1966; Eddie Ray, September 28, 1967; Jackie Elaine, April 5, 1969; Sarah Ann, August 1, 1970; Charlotte Jean, August 3, 1971; Lisa Diane, May 15, 1973; Joseph Bryan, August 18, 1974; Christopher Michael, March 18, 1978.

But anyway, after Glenn couldn't get back in the house, he put all the kids in the car. The one thing I do remember was sitting in the car. I was in a state of shock, but the one memory was Glenn bringing us to the hospital. And those people were letting him drive off there. I've never understood that— people stand around and let someone in that condition drive off. Well, I was told later that when the ambulance passed him, he was doing about 100 miles a hour. I was in the hospital for twenty days. And I wear his handprint, because where he grabbed and was holding my arm scarred in. The scars are still there, and you can see the handprint.

Then we lived up here at Scottsboro. But after that, Glenn never really got over Sarah's death. Five days from the time she died, his stepdad died. And he was very close to him. To Glenn he *was* his dad. His stepdad had raised him, and he had a lot of respect for Mr. Bill. After that, things just kept getting worse and worse. Glenn had a love for bars, fighting, and things I wasn't raised to enjoy. To me, he always thought he could have his cake and his ice cream too. Doris could stay home and raise the kids, take care of them. And he could get out and run around, do what he wanted to; and any time he got ready, he could come back home. And that's about the way it was.

Glenn had a knack for wantin' to run around. I guess you could say he loved women. Glenn has always run around. And he always had a bad temper—he could be abusive. He was abusive to me. He was not abusive to the children. But if he told them to do something, he meant do it. He

Doris Holcomb Summerford

whupped them and they minded, but as far as really beatin' them or stuff like that, no. To the boys, he was a good dad. To the girls, he was indifferent. I don't know if he knew how to be a dad to girls. His sons, he could have a relationship with—hunting, fishing.

He was running around, drinking. And I just got to the point I thought I could make it without him. So I did. On Eddie's birthday in '75 I left and went out to my dad's. I stayed for a while until I got a house; and I moved out, me and the kids. But then he kept comin' back. He'd leave, and he'd come back. And I was the dummy. I still care about the man—I'll still help him anyway I can—but I wouldn't want to live with him. We separated, and he stayed with his mom part of the time.

December the first 1975—he claimed he was drunk—but him and Darlene got married. He wasn't drunk enough that he didn't marry her in another name. He married her in his stepdad's name—we weren't divorced.

The reason they got married was—at that time the welfare had taken her little boy. She had a boy a little over a year old when they took him—I'm not exactly sure how old he was. His name was Bobby Joe. I think they took him because she was runnin' around and doin' things she wadn't suppose' to. But she wasn't takin' care of her son anyhow. Somehow in their head they thought if they got married, they could get him. But that don't work.

But when I first heard about them getting married, I went and talked to a lawyer. That lawyer told me that Glenn could get up to twenty years in prison. But I was angry at that time, so I thought I would cool off before I would sign any papers. And I didn't go back and sign the papers to get him for bigamy. His marriage was on my birthday, whether it was to get back at me or what. I will never be able to forget his anniversary—I was born on December 1, 1946, and he married her December 1, 1975.

I was bad after that. I went through a period of "get even." I went to work with Glenn and Darlene—we worked on a building up here in South Pittsburg, a three-story building. The only way I went to work with him was to find a way to kill both of 'em. That's the reason I say I was bad at that time. We were working in a building up there—it was a burnt building, Lloyd's—we were cleaning it out. Glenn worked for a construction company, doing subcontracting for them. He had got that job, and we were working up there. He had a big dump truck parked down on the street, where we throw'd the glass, the wood, and all that stuff out of this three-story window. Glenn and Darlene were both standing up there close to the front of the window—I won't ever forget it. I had a big board to throw out. And I had intended to knock both of them "accidently" out of that window. That's all I was waiting on, both of them to get up there at the same time. But he turned around and smacked the heck out of her for some reason. What they got into it about I don't know. But anyway, somethin' spoke to my head and said, "Why do you want him back? She's the one who has to take that now." So I walked on. We got through that building, and I worked for them several months. Then I quit and moved back on the mountain. Glenn went to Missouri and Texas with Darlene. And they also went to Florida for quite a while.

I got a divorce in '76—that was one bill Glenn paid for. He'd always told me if I ever left him that he'd take the kids—he'd get guys to lie that I'd been with them and take my kids away from me. He'd always told me that. That's the way he would intimidate you. But he needed the divorce because I had too many kids for me to work and support. And to draw ADC, Aid to Dependent Children, you sign a paper that they can get it out of the husband. I got custody of the kids in the divorce, and he was to pay $200 a month, which was pretty good in '76—even though he never paid it.

After I moved up on the mountain, I got to goin' to church. Glenn's ex-sister-in-law Annette (his brother David's first wife) would come out there and get me and the kids in a station wagon. She'd take us to church and buy groceries—she was a friend and a good one. And I got the Holy Ghost. I was doing real good until Glenn came back, and I backslid and stopped goin' to church. He handed me a line of malarkey about him and Darlene was through. He wanted to come back home, take care of me and the kids, and all that. I found out later that she's in jail—that's the only reason he's over there. Then I got pregnant with Michael, and he got her out of jail, and he flew the coop. Yes, he used Doris for a long time. It takes a little while to realize what you've done.

And after Michael was born, I did move with them to New Hope—all three of us and all of the kids. Course he got us a house. As far as I know, Darlene didn't know about "Glenn and me." If she did, she didn't care. When "anything happened," it was when nobody else was around. But the kids knew, and I figured she did. And it didn't happen all that often. Occasionally things did happen, but not all that often.

We stay out of church for a little while, and then we got back in church down there with—started going over to Mayo's church and then we got to going to church some with Brother Peace, which is the father of two of my daughter-in-laws now. He had a church down there at Crossroad, and we went to it—really got in church, and so did Glenn. When Glenn would go to church and try to do right, he really tried. I mean, things would happen later that he would back

Doris Holcomb Summerford

up—he'd backslide and get back in the world and be the biggest old sinner there was. But when he was goin' to church, he tried. I honestly believe that.

Mom and Dad had decided earlier it was time to keep Glenn from comin' around. But they didn't do nothin' until Michael was born—and I love Michael. It was God's plan, or I wouldn't had him. But then Mom and Dad come to see the judge down here. And when they come to see the judge, Doris just got out of the county. Even if Glenn was her way of goin', I'd get out. The one thing that meant the most to me was my kids. I ain't been the greatest mom. I never was the greatest wife. But my life has been for my kids. God just made me "Mama."

So that's why we went to New Hope in Madison County—to get out of Jackson County. Michael was born in March 1978, and we went down there to Madison County in May or June. We lived down there till '81 or '82. Mom and Dad got to the point that they knew that Doris was going to do what Doris wanted to. So they didn't like it; but they accepted it, I reckon.

Then I moved from Madison County back to the mountain close to my mom and dad. I lived out there, and Glenn moved up here to Hollywood or somewhere for about one year. And after we came back from Madison County, there was never anything between Doris and Glenn. We got in church—that ended. I had been in church, but I had got out of church. Me and Glenn had talked quite a bit on the Bible, and it got to the point I told him: "It's not right." To him, I guess, he considered himself like Jacob with two wives. The way he looked at it—wasn't that much wrong. I said, "Right or wrong, we lie about it. That makes it wrong. So, no more." So after that, there was no more Glenn and Doris in that relationship.

Then Glenn moved to Fackler. He rented a place up there that had two houses on it. He and Darlene moved into the little house, and he talked me and the kids to movin' into the big one. But just before we moved to Fackler, before he found that place down there, he come out to the house a lot. He came out there one day, and two of his buddies—Kenneth Smith and Jimmy Brown—came to the house and said God sent them over there to talk with him. Glenn was drinking that day when they come out there, but they got to prayin' with that man. And, honestly, when Glenn got up, the knees of his pants was busted and he was sober.

Then after that, he stayed in church. He didn't back up no more. He got in church the last of '82. He stayed in church then—he didn't back up no more. He went to church with Brother Aubrey, but mostly he went to Albert York's—he went to different places. But after that time he didn't back up no more until whatever happened, happened.

Rev. Glenn Summerford. Photograph by Ken Elkins.

After Fackler, when Glenn moved that way, I moved the other way. We always went to Holiness churches, Jesus Name churches. And I went to church when he started at the Word Arcade Building, the first church I ever went to where he preached. Then me and the kids went for a while to the one where he was up there at the Chicken Basket. I had carried the kids to church since they were little. And back then, church didn't last until nine o'clock and go home. If you've ever been to a Holiness church back in those days, sometimes you get home at two or three in the mornin'. The kids get up and go to school anyhow. But they slept many a night under a church bench.

Right after he got into that snake handlin' is when I got out of church over there with him. I backed up in '87 and stayed out of church until '92—then Mama got to going back because of Bill, my son. So during that time I didn't know much that was going on between Glenn and Darlene. Several times I'd been in church with 'em—this was in the early '80s—and Darlene'd

Doris Holcomb Summerford

say, she wish he was dead. I went to their house about the kids or something or another; and she'd say, she wish he'd die.

Glenn was never, what you would say, a good provider. He would help to get wood to heat by, but as far as moneywise, he was not a good provider. At times he would work real good and keep a job. And then he would go through spells. But somehow we just always made it. And Glenn was capable of abuse and intimidation. But after he got in church, Glenn changed a whole lot. I mean he wasn't the same run-around person he had been. And that I do know. I watched his life close enough. I knew that. And he had opportunity more there than he had for a long time. But he—I honestly believe there for a long time—Glenn was doing the very best that he could do to live right. And my own personal thing about being in church—it was me that backed up, it wasn't nothin' to do with him. It was just time to get out, I guess, for a while.

After he started handling serpents, I would hear from some of the others. Bill and Junior went to church with him some. Joe went a lot with his daddy. Then Glenn got bit. It was on a Saturday. He got bit around ten that night. My kids came and got me on Sunday morning about daylight. They thought their dad was dying. And according to Darlene, the same snake that bit her was the one that bit Glenn. When I went down there, that man was swelled big enough to look like he was about ready to bust. And he couldn't get up off the floor . . . So you tell me how someone who got bit by *that* snake, and walk around into the video store, and go to this store and that store, and ride around all day—and then get bit again. Darlene may be good, but she ain't that good.

What happened during that day, only those two could tell you—and God himself. As far as Glenn being mean to her, knocking her down—if he was drinkin', I don't doubt it. He would give you a black eye in a hurry. If you opened your mouth and said somethin' and he didn't feel just right, you got it. And if he was backed up on God, I sure wouldn't want to be around. I mean, that's just the way it was. But to give the devil his dues, that gal could do just about anything he could do—and would. Now, he could hit harder, I'm very sure. But I don't think there's anything she wouldn't do—and still ain't.

But when Glenn's got things right with God, when he's livin' right, he tries. And I believe he's got faith—that I do know. (His beliefs is little bit different from mine in some things.) I also believe he would be a *very* rough man too if he wadn't living right—as I say, I wouldn't want to be around him. But if he really wanted her to be dead, she'd be dead. I honestly believe that, because Glenn knows this area too well. He has hunted and fished these mountains till he knows where sink holes is that would never be found. If he really wanted her dead, she'd be dead. But as far as believin' he could have knocked the soup out of her or he could have hit her—yeah, Glenn's capable.

I've made my share of mistakes. I was not no perfect mom. I was not no perfect person. And I don't claim I was, but as I told my kids, "I've made plenty of mistakes, but I did what I thought was best at the time." I can look back, and I can see I made wrong choices. But you don't go back and change it.

Doris Holcomb Summerford

Reverend Glenn Summerford

In Church

Iwas livin' in Jackson County on the mountain when I received the Holy Ghost. I moved to Fackler, and I started fastin' and prayin' 'cause I couldn't read the Bible. And that's why I couldn't live right—it's 'cause one would tell me this, and one would tell me that, and all I knowed is that I was wantin' to do right. But I didn't know how to really live right.

Then God spoke to me that if I'd fast and pray, he'd teach me his word. So I'd steal away. I stayed in the room by myself thirty days and fast and pray and seek God. Darlene, she'd pray, and her and Marty would stay in the other room. And when that thirty days was up, why I come out, and she'd cook fer me and all. And I didn't go to church right then, but I's gettin' my strength back.

At that time I wouldn't drink no water or eat nothin'—thirty days. They say you can't live. It felt like I was rottin' on the inside, you know. I felt rotten. When I come out, you know, I thought I could eat a whole lot. But I couldn't— just eat a little bit. I have fasted since then, and I'd drink water. I've seen people drink a cup of coffee or somethin'. And I have drunk Coke-colie, but not a whole lot—maybe just a mouthful in place of water. But it was like the Lord was feedin' me all the time, you know.

And God spoke to me and said, "Go back thirty more days, and I'll teach you the whole Bible from one cover to the other'n." Then I went back and did it for another thirty days.

After God learned me to read, I didn't want to stop. But the Lord spoke to me and said, "That's enough. Now I'm goin' send you where I want you to go." I didn't know what He meant, you know. So some of the brothers, Brother York and others, was holdin' some house meetin's—them's the first house meetin's I went to. And they wanted me to come, be in church with 'em—they knowed I started back livin' right. And me and Darlene went. They had a big livin' room emptied up. We went in, and they already had the service goin'. This one man, he kept walking around ever'body, layin' hands on 'em. And they'd all shout. I'm standin' there, and I can't feel nothin'. And I say, "Well, Lord, I wish I could just feel somethin', 'cause I've been fastin' and prayin' all this long, and I can't feel nothin'—like I ain't got nothin'." And God spoke to me, and he said, "When he touches you, my Spirit goin' bind him. And you cast him out." I ain't never heared nothin' like 'at, you know.

So that man went around, and when he come by me, he touched me on the back like he did ever'body else. And when he did, he just hit the floor, fell. His mouth was wide open. He was screamin' and a-cussin'. He done changed over, you know. I turned around there and got him by the hand. Darlene turn around there and bowed down with me, and I cast that devil out of him. I went home that night praisin' God. "Boy, I'm proud I didn't feel that."

God let me learn by that—a lot of times people just shout. Somebody just touch 'em on the shoulder, and they go to shoutin'. They don't even know what they're shoutin' to. God let me know to try the spirit. And I said, "God, I don't know how to try the spirit." Then he showed me he was goin' learn me. So he started usin' me in different gifts of the Spirit.

And other ministers and people where we's goin' to church and all, like, they would be jealous of me: "Well, how can this man be this close to God, and he ain't been livin' right all that long?" And stuff like that. But they did know how I'd been fastin' and prayin' and seekin' God. Then Brother York—he was pastoring a church long before I ever went with him—he just took right up with me 'cause he seen two or three miracles right quick—people that he'd been wantin' healed for years. Like, his own daughter had been seekin' the Holy Ghost for a long time. And I called her up and told her, "God's fixin' to give you the Holy Ghost." I laid hands on her, and he give her the Holy Ghost. So it's just miracle a'ter miracle, way God used me.

And then I got with Brother Carl Hazewell. He believed the same way I did. He had this little church, Mink Creek Holiness Church, in Jeffery's Community near Goose Pond. I was assistant pastor. Then we rented that big arcade building near the courthouse. Blacks had services on one side of the building, and we had services on the other. But Brother Carl never did get to hold a service in it with me.

See, we was puttin' carpet in the building. Brother Carl worked for the city, and he went down there on his job to check on those guys that was

Reverend Glenn Summerford

workin'. He said he'd see me a'ter while. And he didn't come back. When I finished gettin' carpet in, why, I went on home. They called me and told me he'd had a heart attack and died. So I had to preach his funeral—the first funeral I ever preached. And I continued as pastor of that church. That was my first church, but later the building was burnt down.

I got a lot of criticism for having Blacks in the services. And that's why they burnt the building, or partly the reason why. But, see, the Scripture says to preach the gospel to every creature. And God said that he ain't no respecter of person, and he said for me not be no respecter of person. So I try to he'p ever'body—it don't matter what color their skin is.

So then we had a church on old Highway 72 near Five Points in the old Bull Durham's store. And after that, in a restaurant building out on Broad Street in Goose Pond. Then the last one was in an old grocery store building on Woods Cove Road near the hospital, the Church of the Lord Jesus Christ with Signs Following.

And I had gone out on Grant Mountain, then on Sand Mountain—in different places, you know. And ever'thing just kept growin'—more people come and more people comin'. And I baptized, like, over 750-somethin' people that I had the record. I baptized that many in the name of Jesus Christ. They's people out of Cullman that takes up serpents now, and they's people over at

Bull Durham's store building near Five Points, an early site of Glenn's churches

Vacated restaurant on Broad Street, site of Glenn's Pentecostal Holiness Church.

Lacey's Spring now that takes up serpents. People out on Grant Mountain—I helt revivals up 'ere and helped them with their church, and they believe in takin' up serpents. I baptized all them. And all down around Paint Rock—it was just growin'.

What I was goin' do was—that land that we had rented and had that little buildin' at Woods Hollow, we was goin' build a church on it. There was a pretty good bit of land that went with that buildin' out behind it. And the man, John Frank, who owned it, he told me he would sell it to me. I had it, like, rent to buy. Well, he died. Whenever he died, why, I heared that the DA had married his daughter. If that's so, see, that would have been a conflict right there. If he did marry Frank's daughter, he wound up with all that land. But I had it in my mind to build a big church.

Now, the first snake that me and Darlene handled together was on Sand Mountain at home. That was way before I was preachin', when I was goin' to church with Brother York. We lived up in a place called Goshen. I'd get up ever' mornin' or go ever' evenin' and pray. I had me a trail goin' upside the mountain. And one mornin' real early I woke up and felt like goin' to pray. So I started up that trail. I was goin' go way on like I usually do, get away from the house and pray.

I started up that trail, and there was a copperhead there. I stopped and started prayin'. The Lord let me pick it up, so I picked it up. Darlene heared me up there—I wasn't fer up behind the house—and she come up there with a hoe. She said, "Put it down, and I'll kill it." So I laid it down. But she felt the

96

Reverend Glenn Summerford

power of God. And she laid that hoe down, and she went to prayin'. Then she comes shoutin' around by me and scooped that copperhead up off the ground and went up that trail a little piece a-shoutin' and a-praisin' God. Here she comes back through there by me again. Look like her eyes just walled back in her head. Look like an angel, you know, shoutin' and praisin' God 'cause that was the first one she ever took up.

Now, I'd been takin' serpents up fer a good while, but I just wouldn't say nothin' to nobody about it. I just believed the word and took 'em up—I never had seen nobody handle one before. I heared about it, you know. When I was young, I heared people talk about it. They had a church one time on Sand Mountain where they took up serpents. It was called Old Straight Creek. One time I went out there, back years and years ago, when I was a teenager, but they didn't take up serpents that night. I didn't even know they took 'em up until a'ter church was over. Brother Uly was who I was with—I'd go to church with him and make music. And we's goin' home, and he said, "Well, Glenn, they didn't have no snakes there tonight." And I said, "Where?" And he said, "There, where we's at." And I said, "What do you mean?" And he said, "Sometimes they bring them snakes in 'ere and handle snakes." And I said, "You didn't tell me 'fore we went." He said, "Well, they didn't bring any anyway."

Me and Darlene handled serpents at home, but we didn't never carry any to church at first. Then a'ter I started pastorin', I started takin' up serpents in church. Down there at Bull Durham's store building near Five Points was, I believe, the first place we carried them in. But I didn't never take snakes to nobody else's church—only places where they wanted somebody to bring snakes.

And at that time me and Darlene hadn't gone to any other serpent-handlin' church. The first church I ever went to where they handled 'em was when Gene Sherbert come to our service over there near Five Points. He invited us to go over there where they was goin' to have some kind of big meetin'. So we drove over there, me and Darlene, over close to Cedar Town somewhere, where Gene and Byron Crawford pastored, near Rome, Georgia. This is before Charles Prince died from serpent bite—that was a long time before he died in 1985.

Well, I guess they was 'bout eight or nine years that me and Darlene handled serpents ever' night, just about it. Didn't nobody else in that area have a church where they take up serpents. Brother Charlie Hall—he pastored the church at Straight Creek—he had got bit and died. Then they quit handlin' 'em out there. We were takin' up serpents at the time, but we kept on with it.

Besides serpents, I've handled fire, but I never did hold lamps of fire under my chin—I never did do nothin' like 'at. I'd just go up in the heater and scoop the fire out in my hands. And it'd be like blue smoke and blue flames comin' up from the coals. And I always wore a long-sleeve white shirt 'cause I had these old tattoos on me for years, you know—I was always ashamed of 'em. And I wouldn't never get no ashes or nothin' even on my clothes. And sometimes, it'd be like oil run out of my hands.

I've also drank strychnine and I don't know what else. There ain't no tellin' what all, you know. People bring in different stuff. Sometime battery acid, I think. I always look at it like it's got a "if" there, you know. "If you do it," the Lord said. Then he'd take care of you so wouldn't nothin' hurt you. Anybody better think about it before he goes to turn that up and drink it—they certainly better know they ready to go to heaven. They won't be no turnin' around if they make a mistake. On serpents, you know, he don't always put poison in somebody ever'time they get bit, I don't guess. But that poison—if you drink it and you ain't ready to go . . . now, that's a bad situation.

I got hit on that poison a little bit one night. It didn't bother me much. It kinda, like, drawin' me a little bit—my skin feel drawin', kind of like muscle cramps draw. It wadn't in my arms or legs or nothin', just my skin in my face. Service was about over, so we went on home. I didn't say nothin' to Darlene about it, you know.

We got home, and I's sittin' on the couch. I got a cramp in my leg. And I's rubbin' that cramp in my leg—I ain't never been gettin' no cramps in my leg before, you know. And when I stretched my leg out to get that cramp out, it's like my foot started drawin', pointin' down. And Darlene said, "What you doin', Glenn?" And I said, "My foot's hung." She looked at me and said, "I know what it is." She went to prayin'. And when she went to prayin', it went away. And I know what it was then.

I laid down on the couch. And she'd gone to bed. I doze off to sleep, and all a sudden I wake up. I got my tongue in between my teeth, and the blood's runnin' outside my mouth where I've shut down on my tongue. It's like I'm locked up, and my hands are drawed. And my legs is drawed up towards my head. I could feel that warm blood runnin' out of my mouth, and I couldn't say nothin'. I was trying to call Darlene, you know, but I couldn't. Then the Lord showed me I was callin' on the wrong one.

It learnt me a lesson, you know. You don't call on nobody but Jesus when you get down. Then in my mind I was prayin' to him and just started relaxin'. I got my tongue where I could speak then, and I started prayin'. All that just

Reverend Glenn Summerford

started relaxin' back out, and I got up and walked around all rest of the night. I'd walk around and pray. Next day I was all right. That's only time I got hit on strychnine.

Gene brought some strychnine one night right a'ter I got bit. He brought some in a jar—that crystal-powder stuff. He put a spoonful in a quart jar, and he put another spoonful. He just kept puttin' spoonfuls in it, and he then just poured it all in—all but a little bit left in the bottom. He put the lid on the jar, and I said, "I ain't goin' drink none of that." "You know," he said, "nobody better even be tastin' that if they ain't got their heart right with God."

The same night a lady got bit by a cottonmouth. I'd took the cottonmouth out and placed it on the Bible stand. She come up and was goin' git it, and the cottonmouth bit her. I was prayin' fer her—and I got exited and drank about half of that jar of strychnine. God lifted her up—she was like foamin' at the mouth and ever'thing. Then when I keep prayin' fer her, I drank the rest of it, the whole quart. They kept lookin' fer me to die. And I didn't even think about it.

Gene, he come over where I's at prayin' for that sister. He knowed that I done forgot about him puttin' the strychnine in there, I guess. He kept comin' up—he was playin' with his cymbals—and he'd lean over and say, "Brother Glenn, you feel all right?" I'd say, "Yeah, I feel like heaven's all around us, don't you?" And so, he'd just shake his head and go on. So God really blessed me and took care of me.

I don't know how many times I've been serpent bit 'cause I've been bit a lot of times when other people would be holdin' 'em and the snakes'd bite me. I've stuck my hand between the snake and somebody to keep 'em from gettin' bit. So I don't really know how many times I've been bit, but I've been hurt 'bout three or four times—one time real bad. Well, I've been hurt twice real bad, but one time was extra bad—July 13, the same time that other brother got bit up in Tennessee, Brother Jimmy Williams Jr. But he died the same night.

That last time I got bit, I stayed out seven days and nights. I didn't know I was in the world. I don't know what I said or what I did. But I know I did a lot of prayin'. I got my Bible back 'ere—it's got blood on the pages where I laid my hand as I's talkin' to the Lord.

And then when I got home, I was 'bout to go all the way out. But I heared the Holy Ghost speakin', and I was whisperin'. Nobody could hear what I was sayin' 'cause I was already gettin' swelled so bad till I couldn't hardly get my voice out. I had my head down, talking to the Lord. And nobody could

Darlene Summerford. Photograph by Ken Elkins.

hear me. I said, "Lord, I knowed that I disobeyed you." And I said, "If I'm goin' die, I want to know if I'm goin' to heaven 'cause I know I've already repented." And prophecy started speakin' through a woman as she come up on the porch. I heared it comin' before it ever come in the house. And she said, "Yea, my son, I say you are a-goin' live. You not goin' die, but you are goin' suffer."

In a way, Darlene caused me to get bit that night, but I didn't blame her. I'd took all the snakes out and laid 'em up on the Bible stand. I emptied up all the boxes—there's about forty-five snakes. They's all on the Bible stand. And this Mojave western diamondback was like a coiled spring standin' up on top of all 'em. And Darlene was standin' beside me, and she punched me about two, three times. I'm clappin' my hands and praisin' the Lord. And I finally lent over fer her to say somethin' to me—I didn't know what she was goin' to say. She'd usually tell somethin', maybe the Lord showed her or somethin'. And she said, "Glenn, that"—she called it "coon tail"—said, "that coon tail's fixin' to bite. Brother Charles said it jumps out at him ever'time he walks by." (Brother Charles was walking by singin' and preachin'.)

And when she said that, I turned and put my hand on top of that snake and didn't even think, and it went all the way down. It was in a coil, and its head was lookin' at me. And the Lord spoke to me and told me to take that snake up then with the same hand and put it in the box—spoke to me just like a person might speak. But instead of that, I retch with my right hand, and that diamond-back jumped out and bit me. It come right out between my thumb and finger of my left hand and bit me between the second and third finger on my right hand. And I'd already just disobeyed the Lord, you know, so I went on and took it up. Then a cottonmouth bit me on the fleshy side of my palm on the same hand, same time—cottonmouth make a dirty bite too. I started prayin'.

So I took the Mojave and put it in the box, but it was too late. And that hand started burnin' and swellin' right then, just like someone blowin' a balloon up. I dropped my head, and I went to repentin' 'cause I knowed I messed up. And I felt anointin' all over me. I retch back in the box and took that rattlesnake back out. And I helt it, and it just got limber-like. I helt it just for a minute, and I looked around and wadn't nobody else handlin' no snake. So I asked the Lord, "What you want me to do with all them snakes?" 'Cause I done see fear all over ever'body. And the Lord showed me to put 'em all back in the box. So I took 'em all and put 'em back in the box.

I felt like havin' victory over the snakebite at that point. And I'm feelin' pretty good, so I'm takin' the serpents out again. And Brother Wayne was wantin' to handle 'em, so him and me both handle 'em just for a minute.

Then we's puttin' 'em back. And I started gettin' down. And I said, "Well, it's time—you-all take me home."

Ever'time I ever got bit is where I disobeyed God. Another time I got bit, I had a big rattler in my hand, and God told me to put it up. I had a little haughty spirit, Look here, this is a big one, you know, without even thinkin'—stuff like that'll hit your mind. So, soon as I realized what I was doin', I take it and put it up. And when I put it in the box, it jumped back out of the box and bit me. But I didn't swell on the outside when it bit me, I swelled on the inside. They say that's worse.

Now, I handle serpents by faith, but it's faith in the anointin'. If I don't feel the anointin', I'm not goin' to fool with 'em. I don't care what they are. Sometimes you feel the anointin' in one hand, and you don't feel it in the other hand. And if I feel that anointin', I'll stick my head in a heater or anything, 'cause I know it's goin' be all right.

But whenever I got bit at church that night by that western diamond-back, in ten or fifteen minutes I didn't even know where I's at. And at home, it's just like I was there, but I wadn't there. Then just a few minutes after the Holy Ghost spoke through that lady and told me I was goin' live and not die—the Lord spoke to me, and he said, "I'll pass by you the seventh day. Take holt of me, and I'll lift you up." And I went out.

I come to once. I was throwin' up, my bowels moved, and all that. And they was Brother Gene and some others of 'em, they was pouring water over me, tryin' to get my kidneys to move. They said my kidneys was locked or somethin'. I don't know if they moved or not. All I know is ever'time I'd come to, I'd just be throwin' up, heavin'. It was like a house was settin' on me. I couldn't get up. I couldn't roll over or nothin'. I couldn't move—like I weighed a ton. But it was all closin' in on me. All I could see was snakes in my face. I don't know if my eyes was open, closed, or what. I couldn't see people. I could hear 'em sometime. It's like I was blind.

And I didn't know how to count the days or nothin'. They had me on a hospital bed in the livin' room. I didn't even know I was on it. They was changin' my clothes and sheets and stuff—Brother Charles and all the brothers was. Wadn't no sisters in there, I don't guess—I don't know. One of the brothers had me in under the arms, holdin' me up. And by him squeezin' me or somethin'—that's how I kind of come to for just a minute. In my mind, I thought it was the Lord liftin' me up, you know. But I found out later it wadn't, it was one of the brothers.

Then on the seventh day, I knew in my mind it was the seventh day. I knowed the Lord had to show me that it's the seventh day, 'cause I couldn't

Reverend Glenn Summerford

count. I was still out. And I felt the Lord when he come in the room. It was like the room started, like, glowin', you know. All I could see was a glow. And it was a brightness, not like the sun and not like a 'lectric light. It was a brightness, though, begin to come over me. And I tried to reach out with my right hand, but somethin' was wrong. I couldn't reach out, you know. And I couldn't reach him with my left hand 'cause he was on the other side of me. I was tryin' to get up to reach out to him, and I heared somebody say, "Grab him, grab him." And they grab me and put me back on the bed 'cause I's gettin' off.

I started comin' to again, but it was the same thing. The Lord was comin' in, and I heared him. I knew his voice above any of 'em. My uncle, he said, "You-all leave him alone. Don't touch him, and see what he does." Said, "Just pray." I could hear him tell 'em that. But I couldn't hear nobody else, you know.

And the brightness begin to come in again. It's like this cloud was goin' away, like I was under a black cloud or somethin'. And it was goin' away, and this brightness was comin' in. It was the Lord comin' in. And that time, whenever I retch, it's just like I retch out and got him. And my eyes come open, and I could see in the room that it was just a real bright glow. And the Lord set me up.

Next thing I knew, I was on my feet. And I's outside runnin' around, praisin' God—just in a matter of minutes. When I kind of come to myself, I was in my pajamas. And I wouldn't never get out like 'at, you know. I seen my arm and hand the first time—it was big as a ball glove. And I was black all across my side and chest.

I didn't go to church that night, and I asked 'em: "How many days I been out?" And they say, "Seven days." Then on the next church night, I's back handlin' snakes. But I was still swelled. All the swellin' hadn't even went out whenever Darlene left.

And it was probably that night after church when I'd gone to bed—it was like I was havin' a bad dream—I woke up, and I was screamin' for Darlene. That woke me up, screamin' for her. And it embarrassed me real bad. I'd never had a bad dream like that-un, me calling nobody's name. That bothered me, you know, for a week or two. I couldn't figure it out.

I always put ever'thing before the Lord. So I was down in the woods prayin'—I'd go pray all the time by myself. I'd stay for hours at a time and pray and seek the Lord. And I'd pray up to a certain point, and the Lord's anointin' be all around me like I's fadin' out into his Spirit, you know. But I couldn't go on as far as I wanted to. So I was sittin' on a stump, where a tree had been cut down right beside another tree, and I'd sit on that stump and lean back on that other tree—talk to the Lord a lot. And I's sittin' there, and I asked the Lord to show me what was wrong. I said, "God, show me whatever this problem is—why was I callin' for Darlene when I woke up?"

I don't 'member no dream I had. It's just a sudden *bam!* you know, like seein' somebody shake you and you holler, "What?" But I wasn't hollerin' that. I hollered "Darlene" extremely loud, and I wanted to know why. And the Lord spoke to me and said, "You not strong enough yet." So about, I guess, another week passed—I'm prayin' again. And I said, "Lord, show me, and make me strong enough." I felt real good in my heart, but he didn't speak to me.

So we went to church that night—I's holdin' a revival. Then we come in from revival. Well, Darlene always had her bed fixed real clean and nice. So we went to bed, you know. She was already in bed whenever I go in. And I said, "Darlene, some grandkids been up here." She said, "Yeah, they's here, but they left." And I said, "Why didn't you put a sheet on the bed?" I said, "Feel like it got sand in the bed." She said, "Glenn, I did." And I said, "Well, it feel like sand. It must be cracker crumbs or somethin'." I couldn't lay there, you know. She put another sheet on the bed. We went back to bed, and it's the same thing. About the third or fourth sheet she put on the bed, it's the same thing. So I laid down on the couch—it was gettin' pretty late.

Next day, I studied about that all day, you know. Two, three days went by. Ever'time I go to bed with her, it's the same way. So I say, "God, I got to have some relief from this. Is this the devil botherin' me—I have all kind of battle with him?" So I get in there prayin' again. The Lord, he ain't spoke to me and answered me, you know, about what I'm prayin'.

But I just keep puttin' it before me. Then it just come over my mind, you know—scripture come to my mind—that the bed was defiled. And I said, "Lord, is this you showin' me this?" I felt the Holy Ghost anointin' come all over me. I said, "Okay, Lord, whatever it is, if you'll show me, make me strong enough—I won't do nothin' about it." So the Lord showed me what Darlene's doin'. He just told me *the bed was defiled.* So I knew what that meant. I knew I hadn't did anything. That's what led me through the whole nine yards of it. Wadn't for that, Darlene couldn't kept tellin' me things she's tellin' me over and over.

I promised God that I wouldn't do nothin' about it, so I put it in God's hands—each time she'd tell me somethin'—instead of me slappin' her, then makin' love to her like she always wanted to do. She liked that breakin' up— do somethin' to you, get mad at you, and fuss on you a little, and then be lovey-dovey, you know. But all that changed when the Lord showed me that

Reverend Glenn Summerford

the bed was defiled. And he showed me that I was goin' have to obey him, and me not cast the devil out of her no more.

As I said, I'd go down there in the woods and pray all the time. Ever'day I had a special time of day. At nighttime, ever' night at a special time, a angel come up and shake me. I'd get up and go pray—ever' night. I've had many, many blessin' of the Lord—and I could tell about visions and God showing me things and God speakin' to me fer a long time. I was real close to the Lord. I was closer to the Lord than anybody ever knew. I was walkin' in all his ways that I could possibly walk in.

I stayed away from ever'body. I didn't listen to ever'body's problems. I stayed to myself all the time. And I talked to people just when it was necessary to talk to 'em. Darlene, she'd take care all the bills. She would go pay her bills and stuff like 'at. She'd go buy groceries. She'd go wherever she want to go. She would take all phone calls. If it was important, I'd talk to 'em. But usually I'd tell her what to tell 'em, and I'd get with 'em or somethin'. That way, I'd keep my mind on the Lord and the Scripture.

I wadn't like most of 'em, havin' go out in the woods and pray to pick up a snake. Some of 'em don't believe in goin' huntin' without wearin' boots— they might step on a snake or somethin'. I wadn't like 'at. I believe God was out there in the woods just like he was down there at the church. Wherever I went, I didn't have to pray him down out of heaven or nothin' like 'at. All I had to do was call on his name, and that anointin'—just all over me.

And that's the way I walked. I'd be threatened—my life was threatened time and time again. People would pull guns on me and ever'thing, even at church, and pulled big knives on me—and the Lord always took care of me. I didn't never have to fight no more.

And I didn't fight Gene Sherbert. I didn't even know nothin' about what was goin' on with Gene until the day I caught Darlene with him. See, I had some little squirrel dogs, and I'd walk 'em around and let them hunt squirrels in them bottoms. But I'd get way back down there where I'd always pray. So one morning early, well—this was close to the end of September—I took the two little cur dogs, little registered curs, and walked down in the woods, went way down on the creek. And I carried my rifle with me, but I wouldn't shoot the squirrels. I'd just shoot up in the air.

I got down there, and they treed a squirrel. And I let 'em stay treed about thirty minutes 'cause I's over 'ere prayin'. So before I got down there to the dogs, I heared a car come in, up the house. And it was loud, but I didn't know who it was. I didn't really care, you know, 'cause I went to pray. So I shot the gun and got the dogs off that tree, patted them real good. And I come on around the creek as it makes a bend, and I'm going back towards my house 'cause I know somebody went up there and I was goin' see who it was.

I couldn't call the dogs to me, so I got to shootin' the gun to get 'em to come. And I kept callin' 'em, you know, and they come on up towards me. But they struck and treed again, and they wouldn't come. So I walked on off and left them and got way on up close to the house. But I didn't go all the way up 'ere. And I seen Gene and Darlene go into the house. So I waited fifteen minutes, I guess, and they didn't come out. But I didn't want a-go up 'ere.

And the dogs treed again on the other side of the creek, so I just turned around and went back to the creek, back down there in the woods and prayed fer a long time. Them dogs treed three or four different times, and I'd go to them just like I was huntin' for real. But I wouldn't go back to the house 'cause I was waitin' on him to leave, you know. I still didn't want a-go up 'ere. And I stayed down there probably a hour.

I finally decided to go back to the house—I figured maybe he left, but he hadn't. And I was really prayed up. When I get up there I went in the house and put the gun up. Then I turn around and come back out . . .

That was like in the last of September. I knew she had been calling him before even he moved to Alabama 'cause I had a phone bill of two hunderd-and-somethin' dollars from Newport, Tennessee. Well, I was hurt. See, I got him to move, and I he'ped him get the job at the cabinet shop. I even he'ped him get the house he rented. And I let him have money, you know. I tried to he'p him 'cause I love Brother Gene.

Later Darlene told me she'd went with Gene before. And I said to her, "Well, it ain't nothin' the Lord can't take care of." At that time I was real close to the Lord. If I hadn't been real close to the Lord, I'd a-got in some real bad trouble. But that time wadn't too long a'ter I'd got bit. And, as I said, the Lord give me a lot of visions and stuff when I was out, you know. And I'd got real close to the Lord.

So I went out to Gene's. I had a horse out there, and I went and got my horse. I'd been lettin' Gene keep him, ridin' him—him and his boy. Gene wadn't there when I went, so when he come in that evenin', he come down at the house and brought my saddle. So I went out there where he was.

Darlene made it pretend like I was goin' jump on him. She said, "Naw, Glenn, don't do it, don't do it!" I just looked at her. And Gene didn't say nothin'. He just stood there. And he said, "Brother Glenn," said, "I love you like Jonathan loved David." And I said, "I know, you said you do." And he talked

Reverend Glenn Summerford

like while I was snakebit, some things went on—as I said, I was out seven days and nights that I didn't know nobody. That supposedly's been the time that they had first went together.

And Darlene started runnin' her mouth, and I started to get in my truck and leave. I said, "I'm goin' leave. Gene can take you with him or whatever you want to do." And she went to cryin', beggin' me not to leave, you know. So I didn't.

Gene knows I didn't never do him wrong in no way. And Gene knows I wadn't drinkin'. If I'd been drinkin' . . . him and these other guys I talked to later . . . if I'd been drinkin', there'd been trouble. 'Cause long time ago whenever I drank, anybody smarted me up wrong way or somethin', why they'd have to fight me. And Darlene and Gene already had it made up if I'd a-hit her, she would've went and got a warrant for me for assault. They'd put me in jail, and her and Gene would have left and took Marty with 'em.

Now, the first time I caught Darlene runnin' around—back in the '80s—I slapped her 'bout two or three times. She got in my face that time and was runnin' her mouth at me real bad, and I slapped her. But that was back when she's goin' with a Coots—I can't think of his first name. You see, his wife had called me and told me that she'd caught Darlene and her old man together. They was down there together at the store at Five Points.

His wife'd been callin' all day, tryin' talk to me. I kept seein' Darlene answer the phone, and she'd get real smart with somebody and hang up. I'd say, "Who's callin' you?" And she said, "Somebody pullin' them pranks on me." I could tell she was real shook up. So I said, "Well, let me talk to 'em next time they call." She unplugged the phone. Then I went and put the phone back up, and she unplugged it again. I plugged it back up, and the phone rung, and I answered it. And it was that sister—her and her old man go to church with us. And she told me, "Brother Glenn, you know, I'm sorry to tell you, but I caught them together. And I've been tryin' to call you all day, and Darlene won't let me talk to you." So when she was talkin' to me, Darlene got right up in my face and went to mouthin' off and usin' curse words. So I slapped her.

The other time Darlene's seeing somebody, I forgot who it was. I never actually caught 'em. It was always somebody tellin' me about it. Both times was in the '80s, and she repented both times.

And this time with Gene, as I said, I was close to the Lord. I almost died when I got snakebit, and I got real close to the Lord. But I think with Darlene things were different and things really got started after I got snakebit that last time. Why, as soon as I got able to go, I was right back in church, and I started

Sign in Glenn's church. Photograph by Ken Elkins.

revival. But I knew she wadn't participatin' in the services like she had been, 'cause God would use her in prophecy and stuff like 'at. And I knew somethin' was wrong with her, but I didn't know what. She told me, like, ever'time we get ready to go to church, she'd say, "Do we have to go?" And I'd say, "Well, I need to go—people dependin' upon me." And she would just drag around, you know, and we'd be late gettin' to church and stuff like 'at.

She was tellin' me all kind of stuff. She'd say, "Well, Glenn, I got somethin' I got to tell you," and then she would change her mind, you know, just act crazy. And I said, "Well, let's just pray," and she wouldn't. She wouldn't do that. One of the sisters come over to the house to pray with us, but Darlene wouldn't pray. Then after the sister left, why Darlene told me again, "Well, Glenn, they's some things I got to tell you before I can live right." I said, "I thought you was livin' right all these years." And she said, "Well, whenever that you got snakebit," she said, "I'd been talkin' to some men." And I said, "Well, it's all they was to it, wadn't it?" And she said, "Yeah." And I said, "Well, the Lord will forgive you, you know, 'cause we had them kind of problems before."

Reverend Glenn Summerford

And she would say things like, "Glenn, you think I'm gettin' fat?" or "Glenn, you think I'm gettin' ugly?" She was just wantin' 'tention. And when I quit givin' her the 'tention that she was wantin', why, then it was like turning through the pages—it got faster. Instead of it's being once a month or so, it would be like ever'day, and it just got worse and worse.

Then followin' that time with her and Gene, she started tellin' me about her and J. L. Dyal. She started tellin' me about her and Willie Southard. She started tellin' me about her and J. L. Lewis—you know, just all way down the line.

So we went to church. I don't remember who all was there, but there was a pretty good crowd that night down there at Woods Cove. They knew somethin' was wrong, you know. And I told the people, I said, "We got a family problem, and I'm goin' let the assistant pastor go ahead and keep ever'thin' goin'." I said, "I might not come tomorrow night. It all depends on if I get ever'thing straightened out." I could see that they was puzzled. They didn't know what was goin' on, and some of the brothers asked me. I just told 'em, "Darlene's not actin' right, you know. She just actin' crazy and tellin' me all kind of old crazy stuff." And I said, "I don't feel like I can do what the Lord wants me to do and try to baby her around. I'm goin' find out what's goin' on."

So I just left it with the assistant pastor for a week to try to get ever'thin' straightened out. And I went and personally talk to each one of the brothers. I'd carry Darlene with me and sometimes the boys. I went and talked with Brother Willie Southard. He's a good brother—went to his house and talked with him. He told me, he said, "Glenn, I didn't want to tell you this, but," he said, "Darlene's been talkin' to me a lot." Said, "You know I've called up there and talked to her a lot, but it ain't nothin' ever really happened. Just talk." And I said, "That's all I wanted to know. She's tellin' me all kind of stuff." So I went and talked to another brother—I believe it was Brother J. L. Dyal—asked him. And he told me, "Brother Glenn," he said, "you know I told you before she'd been makin' eyes at me at church and pickin' at me and stuff." And he said, "I told you before, but she got pretty bad at it." And I said, "Well, that ain't nothin' new. We know how the devil does, you know." I said, "We'll just pray about it." And he said, "Okay."

And durin' that week I went and talked with all the brothers. But, see, I didn't believe nothin' she told me. She just kept on tellin' me stuff, and I'd go talk to the ones. But when we'd get there to talk with 'em, she wouldn't get out. I don't believe I even thought it that she was actually havin' sex with nobody, except one person. But I don't want to do nothin' that would split any family up. Bad enough for me to have to go through what I'm goin' through. If they done somethin', they'll have to answer fer that. No matter what they done or didn't do, God'll forgive 'em, you know.

Anyway, when we went back to church on another night—I think it was on a Wednesday night during that week—Darlene told me that she'd repented and she was goin' get in the altar and pray and get rebaptized. Then we got to church, and she went to the altar, but she wouldn't. She just went and kneeled down for a few minutes, and then she got up there and started singin', you know, with the rest of 'em. So I didn't preach or do nothin', I just stayed on my seat.

The kind of relationship we'd had up until about the time that I got snakebit, it had vanished away. See, I was walkin' more in the Spirit, and the desire to do things we used to do was fadin' away. As far as makin' love, we didn't quit that. But whenever I got snakebit the last time, I completely put ever'thing in God's hands. I'd prayed for her so much till the Lord showed me to just turn her loose, you know. I couldn't keep castin' devils out of her. I got to just put her in his hands. So that's what I did.

Really, she wasn't never the same after she realized that she wasn't goin' to get her first son back. She wasn't the same. She told me how old he was. She said she knowed she wadn't ever goin' get him back. And she kept blamin' it on the people that she said had prophesied to her that she was goin' get him back. And she kept bringin' that kind of stuff up, saying she believed in God, but the people had lied to her or somethin'. I tried to talk to her—that's the only kind of arguments we'd have. I would give her the Bible scriptures and stuff, but she just wadn't the same anymore. So it's like she was livin' right just 'cause she thought she's goin' get her boy back like that. Then when she seen she wadn't goin' get him back, why she just got where she didn't care anymore.

And she had been wantin' me to give the church up and leave with her. But I'd tell her, "I'm goin' turn it over to a devout brother and start another." And she'd get better for a while, and then she'd see I didn't have anybody to completely turn it over to—and God hadn't really told me to. So I'd just hold on.

Whenever I seen in what she was doin', then I started just ignorin' her. When I started ignorin', she just like went crazy, you know, worser, like, ever'-time. She'd say, "Glenn, I know you goin' to beat me up, but I'm goin' tell you. I got tell you. I can't live right to I tell you." Then she'd tell me somethin', and I'd tell her, "I don't want hear no more. If God forgive you, whatever it was, I do too. Just forget it, and put it in God's hands." And then whenever she would just keep on sayin' she couldn't live right 'cause she did somethin', I'd tell her again: "Well, if it's been awhile back, you know, and they ain't no harm come of it, God's punishin' you for it. Pray and God'll forgive you of it." I said, "All the people you've helped, you goin' destroy like 'at. They'll lose their faith and their confidence in you." So she would pray, and then just before she left, it got so she wouldn't pray. Then she'd tell me somethin' else. And that went on, see, for a whole week like 'at.

Some of 'em that she told me about—the ones she would be runnin' a'ter—they'd come to me, but she didn't know it. So I told 'em, "I won't say nothin' about it. Just don't say nothin' about it. We'll pray about it, and God'll take care of it." 'Cause I was hopin' she would straighten up. I wadn't wantin' to just tear down ever'thing that we'd built up.

And they was different men that come to me and told me that they met her in town or the grocery store or somethin'. And they said she would flirt with 'em. One of 'em come told me, Brother Uly's son Earl. He told me that she had met him in different places, just run up on him. And he said that she wanted to get rid of me and get her a real man. But he didn't tell me that until after she was gone. And he said that happened more than once. So I asked him, "What did you tell her?" He said he told her that she had the best man in Alabama—she needed to stay with him.

And Earl knows, when he told me them things, it didn't bother me 'cause I'd been seein' it comin'. Just like playin' ball—you see the ball comin', and you miss it, and it hits you. Well, you can't blame nobody but you. So that's kind of the way I was. I seen things comin', and I didn't do anythin' about it. I wadn't blind to what all Darlene was doin', and I didn't ignore it—I just put it before God.

Most time before, things would work out. I believe this would have worked out if she hadn't of got pregnant. See, I believe that is what really brought it all on. I got a thing from the doctor that she'd gotten pregnant, but that was after she was left. She had went to a doctor, and they had sent me the bill. I got it probably about the week after she had left. I'd be willing to take the child and raise it if I was out where I could, but it's not mine.

When I got this letter from the doctor, why, I think I've got somebody else's mail. I didn't even know for sure she was pregnant until she come to court and I seen her. But on the day of the hearing after I was arrested for first-degree assault—that's when I found out that Darlene was pregnant and it wadn't my baby. (They ain't no trial transcript of that hearing, but my lawyer Gary Lackey, he had taped it on a little tape, and his secretary made me a copy of it.)

At that hearing in front of Judge Grider, Lackey said to Darlene, "You went to a doctor for somethin' beside a snakebite didn't you?" And she said, "Naw." And he said, "You know Doctor so and so?" And she said, "Yeah." And her face got red. And he said, "You went to the doctor for somethin' beside snakebite." She said, "Yeah." And he said, "Tell us what it was." And she said, "For pregnancy test." And he said, "A pregnancy test?" And she said, "Yeah." And he said, "Okay," said, "you still say that is my client's baby?" And she said, "Naw, it ain't his." And he said, "You know whose it is?" And she said, "Naw." But, see, then in the big trial, she tried to make it like it was my baby.

I believe she got pregnant by Gene, but she didn't intend to. And I believe that when she got pregnant, she was afraid that it wadn't mine, and she was afraid I would kill her. That's what I believe.

Only thing that hurt me is the way that she slipped off. It hurt me the most when I realized that she'd been plannin' it a long time. See what she did, and I didn't even tell anybody—I told Brother Uly and his son and some of 'em that was down there: "You-all see anything different in my house?" They said, "Yeah." And I said, "I just noticed it last minute when I's standin' there." And they said, "There's somethin' different, but I can't place what it is." I said, "You see all her family pictures she had on the walls and all? She replaced them with just different types of things." And then in one corner of the bedroom where I'd bought some new saddles, there was a pasteboard box. And she'd took all her picture frames and stuff and took the pictures out of 'em and stacked 'em in the box. I found different things that she, personal stuff, that she had stacked up and had ready to go. So she'd been plannin' it, see, fer a while. She got ever'thing ready, probably weeks before she left. And all she had to do was come back.

Later when Marty come to prison at West Jefferson to visit—late '92—he told me what had happened. He said, "Daddy, Mama tried to get me to leave with her, said she was goin' leave with another man." And I said, "Who?" And he said he didn't know. But she had talked with Marty about runnin' off with her.

But back when I first seen the stuff she had stacked up and then figured it out in my mind, I knew what she had done. I knew she had already made plans with somebody. I knew that I'd fell into that trap. See, God had spoke to me and said Satan had laid that trap for me and I'd fall into it. The Lord had already spoke to me, but he'd also said that I *would* fall into it. So it was already in process then.

But I'll say this, I didn't have no reason to want Darlene dead, and I still ain't got no reason want her dead. I don't want nobody hurt or killed. I just wish I could get the whole world saved, but I can't.

Reverend Glenn Summerford

Dorothy Dyal

A Convert

learnt more about the word of God from listening to Brother Glenn's preaching than I have from any other preacher I ever sat under. We had services on Friday, Saturday, and Sunday nights, as well as Wednesday—'cause Brother Glenn said on the weekends is when the devil is raging and there's people out there doing what the devil wants them to, so we might as well be in church doing what God wants us to do.

And I'll guarantee you that when that man walked in that door—when he was in the Lord—when he walked in that door and raised his hands and said, "Praise God!" and started walking in the aisles with his hands up, praising the Lord—you knew the anointing of God moved in there. And there was no denying—there was no denying it.

And he had some really good healings. My son JJ is one of them. He was in a car wreck. All his face was busted. His jaw was out of place. His teeth was out of place. He was busted all through. He could not eat; he was living off of instant breakfast. And he went to church one night. He was sittin' there, and he went up for Brother Glenn to pray for him—course, the whole church prayed. Brother Glenn laid hands on him, prayed for him. Then JJ went back, and he sit down. About fifteen minutes I turned around, and JJ was crying. And I thought, he was hurtin'. And I said, "Well, son, what's wrong?" He said, "Mama, my jaws feel like they're shiftin'." He couldn't talk plain, but I could understand what he was saying. Well, you've seen the hard, round Certs mints—I had some in my pocket and put one in my mouth. He set there a few minutes, then said, "Mama, give me one of them Certs." I said, "Son, are you sure?" He said, "Yes, ma'am. I'm sure." I give him one of them Certs, and he set right there on

Dorothy Dyal.

that church bench and chewed it up. And that was the first thing he had eat since his car wreck—two and a half months. He went back to the doctor. They had told him before he was gonna have to have surgery, but they wouldn't do it because we didn't have the $500 up front to give 'em. But when he went back to the doctor, the doctors told him, unless he just wanted to, he didn't have to because his jaw was going back in place. And it corrected itself.

And my granddaughter—her little feet was turned in, and her toes would catch. And she could only make maybe one or two steps, and she'd fall. And her little toes would hit each other. The doctors told us that she would have to have her legs and her ankles broke. She'd have to wear braces until after she was eighteen months old or older. And we took her to church one night, and Brother Glenn laid hands on her, prayed for her. We took her back home that night; and to be honest, I had forgot about it. I really had. I didn't think no more about it. We got home, and we set the baby down in my kitchen. And she started walking back and to looking down at her feet. Why, I looked down to see what the baby was looking down at. And her little feet was straight. And they're still straight today. And I told my daughter, I said, "Sandy, look." I said, "Look at the baby's feet." And she looked down, and she said: "Mama, she's walking. She's not falling—she's walking." And I said, "Yes, she is." I said, "Honey, that's just a miracle that God performed on that baby." And we didn't even realize it until we got home. But today she's still walking, and she's never had a brace on. She's never had no legs broke, no ankles broke. She's eleven years old now and doing fine. Brother Glenn's the one that prayed for her. Sure was. It was down there in the brick church near Goose Pond before we moved to Woods Cove.

And Brother Glenn prayed for me one time. I had a real bad, serious sinus infection. And Brother Glenn preached faith to us, you know. Now, I'm not saying nothing bad about going to no doctor. I go to a doctor, you know, when I have to. But sometimes our faith is weak; and, you know, we have to do something. But Brother Glenn prayed for me one time. All my head was infected and everything. And this is a little gross, but about two days later I was home, hanging out clothes. And I went in—I got weak—I went in and I sit down and I thought. I started praying. I said, "God, I know the prayer of faith that's been prayed. Please, if you're going to heal me, Lord, heal me." And the Lord spoke to me and said, "Bend over. Put your head between your legs. Bend over." I did. Now, when I bent over, it was like pouring water out of a bucket. All that infection, every bit of that infection, come out of my head right there on towels and stuff—'cause I went and got me a towel, and I put it down. And every bit of it cleared up. I went back to the doctor. I didn't have no infection. God healed it. And Brother Glenn's the one that prayed for me. He's the one that prayed for me at church a couple of nights before that, and God healed me. And it ain't every time that God heals right then, you know. But sometimes it will be a day. Sometimes it might be a week, but God heals.

Then there was when Aunt Erma got put in that wheelchair. My aunt Erma, my grandma's twin sister, she got down. And she's got high sugar and stuff, but something had happened, arthritis or something—I don't know exactly what. But she couldn't walk. She was in a wheelchair. And she come to church, and Brother Glenn prayed for her. And I guess maybe fifteen, twenty minutes after Brother Glenn got through, my aunt Erma was shouting all over the church.

And my cousin broke her arm, her hand one time—right at the wrist. And we was having house meetings at different places—it was our turn, and she came over to our house that night to have Brother Glenn pray for her. Well, my daughter was carrying our second grandbaby. And she went in labor, and we had to leave and carry her to the hospital. But we told Brother Glenn and them to go on with the services. Well, my cousin come in, and Brother Glenn and them prayed for her. And God healed her hand right then. Right there and then, he healed her hand. She still uses it—does anything she wants to with it. Never had a cast on it. God healed it. Sure did.

And I tell you something else too. My oldest granddaughter—I don't know what was wrong with the cat, but there was this Siamese cat that come in our house—and my oldest granddaughter, when she was about a year and a half years old, was playing with the cat. And the cat bit her. And in less than an hour's time, that baby's hand was swelled. Oh, it was swollen up there really bad. And there was red streaks running up her arm, and we rushed her to the hospital. And they put her in the hospital, and they was giving her all kind of shots and everything else for it. And the red streaks just kept climbing. I mean it wasn't stopping, you know. And it got infected just that fast. The baby was getting to be in real serious condition. And if that had a-continued going up her arm, like it had, and went into her heart—then it could have killed her. And so I called Brother Glenn to come to the hospital and pray for her. And he did. He came up there and he went in and he prayed for her. And by the time Brother Glenn prayed for her—almost by the time he turned that baby's hand loose—the red streaks had stopped going up her arm. They just stopped. And then the next thing, you know, the swelling begin to go down. And I think it was the next day—I believe it was, or the day after—they released her, and we took her home. And she was fine. They didn't have to do nothing else to her.

Then there was the time my son poured alcohol on an ant bed and set it on fire. He was about thirteen. He poured gasoline on the alcohol, and it blowed up on him. It caught his shirt on fire, and it burnt him all across under his arm, really bad. We called Brother Glenn to come to help pray for him. And Brother Glenn and we prayed for him. And the next morning when my son got up, the blisters had done went down. He had second- and third-degree burns. And the blisters had done went down. And the pain had stopped all across under his arm, and he doesn't have any scars. It healed up in a matter of days, two or three days. The only sign of it now is that he doesn't have any hair growing in that area.

And there was one night there—we was at church—Brother Glenn was preaching. He stopped preaching, and he called me up there, and he said, "Sister Dorothy, come here." And I went up there. He says, "I want the whole church to pray right now." He said, "Because Sister Dorothy's son is in danger, in real serious danger." And he told me, he said, "Sister Dorothy, I hate to tell you, but your son is doing something that he's telling you a lie about. And it's

Dorothy Dyal

put him in danger." He said, "And we need to pray, and we need to pray right now." Well, we all did pray. Going on home from church that night, the Lord spoke to me, and he said, "When you get home, you don't stop. You go straight to your son's room, and you pray." Well, I did. I done what the Lord told me to do. And I went in there, and I went to praying. God give me a vision of JJ. I seen him. I can take you to the spot right today. It was at Matheney Bridge. I could see him laying on a flat rock at Matheney's. And he was just laying there and lifeless-like, and he was real white, like he was dead. But then I seen a great big hand, the hand like it was the size of a house. And I knew it was God's hand. And I seen JJ stand up 'cause the hand went up under him. And he stood up in the palm, and he looked straight up. And when he looked straight up, I knew, because the anointing of God went all over me. And I shouted all over his bedroom. I knew God had brought him out of that danger. JJ told me about a week later. I asked him about it, and he first said, "No, Mama." I said, "Son, you will tell me," I said, "because God's done let us know that you was in some kind of danger." I said, "I know where you was at," I said, "but I'm going to wait. You're going to tell me." About a week later he come in, and he told me, "Mama, I was at Matheney's, me and Robert" (a friend of his). And he said, "Mama, there was bullets flying all the way around us. Somebody was trying to kill us." JJ and Robert had rode up there on a four-wheeler, and they had run out of gas. There were some fellers down there with some girls. And they started shooting at JJ and Robert. And JJ didn't know what to do. And Robert throwed his hands up in the air, like, and said, "They're gonna kill us." And about the time he throwed his hands up in the air, the four-wheeler started up, by itself. And here they went. And they rode almost two miles back to Robert's house—and the gas tank was bone dry, wasn't nothin' in it. But like I said, I seen God pick him up—that's what God can do. And Brother Glenn saw that danger. And that happened before JJ's wreck, just before Brother Glenn's trial in February '92.

Brother Glenn was supposed to marry JJ and wasn't able to. And the only reason he didn't marry him is because they wouldn't let everybody that wanted to go to the wedding into jail. That's the only reason he didn't have Brother Glenn marry him. JJ is not a Christian, but he used to go listen to Brother Glenn preach. And JJ says that if Brother Glenn got out of jail—if he had to quit his job—he'd go see him preach. I mean, he thinks that much of him. He says that he's never heard nobody that can preach the way Brother Glenn does.

Now, when Brother Glenn said, "God told me, or God said"—it come true. It was that way. And when a man of God tells you, "God said so and so," and it comes to pass—you know that God told him to tell you that. And I never had Brother Glenn to tell me nothing that did not come to pass. Some of the things that he told me has come to pass since he went to prison. But it still come to pass. Yes, it did. When he said, "God said it," you could count on it. You know it was gonna come to pass. And when he said, "I believe," then you know that's what he believed—it was just what he thought. But when he said, "God said," then you knew to look for it. Because it was that way.

Brother Glenn also converted my husband, J. L. Dyal. And, honestly, you couldn't 'ave got no meaner than J. L. was before he was converted. He drunk all the time, and he'd fight at the drop of a hat. And he started living right and repented and got the Holy Ghost and everything under Brother Glenn. And my husband ain't touched a drop of drink in almost twelve years. Now he's a good husband, and he's a good daddy.

It all started for J. L. about a year and a half after I started to church and got the Holy Ghost there at Brother Glenn's church near Five Points. We had moved then to a little church in a community called Mud Creek. My husband would take me to church, and he'd sit in the car. But Brother Glenn used to walk by the car every night that we had church, and he'd ask my husband, "Might as well get out and come in." And J. L.'d say, "No, I'll sit here." That's all Brother Glenn'd say to him, and he'd go on in. Every church night Brother Glenn'd walk by that car, and he'd invite him into the church. And then my husband got to where he'd park the car close to the door so he could hear the preaching. He'd roll the window down, and he'd listen. Then that didn't satisfy him, so he come in. He eased up on the back bench. And then not too many church nights later he got about halfway. And then after we moved to the brick church near Goose Pond, he got to about the second bench from the front. And then the next thing I knew, he was in the altar. And he's still got the Bible Brother Glenn gave him.

But before J. L. was converted, Brother Glenn would tell me: "Sister Dorothy, God's going to help you. You hold in there and hang on to the Lord. God's going to bring him in. You just hold on, Sister Dorothy." And them words is what kept me going. And it helped me a lot. It helped me go through what I had to go through, and I'm glad I did. It was worth it. It really was. But if it hadn't a-been for Brother Glenn—and I know God showed Brother Glenn because I didn't tell him. I didn't talk to him about it. I didn't tell him nothing that was going on in my home or nothing else. But, when it got to the point to where I didn't feel like I could take anymore, then I would go up to be prayed for. And Brother Glenn would tell me, "Sister Dorothy, I know you're going through a lot. God showed me what you're going through." "But," he said, "if

118

you'll hold on, he's going to bring your husband in. And he'll be a different man." And he is—he is! But if it hadn't a-been for Brother Glenn telling me that, I guess I would have give up. And I would have quit because I was fighting a hard battle. But Brother Glenn helped me through it—him and God. But by Brother Glenn obeying the Lord—and I know God had to show him because, like I said, I didn't tell him nothing—but by him obeying God and a-telling me what he felt like the Lord had told him, what God had showed him—that helped me to hold on to the Lord. And it's made a big difference in my life and in my husband's life too. And in lots of ways, even though they're not in church, it's made a big difference in my kids' lives.

I mean, if it hadn't been for Brother Glenn, I would have quit church several times, you know. But, it was like God showed him, and he knew when I was getting down and when I was thinking about giving up. It was like Brother Glenn knew every time, and he'd tell me, "Sister Dorothy, you hold on." And them words kept me going. And I prayed a prayer one time at my house—I'll never forget that because it amazed me so much. There was nobody at my house but me. I was praying and I was talking to God. And I told God, I said, "God, you don't need me, but I need you desperately." Well, the following weekend, we had church. And I was going through quite a bit at that time. And I was in the altar, and I was praying. And Brother Glenn come up there, and he laid hands on me and went to praying for me. And he told me, he said, "Sister Dorothy, you told God he didn't need you." He said, "But God needs you just like you need him." And he said, "And don't you ever tell God that he don't need you again." And that amazed me because there was nobody there. I know that God had to let that man know it. He had to. I never said nothin' to nobody—nobody. But them's the words Brother Glenn told me in that altar that night. And I know God had to show him. God had to tell him. And the way God used that man. If he hadn't have been standing where he should be with the Lord—God's not going to use a sinner that way—if he's not standing where he should be, God's not going to use him the way he used that man. He just won't—I don't believe. I honestly don't.

And the first time I ever seen a serpent took up, I was at Brother Glenn's church where I started back about 1987—right down below the Chicken Basket near Five Points in that little white building that use to be Bull Durham's Grocery. I didn't know they took up serpents. I saw the snake box sitting up there. But I thought it was a prayer box where you put the names in, you know; and you get the names out and pray over them. And I seen Brother Glenn go over there and open up the box, and I thought he was going to get a handful of names out of the box. But instead, he come out with this rattlesnake about as long as I was tall. And I set there, and I thought, My God, what is he doing? I wanted to leave, but yet I wanted to see. I got to watching him. And he got to preaching, and he was preaching all around that Bible stand up there. The next thing I knew, he took that thing, that serpent, and he hung it around his neck. And he was doing some good preaching. And I said, "Now, Lord"—he was preaching about taking up serpents—I said, "Lord, if it's really meant to be, I want to do it too. I want to obey your word." And Brother Glenn kept preaching. And further on in there he says: "If you want the power of God in your life, fast and pray and ask God for it because he's promised it to you after you receive the Holy Ghost. He's promised you power. Fast and pray, and the power of God will come in your life like it should. If you want to do this, fast and ask God to let you do it— and you can do it." And Brother Glenn didn't know what I was asking God because I wasn't asking out loud.

And I went home. And I begin to fast, and I begin to pray that God would let me do it too, if it was meant to be. Then later after we had moved from that church to the brick church, we was up praising the Lord. And I was standing there, and I said: "Lord, if it's meant to be, let me do it." I had been fasting and I had been praying. I said, "Lord, if it's meant for me to take that serpent, let Brother Glenn hand it to me." And Brother Glenn was up there— he had the serpent—and he didn't hand it to me, but he turned around toward me and held the serpent up. And God let me know that I could go take that serpent, and I did. And I've never felt nothing like it. That was my first time to ever feel the anointing to take up a serpent. And it was—to me it was different than anything I'd ever felt, you know. My hands felt like ice. They was cold as ice. But the snake felt warm. It really did. It felt warm in my hands, but my hands felt like they were cold as ice. And it was a great big rattlesnake. As a matter of fact, I think it was the same snake that he had the first time that I ever seen him take up a serpent. Then, you know, I just went from there. When God let me, I'd do it. I still do when God lets me. I still do.

But Brother Glenn was the first time I'd ever seen it done. And I knew it had to be God. Because you know it's real. And you know there ain't nothing wrong with it. If it ain't the power of God, a man ain't going to take that rattlesnake and stand there and hold it and put it around his neck and preach with it—and its head going just anywhere it wants to go. I mean, I've seen Brother Glenn walk up and down with serpents preaching—four or five at a time. I've seen Brother Glenn pick up a serpent, and the anointing be so strong that it would kill that snake. It would literally die. And it would just

Dorothy Dyal

Dorothy Dyal handling a rattlesnake. Photograph courtesy of Dorothy Dyal.

turn upside down in his hand. I've seen it several times. And it was just the anointing of God that killed it—nothing more.

I can remember seeing Brother Glenn be up there preaching and be under the anointing and walk up and open the door on a wood stove and reach in and grab the coals—and them flaming in his hand—and walk around and preach a little and never get burned. I've seen him do it. I've seen him pull the ash pan out, and there'll be coals in the ash pan—take his shoes off and stand on 'em while he preached.

Brother Glenn had quite a few gifts in his life from God. He would go off in the woods and seek God and pray. He had the discerning of the spirit—he could discern the spirit. And he preached like none I have ever heard. The expression "fire and brimstone"—that's pretty much Brother Glenn. He didn't hold nothing back. He didn't hide nothing. He didn't cut nothing out of the Bible. He preached it from beginning to end, the way it's supposed to be. He preached from Genesis to Revelation. He wasn't scared to tell you about the end of time or burning in hell no more than he was telling you about going to heaven and getting the Holy Ghost. And he did not try to change it, and he would not back down on the word of God—not for nobody. He would not compromise on the word of God for nobody. He wouldn't do it for his mother, his brother, or nobody else. When Brother Glenn was really in the Lord, he stood firm on the word of God. He really did. Like I said, I've never heard one like him, you know. I really ain't. He would preach it and teach it at the same time—is the way Brother Glenn would do it. And he would preach it in a way that a child could understand what he was talking about, you know. But, you knew, too, that it was the word of God. If anybody can teach you how to get to heaven, he can. And you knowed when Brother Glenn preached— you could tell—he was believing every word he said, wholeheartedly. You knew he was a man of God.

And I've seen Brother Glenn come in the church house, and church would start. And Brother Glenn would raise his hands, and he would start walking up one aisle and down another. And he wouldn't make over two or three walks up and down that aisle until you could feel the anointing—it was like electricity— jumping off of him onto you. 'Cause you could feel the anointing of God just bouncing off of the man—I don't know another way to put it. But you knew that the power of God was on that man.

And I was there the night that Brother Glenn came to the church and apologized to the church and asked the church to forgive him. That was after him and Darlene had separated. He said he had done things that he shouldn't have, and he prayed and asked God for forgiveness. And he said he had to ask the church first. And he come to the church, and he asked everybody to forgive him for it. And we all told him we would forgive him. He got into the altar, and he prayed until he felt like that God had forgive him. And when he come up, he come up speaking in tongues. He went to the river and was baptized over, right then. Brother Carl Porter baptized him. And we went down to the baptizing and seen Brother Glenn baptized. And then I think it was the next day or maybe the day after, I'm not sure. But, anyway, shortly after is when they picked him up and locked him up.

Brother Glenn asked my husband to keep the church going for him and to do the best he could, you know, to keep the church going—and which my husband did. And it was a battle, and it was a struggle; but my husband done the best he could do at it. And we kept it open as long as we could, you know— or he did, I should say.

I guess it was about two to three weeks before Brother Glenn let the church go, I seen Darlene doing a lot that she shouldn't have been doing. And, you know, I don't know if Brother Glenn seen it and chose to ignore it, or if he didn't see it and didn't know. But I did. And you know, I'm not the only one—I guess everybody in the church seen her, you know, doing things that she shouldn't been doing. It started out with just little things, you know, that you thought, well, maybe I was wrong—maybe it was just a trick of the devil, you know, trying to show me something on my sisters that wasn't happening.

Dorothy Dyal

('Cause the devil will fool you like that.) But then it got to the point where you couldn't ignore what you was seeing. You had to believe what you were seeing. And it just sort of got worse. And it was only a matter of time, I guess, that, you know, Brother Glenn confronted her with it. I don't know. I wasn't there, so I can't really say. But most everybody in the church knew, and there was other people outside the church that knew. And there were things she did right there at the meetings that a lot of people didn't approve of. And we heard a lot of rumors, different rumors, you know. But I think that's what they were—most of them were rumors on him, and a lot of them was on her. I can't say which was the truth and which wasn't because I wasn't there. So I don't know. And I won't speculate on what was.

But I do know that Brother Glenn come to the church one night and said that the rumor had got started that he was going to get married again. He said, "And I want to tell the church right here and now, I am not going to get married." He said, "I am married. Darlene is my wife." (And this was after they had separated.) He said, "Darlene is my wife." He said, "And as far as I'm concerned, she will be my wife. There will be no other." He said, "Now, if me and Darlene gets back together," he said, "then I'll be with my wife." He said, "But if not, it will be me and God," he said, "because I am not going to get married again." And we all took him at his word because we didn't have no reason to doubt it.

I believe that there was one time that Darlene was doing all she knowed to do, you know, to live for the Lord. And I believed that she was living it at one time. And I don't know what happened—it's hard to say, you know, what happened—but my guess would be that she picked up some bad spirit somewhere, you know, and she just give over to it. And, it caused her to back up on God. And that will happen, you know. I would truly love to see Darlene back in church and living for the Lord like she's supposed to and doing like she's supposed to do for the Lord. I would truly love to see it with all my heart—I'd love to see it.

I think there was a period that Brother Glenn backed up on God. I think that it happened when he caught Darlene with another man—everybody knew what happened, you know. I mean, it spread like wildfire. I believe that's when it was more than Brother Glenn could handle. I mean, that's a lot for any man to face, you know. A preacher is only human, and they can only stand so much. And I know that the Bible says that God won't put more on us than we can handle, you know, that we can stand. And he won't. But sometimes, we don't always turn to God at that point. And I think that's what happened. But I do believe that if he was going to kill Darlene, it would have been then. Because they were in his house; and, you know, that was his wife. So if he was gonna kill her, it would have been then. He wouldn't have waited until all that time and then done what she said.

But Brother Saylor, Arnold Saylor, prophesied to Brother Glenn not too long before that happened. And he told him that the devil was going to lay a trap for him and that if he wasn't careful he would fall in—and that it could destroy him. And I remember it so well because when all this did take place, I remembered the prophecy that Brother Arnold Saylor had spoke to Brother Glenn. I heard Brother Arnold say it down here in Woods Cove. And it wasn't too long after that until all that happened. And I believe that's when Brother Glenn—you know, it was just more than he could handle.

But when Brother Glenn did back up on the Lord, he did come to the church and apologize to the church. And he told the church that he had been drinking. This was after he had caught Darlene and another man. And Brother Glenn apologized, and he said that, you know, he wanted us to forgive him. And I believe God forgive him for it. And that's when he asked Brother Carl Porter to baptized him again. I'll say most of the church—I can't say everybody, but most of the church—forgive Brother Glenn for it and don't hold it against him. And I don't hold it against him. And he did pray until I do believe God forgive him for it. And, yeah, he might have fell away from the Lord, but I believe with all my heart that he come back to the Lord.

And I do honestly believe that Brother Glenn is a God-called preacher. I believe that with all my heart. I honestly do. And I do not believe that he would've done what they accused him of doing. I don't believe it. I will never believe it. I didn't believe it then—I don't believe it now. I don't. Because he might have done things, some things; but I don't believe he did what he was accused of doing.

And the trial he had wasn't nothing but a kangaroo trial. My husband was supposed to testify for Brother Glenn, but they didn't let none of Brother Glenn's witnesses get on the witness stand. I could have done a better job defending him. I really could have. It was awful. It really was. It was awful. And I think, really, they decided that they would go ahead and make an example out of Brother Glenn. And they figured if they could get him gone, they could take the serpent handling out of Scottsboro and probably out of Jackson County. You know, they could put a stop to it. But it don't work that way. Yeah, there was a good man took, you know, done wrong. And that was Brother Glenn. But God's word is still God's word. And it still holds true, you know. And it says you shall take up serpents; and if you believe it, you'll take them up. They didn't stop it. They might've hindered it for a little while, but they didn't stop it.

124

Glenn

In Turmoil

The last day or so of September I knew that somethin' was wrong with Darlene 'cause she'd get real mad easy at my sons Marty and Mac—that's Michael, but we called him "Mac." But she'd just fly off the handle, so I knew somethin' was botherin' her. I'd try to talk with her at different times, and she'd say, "You'll find out what it is later." But she never would tell me what her problem was.

So Marty and Mac had one of their friends spendin' the night with 'em—I believe his name is a "Moore," I'm not sure. My oldest daughter Jackie was goin' take them to the lake that weekend. So their little buddy come down and spend the night with 'em, and they'd ride the four-wheelers and stuff. When they would come in, why, she would be real smart with 'em, jump on 'em about gettin' out and gettin' muddy and all. And I'd try to talk to her, and she just act crazy. So she'd get in the car and leave and stay gone for a while and come back. See, Darlene always went anywhere she want to go. She had her own vehicle, and I had a truck. Well, she'd go to the store or somethin'. And when she'd come back, she wouldn't act right. So I just go ahead and feed my animals. And I wouldn't really pay no 'tention to her 'cause, you know, more 'tention you give a devil, the more he'll act up. So I knew it was the devil botherin' her.

She really showed out that evenin' when Mac come out in the yard and told me—and then Marty followed him on out there—said, "Daddy, Mama's took a whole bottle of some kind of pills." And I said, "She has?" And he said, "Yeah." And he handed me a little box, you know, showing me what it was. I didn't take time to read it, I just went runnin' in the house. And I said, "Where's them pills at?" And Darlene said, "What pills?" And I said, "Them pills you just took." And she said, "You'll know a'ter while." You know, just crazy stuff like 'at. And Mac said, "She took 'em all, Daddy. I seen her, and Marty did too."

I said, "Get a glass of warm water." And I told Darlene, "You drink that warm water. I'm goin' pray fer you, and the Lord—you'll throw it up." She didn't want to—she kept arguin' about it, you know. And she started out the front door. And I grabbed her by the arm, told her to just hold on, drink that water, or she's goin' to the hospital. You know, we's goin' take her and have her stomach pumped out. So she drank it, and I started prayin', prayed over the water even before she drank it. Just in a few minutes, why, she run out on the front porch and throwed up in the yard. And it looked like blue paint.

So I don't know to this day what kind of pills they really was. But then I sat up with her all that night, but I don't remember what the day of the week or what day of the month it was either—it's been so long. I sat up with her that night to make sure she wouldn't go to sleep. I always heared if you take any dope or anything like that, you're not supposed to go to sleep. I'd talk to her and try to get her to pray and stuff like 'at, and she wouldn't.

She went to actin' up again. And me and the boys was in the house. I'd been down there feedin' my horses, and I come back to the house and was sittin' on the couch. Mac and Marty had just come up on the four-wheelers. They come in, and they said, "Where's Mama at?" I said, "She's outside some-where." So she come in, and I's sittin' on the couch behind the coffee table. I'm there just tired, you know, drinkin' me some Coke-colie. She come in, and she said, "Here, Glenn." She stuck her hand out over the coffee table, and I stuck my hand out 'cause I didn't know what she's wantin' to give me. Then she dropped .22 shells in my hand. She said, "I decided not to do it." And I looked at her. "What you talkin' about?" I just held the shells. And there's a little vase sittin' there, so I dropped 'em in the vase.

And she went through to the bedroom, and a little while I went in there. She didn't have no gun then. She done put it back in her pocketbook. She was standing in front of the mirror cryin'. She'd get in front of the mirror and cry, comb her hair, and take another mirror and look behind her and all that. She'd ask me if I thought she was gettin' fat and stuff like 'at. I told her, "Naw," put my arms around her, and tried to tell her that I loved her and she needed to pray. She was wantin' 'tention like she had on the other times. But I could tell that she was really upset.

Well, as I said, she'd told me about different brothers of the church that she been talkin' to, you know, at church and on the phone, just talkin' love stuff or whatever. Then she told me somethin' on another one of my best friends, the best friend I ever had. And I believed her, you know, because of that stuff with Gene. So I'm thinkin' maybe she is doin' these things and I don't know about 'em.

So she told me that J. L. had called her. And she went down there to get some money. He wadn't goin' get to come to church, so he wanted her to come and pick up some money that he was goin' give me. And she said her and Marty went down there.

Now, J. L. Lewis is a real wealthy man. And like I said, me and him's been like brothers for twenty-five, thirty years. She said her and Marty went down there to his office—he runs a business in Huntsville—said, when they got down there, J. L. give Marty some money and told him go out to the store and get 'em some Coke-colies. And I said, "You-all didn't send Marty down the store, down that parkway—you-all ain't sent Marty down there?" He ain't twelve year old then, you know. "Yeah," Darlene said, "I didn't, but J. L. did." I said, "Well, why'd you do that?" She said, "Well, give me time, and I'll tell you"—you know, real smart, like 'at. I said, "Well, I want to know."

She said, "J. L. pulled a couch up agin the door, and," said, "he's makin' love to me. And he sent Marty down 'ere at the store." She said J. L. had sex with her, and when Marty come back that J. L. cracked the door and retch out there and slapped him, told him to get out there and sit down. So that broke me down. Gene didn't break me down—that broke me down.

Then a'ter that she told me J. L. was callin' her, tryin' to get her to meet him somewhere. Well, I know she wouldn't talk long and she'd hang up. And she said, "That's J. L. callin'." Says, "He keeps callin', tryin' to get me to meet him. He said he rented a motel room or somethin', tryin' to get me to meet him." I said, "I don't believe that." And she said, "Well, you go with me, and I'll prove it to you." She said, "But you'll go down there and talk to J. L., and you won't do nothin' to him." Said, "You-all's good friends. You won't do nothin' to him. All you'll do is jump on me." I said, "Naw, I ain't goin' jump on nobody."

And I said, "Where we got to go?" And she said, "Go down to his office." And I said, "I thought you said he had a motel room." She said, "He has, but he's went back to his office. He's called me from down there." So that's when I went down there. And I pull into the parkin' lot, and he pulls in and gets out of his truck. He tells this boy there to go park his truck. J. L. walks in front of my car and walks around on that side where Darlene is. So I'm in front of the car and raise the hood 'cause the battery cable is bad to get loose. I had a piece of a timin' chain with some tape wrapped around it, down in beside of the battery to help hold the battery in tight. I was goin' to put new cables in it

Gene Sherbert handling a serpent. Photograph by Ken Elkins.

before winter, but I just hadn't. And I'd take that timin' chain and peck the cable down to make it crank, you know.

Well, we just started talkin' normal like we always do, and J. L. was doin' all the talkin'. I was waitin' for him to get through so I could talk with him. And while I was standin' there, I just got madder and madder about what he did to

Marty. See, I believed her. Now, I don't believe her about it—right then, I believed her. And he kept talkin', talkin', talkin', and it just overcome me. He got smart. And when he did, I took that timin' chain and whupped him upside the head. I didn't hit him real hard, but I got his 'tention.

Then we got down to business about what I wanted to talk with him about. I said, "You claim to be my friend. And you foolin' with my old lady all the time and send Marty up the road here to the store." I said, "You bad with the kids, want to slap them around—won't you slap me around?" And that's what I told him.

And he said, "Huh?" You know, he couldn't believe what I was sayin' 'cause I was sayin' what she said. He turned around and looked at her, and he said, "Glenn, she's goin' get you killed." Said, "She'll tell you anything on anybody. You goin' have to straighten that woman out." And then I hit him in the face, I think, with my fist—he's supposed to be talkin' to me, not her. And J. L.'s a real good fighter, too, but he just didn't fight.

I know now that Darlene was settin' J. L. up for me to get into it with him. She said, "J. L., you know you pulled that couch up agin the door, and me and you was huggin' and kissin'." And I's fixin' to fire him up with my fists, but he throwed both hands out. He said, "Glenn, she's lyin' to you." And when I heard her say that—"me and you was huggin' and kissin'"—it just put a stop on everything, you know. My mind just went blank: "She's lyin'." I felt it, you know. She was lyin', way she said it—'cause she wadn't blamin' it on him then. But when she told me to start with, she's blamin' it all on him. I knowed she was changin' things around from what she first said.

And that's where I messed up. He was my best friend. And I hate it, but I did it. I didn't hit J. L. on 'count of Darlene. I wadn't goin' do nothin' to nobody on 'count of Darlene. I was gettin' a divorce from Darlene. See, my kids is always, like, special to me. I always watched a'ter 'em. When she told me that J. L. has sent him up that highway to that store up there—see, I'd seen a kid about eighteen, nineteen year old, get killed up there on that highway right close to that store one night when I was down there huntin'. Somebody'd hit him, killed him. And when she told me J. L. had slapped Marty, that just tore me all to pieces, broke me down. And when I started talking to J. L. about it, well, I just flew real mad. I grabbed that timin' chain and hit him upside the head. And I wadn't drinkin' or anything. It was just the devil. I know *now* what it was—I knowed *then* what it was.

I just wanted to lay down and die. But I fear the Lord more than anything. And at that time I was closer to the Lord than I'd ever been. I come to myself, and I knew I was wrong by even goin' down there and sayin' anything or goin' down there to do anything 'cause of what he did or didn't do.

So anyway, I went on home, and I hadn't been there but just a few minutes till the phone rang. And Darlene was on the phone talkin'. She hollered for me to come in the house, said J. L.'s on the phone. So I go to the house and went in. I said, "I don't want to talk to him." And she said, "He's wantin' to talk to you, Glenn." Said, "He's comin' up here if you don't talk to him on the phone." "Okay, I'll talk to him." So I took the phone. I figured he's goin' cuss me out, you know. But he didn't. He said, "Glenn, look, somethin' I've got to tell you." Said, "Your boys is needin' to tell you. I want you to come down here and meet me at the oak tree at New Hope." I said, "Well, you're wantin' get down there, and me and you to get into it again, ain't you?" He said, "Naw, Glenn," he said, "I ain't goin' say nothin' out of the way." And I said, "Look here, J. L.—man, I hate it. Somethin' may happen before I even get down there, the way I feel. I want you to forgive me 'cause I done wrong. I ort not to jumped on you." He didn't never say he forgive me, you know. But I asked him anyway.

He told me before I left that he's goin' by my son's house over 'ere and get Junior and Bill. And he said, "They's somethin' that I got to tell you. And you can get the whole thing straightened out before it gets out of hand." Why, I didn't know what he's talkin' about. So I got in the car, and me and Darlene went down there. My two sons's sittin' there in a pickup. So I pulled in 'ere in my car. Junior and Bill got out of the pickup and stood beside the car.

Well, Darlene's sittin' over there turnin' and twistin' all the time. So I ain't said nothin', you know, except, "What is it that he's wantin' to talk about? Is he wantin' to get into it again?" And Junior said, "Naw, Daddy, He won't fight you noway. He knows that you messed up." And I said, "I really messed up." Junior said, "He called us and told us to come up here and meet you, that he's comin' on up here." And about that time J. L.'s truck come by, but he didn't stop.

J. L. went down the road and turned around. And when he started back, Darlene jumped plumb around there and said, "Junior, Bill, you-all tell your daddy." Said, "Haven't I been havin' sex with you-all." She said it happened when they were thirteen- , fourteen-year-old kids. I didn't know what to say. And she just act crazy. That's all I could figure is she just needed help, you know what I mean. And that's the honest God's truth. I told Junior and Bill, I said, "Boys, don't let that bother you-all." I said, "If somethin' like that did happen, I wouldn't never hold it agin you-all 'cause you-all was kids." They didn't say it did or it didn't happen. Their eyes bugged out. So J. L. he come back by, and he waved, but he didn't stop.

See, the day she told me that, I didn't even ask them anything. I just said, "Boys, I don't know. All I know is I'm goin' get a divorce." I told 'em, "Don't worry, you know, 'cause I love you and you ain't got to worry 'bout nothin'. I ain't goin' say nothin' to nobody 'bout it." And that's the last thing I told 'em. But it hurt 'em real bad whenever she told it. She thought J. L. was goin' tell me when he come up. But see, he didn't pull in. By him not pullin' in, she'd already run her mouth and told it, you know.

I still didn't never believe her until I got a letter in prison from my son Bill. He wrote a letter to the parole board and told them that Darlene would get them in bed with her when I was gone and have sex with them. And Bill give the letter to his mother Doris to mail fer him, and then she rewrote it and mailed me the copy of the one he sent to the parole board.

Anyway, a'ter Darlene said that about the boys, Junior and Bill was goin' go back home. So I told 'em we'd follow 'em. We thought J. L. went back over Junior's. So they went home, and we followed 'em. And I got around there, and I run over somethin' and cut a tire and had a flat. So they went and got me a spare.

Whenever we went down to Junior's, we'd stop and bought orange juice. I like orange juice. And that's all it was, orange juice. There wadn't no alcohol. I never did buy no alcohol for nobody. Whatever Darlene had drinkin', she bought it when she went out. See, Darlene drank for years. She drank all her life whenever she was growin' up. They was always partyin' at their house. So, it'd be pretty hard to tell when Darlene's drinkin' without she's real drunk, you know—without she taken dope or somethin', 'cause she used to do that too.

We stayed around there talkin' to the kids and all, my grandkids and everything, at Junior's house. We was there probably an hour, hour and a half. But J. L. didn't never come by there, so we got in the car and went back home. And I'm hurt real bad on account of way I've done J. L.—that hurt me worse. All the other ain't hurt me like that right there.

I went on home. And when we got there, why, I told her then: "Darlene, I'm goin' go down there and get Tommy Armstrong to file for divorce." I said, "I'm just goin' get a divorce this time." And she said, "Well, I don't want a divorce." And I say, "That's the only thing to do. I can't keep livin' with you and you doing these things like this. I'm goin' get a divorce Monday morning. And I want divorce on adultery, and I'm goin' keep Marty. You ain't goin' get nothin'. Just go take your clothes and leave."

And J. L. called again—phone was ringin' just a'ter I got home. And I knew that was him. So I went and answered the phone, talked to him. He told me the reason he didn't stop is 'cause I brought Darlene with me. He said he couldn't talk to me as long as she was with me. I said, "Well, J. L., she was the one was tellin' me. And I ain't asked her nothin.'" I said, "I don't know what's wrong with her." He said, "Glenn, that woman's goin' get you killed."

It was probably that same day when Darlene called and told my daughter Jackie and her husband Kenneth to pick the boys up. And before they picked 'em up, Darlene went in the kitchen. (We had a pet coon, a big coon, and it got so old it died. And we got another one that my son-in-law had give us, a real little one. And we'd raised it up till it 'as about half grown, and it was bad to get on the table. And she'd train it with a fly swat to make it get off the table. And it was doin' pretty good, but if you'd ever grab it, it would bite you. Well, that day, instead of Darlene takin' the fly swat and whuppin' it off the table, makin' it mind, she grabbed it. And it bit her. The boys was laughin' at her, 'cause it bit her, and she got real upset then and said some pretty bad words.) So anyway, Jackie and them come on and picked the boys up and took 'em down to their house.

And so that's the night, Friday—best I remember it—we was goin' go back to church. She wanted me to go out there to the buildin' to handle serpents. She'd keep tellin' me, "Glenn, I've repented—I'll show you if you'll come on." She had been talkin' to different people on the phone and was ready to go back to church. And she said she was goin' get Brother Rayford to baptize her. But anyway, that night Darlene said she got bit by a serpent.

And whenever I went out there to the buildin' to get the serpents, well, she was wantin' me to hurry 'cause I took a bath and I was a little bit late. And she was goin' go ahead and get ever'thin' fer me. Like, if I was late, why she would get the snakes out—if I told her which ones to get or if I told her to get whatever she wanted to get, you know. See, we had a lot of snakes in different boxes and cases. We had a snake catcher in there that had a handle on one end and a fork on the other end, and you could pick 'em up with it. Well, she had already put some in a box. I walked in by her, and I pick another box up 'cause I seen the ones she had. So I retch in there—I never did use a snake catcher most of the time, I'd just stayed prayed up. I'd just reach in there and get 'em out and put 'em in the box.

And she said, "Glenn, I decided I don't want to go to church." I said, "Why?" And she said, "I got bit while ago." And I said, "What?" She said, "I got bit." And I said, "You didn't neither." She said, "Yeah, I did, right here." And I looked at her hand, and I seen her thumb like it was swelled a little bit. So I just took the snakes I had and just dumped 'em back in the big case and let the

132

Glenn

lid down. And I just knelt down right then, you know, without saying any-thing and begin to pray and talk to the Lord. And I figured the anointin' would come on me to lay hands on her. I never did feel the anointin'. So I got up, and I just kept my mind on the Lord and kept praisin' the Lord. And I still ain't feel no anointin'. And I took her hand and looked at it. And it didn't look like no snakebite. Only place I seen on her hand was where that coon had bit her. Even if she'd got bit by a copperhead, she'd a-swelled real bad. I figured she just startin' that crazy stuff again.

"Why," I said, "if you want to, we won't go to church tonight. We'll stay at home and pray." She said, "Well, what about takin' me out to supper if we ain't goin' to church." And I said, "We'll go down here somewhere and get somethin'." So we went to MacDonald's. She ordered McRibs and I got chicken breast or somethin'. Then we go on back home. We sat around and eat supper. I tried to get her to pray, and she wouldn't. So I left and went down in the woods and pray like I always do. And I come back to the house.

Then we watched video all Friday night. The ones we watched is the ones I had borrowed—they's real old westerns. They belonged to Paul Hancocke—he'd taped them. (Me and my boys like them old westerns.) So me and Darlene put one of them tapes in the VCR, and I sat there and watched it. One played about six or eight hours, I guess. And I watched Darlene all during the night to make sure she wadn't sick. She could have bought some pills or somethin' 'cause she was sleepin' awful good. I believe if I'd a-went asleep that night, she would have done probably the same thing she did on Saturday night.

We had rented some other movies for the boys 'cause while we was goin' to church, they'd stay at home most of the time—Mac and Marty would. They watch Walt Disney movies and this movie about ET. Anyway, we rented tapes at three different places, but we'd already carried some of them back. But the ones we got at Lakeside, we didn't take 'em back until Saturday.

So whenever Saturday come, we went to pay our bills and get ever'thing take care of. And I told her I was goin' down to talk to the lawyer 'bout the divorce. And she said again, "I don't want a divorce." And I said, "What do you want to do?" And she said, "I'll go back and stay with Mama, but I don't want no divorce." Said, "I don't want people find out that we divorced." I said, "I'm not goin' live with you no more—that's just it. I'm not goin' to. I forgive you, 'cause I know the Lord'll forgive you, but I can't live with you no more. I want a divorce." She really went off the deep end then actin' crazy.

We went shoppin', you know, different stores and stuff. We were in her car, a black Chevette. I was drivin' the car 'cause it was an automatic. See, at that time my hand was still swelled up, you know, from being snakebit back in July. And it would bother me—I almost lost that arm from what they said. So if I drive a car, it's automatic. My pickup—I had a Ford pickup, and I had a Dodge pickup, and both of them's standard shift.

And she would go in the stores, or I would go in. We went to Lakeside Grocery. They had a store on one side and a video place on the other side. When I pulled up there, why, I bought some gas and went in to pay fer the gas. I bought some Coke-colies while Darlene carried the video back. I had to buy some huntin' stuff. And I had to get horse feed and dog feed, so we went to Pendergrass Feed. I bought some horse feed there. Then we went down to the Farmer's Co-Op in Scottsboro, and I bought some dog food. We carried it home. Then we went again.

She acted happy 'cause we's just out ridin' around. She'd act different when we'd be out goin'. That's the reason we'd get out and ride around—like she's bored sittin' at the house all the time or somethin'. She was callin' differ-ent people on the phone, and I figured she's gettin' better.

We went to a lot of places. We went to the other stores almost in front of Lakeside. It's a new place over there. We went over there to get a video. We's goin' rent one, you know, and she went in to check. But we left there and got us somethin' to eat for supper—for dinner, really, 'cause we went back home then and eat.

I had a mule over there that I just had got. So I went and saddled the mule up and rode him around awhile, 'cause I never had rode it but two, three time. And I go way back there in the woods and see how the mule'll go through briars, and cross creeks and stuff, 'cause I like to coon hunt on mules and horses. That's the last thing I did before I went to sleep, 'cause I stayed back 'ere a long time goin' through a lot of big briar fields. So it was pretty late in the evenin' when I laid down on the couch and went to sleep. It wadn't dark. I 'member that. But I don't remember what time it was, 'bout four or five o'clock. That's the night she left, a'ter I went to sleep—on Saturday night.

When I woke up—it was probably 9:30 or something like 'at whenever my sister Charlotte and Mama and my brother-in-law Joe woke me up. They come in the house, and I'm laying there lookin' up at 'em: "You-all gets you a seat." And I didn't even really know what time it was, you know. I didn't even think about it being that late 'cause, see, I'd lost that sleep the other night sittin' up with her, you know. Anyway, my sister said, "Where's Darlene at?" "She's in yonder, I guess." And she said, "Naw, she ain't in there." And I said, "She may be laying on that other couch."

See, we had two couches in our livin'room. And it looked like Darlene layin' on the couch 'cause she'd took and put a piller or somethin' and laid a coat or somethin' over it. She was sittin' on that couch when I laid down there—we was watching TV. And Darlene had asked if I wanted anything else to eat, and I said, "Naw, not right now." I drunk me some Coke-colie, 'cause I was bad on them Coke-colies, on them Sprite—I drank Sprite all the time. Anyway, I drank me some Sprite and laid there and watched some kind of news. It wadn't regular news that come on ever'day. It was some kind of sports, 'cause it was on Saturday. Anyway, I just dozed off to sleep.

Whenever they woke me up, well, my sister said, "You know Darlene got snakebit." And I said, "I know she *said* she got snakebit Friday, but," I said, "she didn't."

Then I call, "Darlene, come here." I thought she was in the other room, you know. I got up and look for her, and she's really gone. But my sister said, "You know she locked you in the house?" And I said, "Naw." Darlene had locked the door from the outside and left the key in the lock.

Charlotte said, "Where's your phone at?" I said, "We got three. Which one you talkin' about? One's outside on the wall, one's settin' over there." And I said, "Naw, that un ain't sittin' there. Where's it at?" And she said, "It's in there in the kitchen." And I said, "What's the phone doin' in the kitchen? You-all take it in the kitchen?" And she said, "Naw," said, "Darlene went in the kitchen and used the phone to keep you from hearin'. She called the ambulance and had 'em come get her." Said, "She told 'em she got snakebit." And I said, "Well, look, you-all go with me down there then. Let's just go see." And she said, "Ain't no need of it." Said, "Darlene told 'em she wanted to go to Birmingham, that they couldn't treat her for the kind of snake she got bit by."

And right then I really thought Darlene had gone out there in the shed and got snakebit for real 'cause she'd been tellin' me, "Glenn, I done prayed." Whenever I rode my mule back there, when I first come back, that's the first thing she told me: "Glenn, I done repented." She said, "I was prayin' and somethin' come out of me. I'm goin' be all right." And I said, "Well, praise the Lord." I'm thinkin' she's actin' so much better, 'cause I went on to sleep, like I said. And what I really did think was she got to prayin' and handlin' snakes and got bit.

And I went to tryin' to call around. And I called the Jackson County Hospital, and they wouldn't tell where's she's at or nothin'. Course my sister done told me they carried her to Birmingham. So I went to callin' Birmingham, and she hadn't got there yet. I had 'em call me soon as she got there.

So soon as she got to Birmingham, they called me. And it was probably . . . I guess it was twelve, one o'clock then when they called. I asked how she was doin', and all they said was that she was doin' okay—said they put her in a private room. And I said, "Well, can you give me the number?" And they said, "Yes." So they give me the phone number. And I called, but I couldn't never get through, not right at that time.

So it was over in the morning. I turned TV on, and they was already runnin' it on TV that I'd try to kill my old lady. I said, "Well, somethin' got be done about this." So I called again, and that time I got through to the hospital room. Darlene's sister and some more—I could hear 'em talkin'—was there. Her sister Dean answered the phone, and I asked her how Darlene was. And she said, "She's okay. You want to talk to her?" And I said, "Yeah." So Darlene took the phone and said, "Glenn, I left while you's asleep. How'd you know where I's at?" And she hung up. And I tried to call bunch more times, and I couldn't. So I had Brother Carl Porter call. And I called other church people and give 'em the phone numbers so they could call and talk to her, see what was goin' on.

I sat around the house there and some people had come in a'ter church and left. And it was gettin' pretty early on Sunday morning. It's already daylight. I eat breakfast and fed my horses. Well, the phone rung, and I picked it up, and it was Darlene. And she said, "Well, Glenn, I've decided to come home. You can come get me." And I said, "Where do I come to?" And she told me how to get there. I say, "Okay."

So I went down there to Paint Rock Valley to pick Marty up at my daughter's. And I asked him if he wanted to ride down there with me, "I'm goin' down there to pick your mama up." And he said, "Yeah." My daughter said, "Naw, Glenn, don't take him with you." And I said, "Why not?" I said, "He wants to go—that's his mother. He can go with me to pick her up, and we goin' on home whenever we leave down there, anyway."

Well, me and Marty stopped and bought gas, bought us some Coke-colies. I bought me a pint of milk and a cake, and he bought him a Coke-colie and peanuts or somethin', might have been Cracker Jacks or somethin'. And so we got way on down—that's a long drive from Jackson County all the way down there out of Paint Rock Valley—so we stopped at another place. That time I bought me a Coca-Cola or somethin'. I don't think I could get the kind I drink, Sprite. Got me a candy bar that time. Marty, he got him, I believe he got him ice cream or somethin'—anyway, we went on down there.

I missed the place and had to drive around a little bit to find how to get in the hospital parkin' lot. And whenever we pulled in, they raised up the gates, and I drove in. It was like you drive up in the buildin', but it was on the bottom floor there. The other gates was still down. I looked back, but I didn't see nobody. They ain't nobody in that little buildin' where they let the gates up and down. I heared somebody hollerin'. And I looked around. And they had guns pointed at me.

So they's fixin' to ambush me, and I said, "Wait a minute! Hold up! You got the wrong one!" you know. There was a bunch of 'em. And the police cars run in there then. And they jumped out of their police cars. And they told me to get out and walk around the car and put my hands on the back of the car. So I did. I said, "Don't you-all shoot—my little boy's in the car." Anyway, I put my hands on the car, and one of 'em told me to spread my feet out and all that. And I laid down on the trunk like he said.

Then one come runnin' up and jammed that gun in back of my head and just scooted my face across the trunk. He said, "If you got a knife or a gun in your pocket, you're a dead man." I said, "Don't kill me in front of my little boy. You-all get him out of the car. If you're goin' to kill me, don't let him see it." And he just kept punchin' that gun—it was one of them square kind of guns. So I'm just layin' there, you know, my heart poundin', thinkin', Well, Lord, I'm in your hands, you know. You said you'd take care of me.

Then the cop said, "If you got a rattlesnake in this car," said, "you're a dead man." I knew then what was goin' on. I knew I done been set up. He said, "You smell like a beer brewry." I ain't arguin' with him or nothin'. I'm just laying there, 'cause I'm expectin' that gun to go off any minute. And in my mind I'm prayin', you know. So the other polices search the car, and one said, "He ain't got no gun in here or nothin'."

Whenever he took the gun off back of my head, well, I could see Darlene's pocketbook was sittin' in the back floorboard. I didn't even think about it being in there. I hadn't even thought about it. And I said, "They is a gun in the car, too. That's my wife's pocketbook in my car there. It's probably got her gun in it, but she's got a permit fer it. That's her gun. He jammed me with that gun again. He said, "Where's the snakebox at?" And I said, "They's a snakebox there in the trunk. You can see it if you look in there." They's always a snakebox in the trunk, but there wadn't no snake in it.

Anyway, they arrested me for DUI. But they didn't stop me for drivin', and I wadn't drunk, you know. They didn't even give me no test or nothin'. So they drove me over there to the jail and locked me up, put me in the regular bullpen, you know, with everybody else. And they was a pay phone in there. I had change in my pocket, but I didn't have my wallet. I called home, and I couldn't get nobody at Mama's. And I called my house, and my sister Carolyn picked it up. And I said, "I sure am proud you's there." They's waitin' on for me to come in, and they didn't know where I's at. I told 'em, "I'm down here in jail." Then my sister Barbara and her husband Kenny come down there and got me, made my bond.

When I got out of jail in Birmingham, I come to church, and Brother Carl baptized me after the service—the next service night after I got out of jail. I repented and was rebaptized. I backslid when I did to J. L. what I did. And whatever that I sinned agin God in anyway, he forgive me. And I've been stayin' straight ever since then.

All this was like a nightmare to me. And I'm tellin' you the honest truth, her leavin' and her lyin' like she did in court is just like a nightmare to me— 'cause the night that she left, they wadn't no fussin' and fightin' or nothin' goin' on. Not the night she left. All that was supposed to be done over. She's supposed to done repented, and God's forgive her.

Darlene, the way I understood it, she stayed into the hospital in Birmingham there about, I think, three or four days, and she got out. She'd supposed to went in intensive care. That's the way they said at Scottsboro during trial, but she didn't. They took her to Birmingham to the emergency room where they unloaded her. They put her in a private room, just in a regular room. She gets out and goes to her brother's and stays out there with somebody for two weeks. Then she went back to Birmingham hospital and let them do some kind of surgery on her thumb. And she stays down there then two, three more days.

See, they was tellin' it in trial like she was afraid fer her life and she was under protective custody and all that, and couldn't nobody call her. But all the church people was callin' in the hospital, and Brother Carl Porter even talked to her on the phone. Her life was never in no danger.

And at the trial Darlene, she said I made her write a note to Marty. But my sister found that note, and later another sister, Barbara, give it to the lawyer. The other note, a whole page, that Darlene wrote her sister, the one married my brother David—I found that note behind the couch a'ter she was gone, wadded up. I thought that coon's been under there pullin' this paper and stuff up. So I'm goin' clean up after him, you know. And I took the broom and sweep it out. And it was just a wadded-up piece of paper, and I picked it up and started readin'. Darlene was telling her sister that she'd had sex with my brother David, and first one thing and 'nother. And I think, My goodness, Darlene's trying to cause them trouble now. So I throwed that one away. But they got it out of the garbage can, and I don't know what they did with it. Later on they told me that some of 'em had got it 'cause they wanted it for some kind of proof of somethin'. But it never come up in trial.

The one Darlene wrote Marty, she put in the microwave. I never did use microwave, and Darlene knew Marty would use the microwave. That DA tried to make it look like it was a suicide note or somethin'. But it wadn't no suicide note, the way I read it. It's tellin' it just about the way I'm tellin'—said she got snakebit and daddy don't know nothin' about it; said he's on the couch asleep.

I believe she went to get a snake and was goin' to kill me with it while I's asleep. I believe she's really goin' put it on me. Darlene wadn't skeered of no snake, not even when she wadn't prayin'. She fed the snakes and watered the snakes. She'd move 'em around from place to place. She wasn't skeered of no snake. I believe she could've went out 'ere to get a snake, and it bit her. And she come back, called the doctor, and left.

The only thing I could think of, the reason she's wantin' to get rid of me is 'cause she knew if I got a divorce, that ever'body was goin' find out why I got the divorce. See, I was goin' get it on adultery—on what I knew, what she'd told me, and what the Lord had showed me. And she didn't want me to have her mentally evaluated. She's afraid she'd go to jail fer that stuff with my boys. She'd been in jail a lot of times—she didn't want to go to jail. That's what it was, I believe. That's all I could ever think of, but I'm not sayin' she did it like 'at 'cause I don't know. If I knowed exactly what happened, you know, I'd feel better.

I don't know how she done it, but I believe Gene told her how to do it. But I don't know. I know ever'thin' that happened up to the point where that I laid down and went to sleep. And when I went to sleep, she was watchin' TV.

I know whenever they come in and woke me up, I didn't even know she was gone. And I know she wadn't snakebit. She told me that she had been bit, but that was like a day or two before then, when she said she repented and all, and she wanted to go back to church. I didn't see her get bit, and I didn't see even a place on her hand. I didn't see no blood in no place. And if she'd been snakebit, she'd a-been swelled up. She wouldn't been goin' and eatin' or doin' things that we were doin'.

She kept on, kept on, about men she went with and her foolin' with my boys even when they's little. And she thought that I'd beat her up, and she'd get me put in jail for assault for beatin' her up. So I wouldn't beat her up. I wouldn't even touch her. I wouldn't have nothin' to do with her. And she just act crazy.

And really she was drinkin', but I wadn't drinkin' like 'at. There ain't nobody seen me drink nothin', not nobody. I got off alcohol a long time ago. If

I'd started drinkin' and got on alcohol, I wouldn't 'ave just whupped Darlene, I'd whupped ever'thing around. I wouldn't have went out like that. I wouldn't have went to court. I wouldn't went on to church. I tell you what I'd a-been. I'd been a devil. Ever'body knows it, too. For me, it ain't in and out and playin' around. This thing's for real, forever. And whenever I changed my life, I'd went straight. And I made this one mistake with J. L.—I failed God in it—God'll punish me fer it. I failed God, and I got rebaptized.

I didn't do any of the things she said I did. I never did even have the gun in my hand. I didn't at no time point no gun at Darlene and tell her I was goin' kill her. If I'd a-pulled a gun on her, I'd a-killed her—if I'd got that far. That's why I put the rifle up when I did the day Gene was there. I was prayed up. I don't care what they think or what they tell—God was with me. I didn't have no reason to kill Darlene. If I'd be goin' to kill her, I'd just give her a drink of strychnine.

And if I'd did anything to her, I would have beat her about half to death—that's exactly what I'd a-did to her. But I didn't do that. I'd give her a good whuppin' and that would have straightened her out. But, see, I wadn't goin' to straighten her out no more. I'd straightened her out so many times till I was just goin' get divorce.

I knowed I wadn't guilty. I didn't beat her up. God knows I didn't hold no gun on her to make her stick her hand in no snake box. Only time she was even with me around any snakes was when we was goin' get 'em out and go to church that night. And I believe she was goin' kill me, just while I was asleep. But I ain't got no proof of it.

Glenn

Junior and Virginia Peace Summerford

Glenn's Oldest Son and Daughter-in-Law

Virginia Peace Summerford

It was at night when Glenn and Darlene come over to the house right before all this happened. They had had a flat. They both came, and they were drunk. And Darlene said she had to use the restroom, and I told her to come on in. I went in there with her 'cause she said she wanted me to. And she told me that Glenn was really mad 'cause of all the stuff she had told. She'd told him about sleepin' with several men in the church and that his own sons, Bill and Junior, had slept with her and that J. L. Lewis had slept with her.

She'd done told Glenn so much stuff that she said that he was goin' kill her. And I told her, no, he wadn't goin' to kill her. And she said, "Yeah, he is too. He's done told me he's goin' kill me. He's goin' to kill me tonight." I said, "Darlene, you're talkin' stupid. He may be mad, but he ain't goin' kill you." I said, "He might beat your butt, but he won't kill you 'cause he don't want to go to jail. He ain't stupid." We stayed in there a few minutes, and she said, "Well, I better get back out there 'cause if I don't, he'll probably come in the house after me." I said, "Well, come on."

We went back outside, and I got to talkin' with Glenn. I asked him what was goin' on. He told me that he was just hurt that she had told him so many things. He didn't know what was true and what wadn't true. But he had sent

Junior Summerford.

Virginia Summerford.

Marty over there at Kenneth and Jackie's so if they got into a fuss or anything that Marty wouldn't be there and have to hear all the crap. I stood out there with him for about, I guess, an hour or longer and talked to him.

And I asked him to let me call my father, which is Walter Peace—he's a preacher too (he's the man that Glenn had got saved in under)—and see if my father couldn't come down and talk to him and pray for him and help him get over it. He said he didn't care. And I asked him if I could come over there that Friday night. He said, "Yeah, come on. Go on in there and get ready, and you come on to the house." Said, "We can talk."

I said, "Glenn, I don't want you to do nothin' stupid." He said, "Aw, I ain't goin' do nothin' stupid. We just goin' straightened stuff out. And it's goin' be tonight, goin' be this weekend. I don't know how long it's goin' take us—if it's goin' take us all weekend or just tonight. But we're goin' talk things out and get everything out in the open. Things are goin' change one way or another. We goin' get all this stuff straightened out." And I said, "Are you sure?" And he said, "Yeah, come on. You come on to the house." Then, we talked a few minutes longer. He told us all he loved us. And they got in the car and left. I got involved with some other stuff and didn't go. And I didn't hear no more till the next mornin' when they said she'd got snakebit.

You've got to realize that this had been goin' on for like . . . God . . . for months. Then, like two weeks before she supposedly got bit, she told him all kind of stuff—she'd been tellin' him stuff all along, just trying to get him aggravated and mad. She told him about her sleepin' with Bill and Junior. Glenn hadn't heard anythin' bout Junior, only Bill—and according to Junior, it did happen with Bill, but not with him. But she wanted Junior to tell Glenn, yeah, he did it. And she told Junior to tell him. And Junior said, "I ain't tellin' that 'cause you know you tellin' a lie—I never slept with you." And she said, "Junior, tell him. He thinks I'm just makin' up all this stuff." Junior said, "I ain't tellin' my daddy I slept with you 'cause I didn't sleep with you."

She was tryin' to get trouble started between Glenn and his son, 'cause she figured it if she got enough started that they'd start fightin'. And one or the other of 'em would die. Hopefully, it'd be Glenn. It just didn't work out the way she wanted it to. And she knew if Junior told that he slept with her, that would just kill Glenn—that would just kill him. That would be the breakin' point. That would be where he come unglued. See, she knowed how to make him crazy. And, buddy, she used it too. This woman was trying to do whatever she could to get Glenn to kill his son, get him to kill his best friend,

Glenn's Oldest Son and Daughter-in-Law

whatever she had to do to get Glenn in prison. She thought this thing out. I know she did.

My two sons Chris and Joshua stayed all the time over there with Glenn and Darlene. And they told me that Darlene had gotten coon bit by a coon that they kept in the house—that she was not snakebit. But, see, she wouldn't go to the doctor. One time she got bit on the right breast by a snake, by a rattlesnake, and didn't go to the doctor or nothin'. She was not afraid of the snakes. She handled ever' one of 'em. I know—I went to church with her all the time—she was not afraid of those snakes. And she was not afraid of drinkin' anything anybody in that church drank. I just can't believe—she fed them snakes ever'day—so I just can't believe, you know, what happened the way she said it happened.

She had told me back before, when Glenn got bit, that she hated his guts and she hoped he'd die. I said, "Darlene, you better shut up." She said, "Why, I don't want to live with him anymore." And I said, "Well, divorce him." She said, "No, I can't divorce him. If I do, he won't give me Marty." I said, "The law'll give you Marty." And she said, no, because she lost Bobby Joe, her first son—the welfare took him. She said she wouldn't have a chance. And I said, "Well, Darlene, that's stupid, livin' with a man you hate." She said that the only way she could get Marty was if Glenn died or if he went to prison. He didn't die, so now he's in prison. And she still didn't get Marty.

After she got bitten and Glenn went to jail, we didn't have much to do with her. And she didn't have nothin' to do with us. She wouldn't even talk to us. I know back then she tried to kill herself several times with pills 'cause Chris had told me while he was there that she had done that several times. You see, my son Chris stayed with them all the time. I'd go get him one day, and he'd get mad at me and cry and call his pap-paw. Then I'd have to take him back. He's a grandpa's boy.

Now, Glenn got saved about eighteen years ago. That's when I met Junior, the night Glenn got saved. They come to our house. I lived with my mama and daddy, and they come to our house. When Glenn come up and knocked on the door, he had two rifles and a shotgun in his hand. And he told Daddy that he come to get saved, and Daddy said, "Well, son, you don't need them guns if you come to get saved." So they just handed them to Mama. They prayed for hours and hours and hours. I think like four o'clock in the mornin'—or two o'clock in the morning, one—Daddy took him to Guntersville to the river and baptized him. It happened in '81, I think—'80 or '81. Glenn stayed in church that long. And I mean, after that he hadn't had a cross word with nobody.

Junior and Virginia Peace Summerford

Junior Summerford

I'll just be honest with you. Daddy didn't do all what Darlene said he done. He did some of it. If he'd wanted to kill her, though, he'd killed her when he caught her in bed with that feller, probably got away with it. Said he went off huntin', come in, saw Gene's car up here and went in the house, and she was in bed with Gene. He didn't do nothin' then. And Darlene even told us that that happened. Sure did. Daddy made her tell us. He told her he wanted her to tell us, wanted us to hear it from her, not from him—and she told us. Daddy didn't do anything then because he was close to God.

I went around Daddy and Darlene, but I never did go to church or nothin' with 'em. I didn't believe in handlin' serpents and still don't. He got away from God when he got to drinkin' and carryin' on. He may say he didn't, but he did. He come out to the house drinkin'. Darlene said later he couldn't get a divorce and stay a preacher, but he could have got one on adultery and been all right there. He could have gotten a divorce anytime he wanted. And he was always real jealous of her too. He probably slapped her around a little. But he didn't go as far as make her stick her hand in no snake box.

She thought that was the only way she could get Marty. In some situations like that, she's probably right. But she still didn't get Marty. She was just trying to stir up trouble. I think she was just tryin' anything to get away. She was scared of him. Back before he got in church, he's mean to her, mean to Mama too. He was just mean to anybody. He was pretty abusive till he got in church. But after he got in church, he was a different person. It just took God to change him—man sure couldn't.

When I really knowed of him drinkin' is the day that him and J. L. got into it. That's the first time I know, or even suspected him, of drinkin'—was that day. I knowed it that day, which he told me he had a bottle of vodka. Darlene got J. L. talkin', and Daddy knocked him in the head. Yeah, I saw Daddy that morning. He told me, not go down there to work, go in late—he had to go talk to J. L. about somethin'. I don't guess somethin' went right.

Then Bill and me talked to him at the oak tree on the same day he hit J. L. I went into work that day and me and J. L. called him at home. Him and J. L. talked mostly. I just told him, I'm goin' talk to him. I didn't have to work, so I drove out here and met him at the oak tree. I got him to meet me down there, and I think Virginia went with me. And I's goin' try to talk some sense into him 'cause I knowed some things on Darlene. She fooled around with everybody at church, and he never even seen it—near anybody was there at

Glenn's Oldest Son and Daughter-in-Law

church. And he wouldn't pay any attention to her. It wasn't just Gene Sherbert, it was any man that would have anything to do with her. There was even a couple who quit goin' to church because of it. There's one, he actually come and talked to me, Daddy's first cousin, I guess—Barney.

So he come down there to the oak tree and talked to us. Daddy wadn't drunk. He hadn't drank much more than a sup out of that bottle of vodka. He wadn't talkin' stupid. But the first words out of Darlene's mouth was, "He's goin' kill me." I think she was scared, but not that he was goin' kill her. She'd always say stuff like that, though: "Glenn's goin' to kill me" . . . little stupid stuff. She'd always say stuff. But at that point, I believe she was scared. That was just a day or so after he caught her with Gene Sherbert. And then she told him she was sleepin' with J. L., with me, Bill, Daddy's brother, and everybody else that he cared about.

Daddy left the oak tree and came over to the house. Then he started home and had a flat tire and came back to the house, and stayed at the house for three hours I guess. We sat out in the yard and talked about huntin' and everything. Darlene's brother Gary was there. I never seen Daddy drink a drop at the house. He said they had some things they had to work out and probably was goin' get a divorce. I don't know what went on later that night. There ain't nobody knows but them two and God. And if God don't tell us, I don't figure we'll ever get a straight story. And I didn't see him for a day or two. That's when we heard he done made her stick her hand in a snake box.

They always had problems. Darlene, she told everybody she wished Daddy was dead. She tried to poison him. That wadn't no big secret—she told everybody. She said that she used rat poison. That's what she said. My son Chris also tells about him, Marty, Michael, and Josh catching fish down there in the creek—and Darlene cooked the fish. And she wouldn't let them get two certain pieces of fish, wouldn't let them get 'em. Then after they got their fish, she got the two pieces and put 'em on Daddy's plate. And he got real sick. He was throwin' up, but it just lasted for the night. And Michael told me about the blue pills—I asked him if Darlene tried to kill herself, and he said, "Yeah."

Darlene never was no good. She wasn't when Daddy married her—she still ain't. She was good to us, I mean, as a stepmother. She never mistreated me in any way. But I know about things she done. And she's been in more trouble since Daddy's been in prison. She's always in trouble—DUI, startin' trouble in clubs—she's in and out of jail all the time.

And at the trial there's a lot that went on that wasn't told. A lot was added to it. Darlene was just tellin' anything she could 'cause she's scared of

146

Daddy—to get him sent off. I don't know what all was told. I never was in the courtroom, never went in. I was in the witness room. And there was a witness room full of people, but there weren't but two or three that ever went on the stand. It was full: Joe and Charlotte, me and Bill, Leslie (Virginia's brother), Carl Porter, Bobbie Sue Thompson, Tammy Flippo.

Sylvia Ingram, she sat in the courtroom through the whole thing; then she blowed up in the courtroom, and they put her on the stand.

One thing, Daddy didn't have a lawyer. A good lawyer, I feel would have got him out of it. He didn't have no lawyer. It wasn't his choice though not to testify. I was in there when the lawyer told him. The reason the lawyer didn't want him to testify, Daddy couldn't keep the story straight—he couldn't tell the same story. He's always been that way—I don't care what it's about. The lawyer said, "I'd rather not put you on the stand." Said, "If you insist, that's your choice; but," he said, "that's my opinion. I'd rather not put you on." Daddy said, "Well, he's a lawyer."

Before the trial we talked to the lawyer—he talked to everybody that's a witness. We went up there weeks ahead of time and talked with him—had to meet with him two or three times. I had to talk with the district attorney and all kinds of stuff. Only thing the district attorney said, they'd heard that Daddy told us he's goin' kill Darlene—he never did tell us that. He told us *if* he wanted to kill her, he could have killed her and got away with it when he caught her in bed with Gene Sherbert. He loved her and didn't want to kill her. He wanted to work it out, but he didn't think it was goin' happen 'cause he couldn't trust her no more—that was a day or two before it happened when we was at the house and at the oak tree.

Daddy was never really a daddy to me. I was never proud of him—until Daddy got saved. And then I was proud of him. He was abusive to my mother (Doris)—he was never abusive to me. He was a mean man. He'd fight at the drop of a hat. But when he got saved, he changed. And I was proud of him. As I say, it took God to change him, because man couldn't do it.

Bill Summerford

Glenn's Second Son

At the point of time where Daddy got snakebit real bad, before anything come up at church and things, I thought him and Darlene had a real good life goin'. When we'd go up and visit, it'd be just like, you know, ever'thing was okay—up to the point of time when he was down real bad from the snakebite and hurt real bad from it and swollen up real bad. We all thought he was goin' to die, and the family gathered around the house. Then they was a kind of conflict between him and Darlene that us kids saw that I'd never seen.

I think the bite was from a Mojave Desert rattler. Daddy was in the floor in the house fer three or four days. They was different people takin' care of him. And, you know, the family didn't know whether he was goin' live or he was goin' to die 'cause he was just in and out. He was swelled up. His shoulder was swelled real thick. And he busted all under his arm and down his arm, just busted wide open like someone that'd been in a house fire or somethin'. The flesh on his body was just mangled and had like a burnt look to it. His arm had big blisters that just hung off it and dripped down. It just looked pitiful.

What I'm tryin' to say is when he got down and got sick from the snakebite, Darlene, she was all time runnin' in and out with her sister, kind of flirtin' with the men—some of the different people that was around—more than she was helpin' out with Daddy. I knowed that she'd flirted with different ones of the guys because I got a brother-in-law that she had actually flirted with—Leslie Peace.

But she kind of stayed her distance from me at that point of time. I don't know why. She kind of drawed to other people. I guess because I was kind of drawed to Daddy and different ones myself, kind of hangin' around with

Joe, Bill, and Michael Summerford and the author. Photograph by Donna Rizzo.

Uncle David and with different ones talkin'. But we heard all kind of rumors that took place at that time. I think they was just situations in their family that rose up that was causin' conflict between Daddy and Darlene.

One situation was with Gene Sherbert. What happened between Gene and Darlene, I really don't know. Daddy said that he thought that they had been together because he left the house and he come back and she had changed clothes while he was gone. He caught Gene there, and he could tell from Gene's actions that somethin' had happened. You know, what might have happened, I don't know. He said he caught Gene with Darlene in a situation where that if he had wanted to at that point of time, if he had wanted to kill either one, he could have. He could have killed Darlene and Gene both. I don't know how much he caught and how much he saw. But he said he didn't get mad at Gene or nothin'—he just talked to Gene. And I think him and Daddy worked things out and fixed things up between them two.

I think there was another time, another situation between Darlene and another brother in the church, I believe Brother Willie Southard. I reckon him and Daddy had talked. And they had worked things out, far as I know, 'cause I've talked to Willie since then; and Willie said him and Daddy had talked. He said they'd still be brothers in the Lord.

There was also a time some years before this. I don't know what year it was, but it was when they were in the church right up there above the Chicken Basket. There was a situation come up with Junior Coots. And it was a pretty big situation. They never did let it out. Don't know what all happened. But we do know there was some conflict there because they had brought Marty down to stay with my brother Junior. And Gary, Darlene's brother, and Eddie, my brother, was stayin' up at Daddy's—they even come down and stayed with Junior. I don't know what all happened. I just know there was some conflict come up then. I do know before they got in church, even when us kids was small, there was things happened that even Daddy didn't know about.

There was a situation that I'd got in when I was, I think, fourteen year old. I'd been with Darlene myself. I was young and just sex crazy. And it was just somethin' dumb that shouldn't never happened. It was just a situation that come up between me and her. And there was a time after it when Daddy kind of caught on to what was goin' on. I knowed he'd caught on to what was goin' on, and she did too. I just went to Daddy, told him I had to talk. And we talked. I let him know how things was done. And he really didn't even hear the story 'cause he already knowed in his heart what had happened. But he forgave me of it. He said, "Son, I've done crazy things in my life too." He said, "I forgive you." And we both cried and talked and worked things out between us. I didn't want no hard feelin's, and I didn't want him to have no hard feelin's toward me. He's always said, "Son, I forgive you of it then—I forgive you of it now."

I think Daddy talked to Darlene about it—she said that he said some things to her. But as far as hittin' her or somethin' like that, as far as I know, he didn't. With me, he didn't hit me or nothin'. And I don't think he got real aggressive with her 'cause, you know, we was at the house with Mama, and Darlene and Daddy would come over—and, you know, they just kept comin' over. That's when we lived down here at New Hope. We lived at foot of what we called Morris Hill, which is off Main Drive in New Hope. And Daddy lived on Gurley Pike. There was one road that connects Gurley Pike to Main Drive. We was probably six, eight mile apart. And they'd still come and visit, still come to carry Mama to the store—carry Mama wherever she needed to go.

Later at the oak tree situation, I don't know whether Daddy had all the story or not. When we lived on Sand Mountain, that's when he found out some things on me and her, and I talked to him. We had moved from New Hope to Sand Mountain. Then later when all that stuff came up in the church and she was with other men, he wanted to talk with me and my brother Junior. He knowed on me, and he had heard some things on Junior. But at that point of time he didn't know on Junior. And he asked us to meet him and to talk to him at the oak tree.

Daddy was actually coming there to see J. L.—and to talk with me and Junior too. Junior was kind of little bit scared to go talk to Daddy 'cause he knowed how Daddy was before he got in church and how rough he was. But I'd talked with Junior and told him how Daddy was with me when I'd went to him. And I figured Daddy'd be the same way with him as he was with me.

J. L. was suppose' to come and meet with Daddy that day, but J. L. never did show up. I think he might have rode by, but I don't think he ever stopped. I think he was a little bit 'fraid to come and talk to Daddy too 'cause he knowed how Daddy was before he got in church.

Darlene come with Daddy. And me, Daddy, and Junior got to talk a little bit waiting for J. L. Daddy was just more or less talkin' to us about what had happened with J. L. And, you know, Daddy was just a little bit hurt 'cause J. L. wouldn't meet him and talk to him.

Actually, I think it was Darlene brought it up about me and Junior. And Junior, he more or less denied ever bein' with her. Course I'd been with her, and I couldn't deny that I'd been with her. And there was also some situations brought up with Uncle David, that maybe Uncle David had been with her. And I don't know that he had—I think Darlene was sayin' that. I don't really know what all she was sayin'. It's been so long I can't really remember.

But Daddy didn't get furious or cussin' mad. You know, we could tell he was hurt 'cause he was cryin'. He just kind of broke down. That's just kind of the way he was dealin' with it. But as far as bein' furious and mad, maybe takin' it out on somethin' else—he wasn't doin' that. He was just like he had a ton of weights sittin' on his shoulders. And at times he had tears runnin' down his face.

When we left the oak tree, we went to the house. Me and Junior stood out there and talked to Daddy. And I think maybe Eddie and Gary may have come by. Daddy had a flat, and some of us went and got a tire and fixed his flat. I don't know that Daddy had been drinkin' or what point he may have. When he come to the house that day, I felt like that maybe he had. But as far as knowing for sure, I really don't know that he had been drinkin' at that point of time. I never have seen him drink. I think he had some kind of juice in a plastic container. I don't know if it may've had anything in it or not. I don't know. As far as seein' him drink, I never had—not while he was in church.

Darlene had got out and went in the house and was talkin' to Virginia, Junior's wife, and Rita, my wife. Darlene had been in the house quite a while, and we had been outside talkin' to Daddy for a long time 'cause, you know, we

Bill Summerford

didn't want to see him out of church. Really the best father that we had was from the time we was probably fourteen, fifteen year old, from the point of time he got saved and got the Holy Ghost. The best father we ever had was while he was in church.

But he was always a good father to us. Me and Junior and Eddy—the old-est boys, anyway—we all time hunted with Daddy a lot when we was kids. I guess when we was learnin' how to walk he was carryin' us huntin'. I remember times in the woods—probably three or four year old—be out coon huntin', fishin', huntin' somethin', doin' somethin' all the time. We all time enjoyed spendin' time in the woods with Daddy, especially on coon hunts, time when the men got off together and just had a wonderful time, listenin' to dogs bark, tree coons, shoot 'em out on dogs and watch the dogs fight 'em—it's just fun. And after he got in church, he was the kind of a person I'd look up to, you know. We could go to him, talk about our problems, talk about things we was goin' through. And he'd kinda help us with 'em and kinda work things out with us. He was a lot of help to us 'cause a lot of things he'd already been through.

And there at the house, we's just talking, "Daddy, we don't want to see you out of church, don't want to see you quit church. And we know what you done to J. L." He was talkin' like he was goin' go back to church and fix things up that night. And I don't know, whenever he left there, I don't know whether he went right back to the church or not. But he talked like he was goin' go back to church then.

I don't know why he exploded with J. L. and not the others. I don't know unless it might have been . . . see, Junior worked with J. L. for a long time. And they was a lot of times there'd be like two or three weeks before Junior'd get his money from J. L. Maybe that had a lot of buildup on pressure toward J. L.— when he went and hit J. L. 'Cause I think he might have been in a lot of ways takin' up for his son—and in a lot of ways whatever else that had happened. You know, that was on him too. And Marty was part of it—that probably built pressure somewhat. Daddy, he lets a lot things build up on him. When it builds up, it's like a bomb explodin'. I do know with Daddy, he always liked to get to the very bottom of things. Whenever things happened, he liked to find out every incident and get to the bottom of things.

And I think whenever he come to meet J. L. at the oak tree, I think maybe he was wantin' to talk and really get J. L.'s point of the story. I think the way Daddy, Willie, and Gene worked things out and forgave one another—I think that's what he was really wantin' to do with J. L. But J. L. just never would meet and talk to him.

Glenn's Second Son

Now, the night Darlene got bit and got away to the hospital, me and my wife was at Uncle David's, Daddy's brother who's married to Darlene's sister Kathy. Well, Darlene called Uncle David's—I think it was her called from the hospital, or my aunt Charlotte had called Kathy and talked to her. So me and Uncle David and Kathy left from there, and we went down to the hospital. Aunt Charlotte and Uncle Joe was already there talkin' to Darlene.

There was a program come on TV a while back. And they said a officer of the law had met a high-speedin' car comin' from Daddy's house. They stopped it on the side of the road goin' to the hospital, and it was Kathy carryin' Darlene to the hospital—a officer of the law tellin' somethin' like 'at. I couldn't believe that. I couldn't believe it at all. I can't even remember a officer being there at the hospital that night.

But when we got to the hospital, we went to the emergency room. Darlene was there. Her hair was frizzed up, like maybe she hadn't combed her hair in a while. But as far as lookin' like she'd been beat, she didn't look like she'd been beat, didn't look like she'd been kicked, stomped, or nothin' like 'at. And she had one mark on her thumb, and her thumb wasn't swollen like what I'd seen from a snakebite. See, since I got in church and got to goin' out to Brother Jimmy's, I seen Brother Jimmy bit one night by a little old copperhead. It just tapped him on the thumb, and his thumb swelled up—I mean just enormous in a matter of a few minutes. But it didn't look like Darlene'd been bit by no snake, the way she looked there at the hospital.

Then they took Darlene by ambulance from the hospital there at Scottsboro and was takin' her to Birmingham. Seems like Kathy may have rode with her. I rode back with David to his house and got my wife. And me and my wife left from there and went over to my sister Jackie's, who lived in Paint Rock Valley, where my little brother Marty was stayin'. And we talked to Marty, Jackie, and my brother-in-law Kenneth about ever'thing—the call up to Kathy's sayin' that Darlene was at the hospital, and about goin' down there.

Daddy was suppose' to be at home, and didn't none of us really right then go over there and check on him. I don't know why. I reckon 'cause the way he was in the past, when he'd get drunk and was mean as he would get. I was actually scared to go over there 'cause what Darlene was tellin' her sister Kathy and David and them about what was goin' on. I was really a little bit 'fraid to go over there. I was just lettin' Daddy work things out on his own. At that point of time I actually thought maybe what she was tellin' was the truth. She was tellin' stories, you know, and it was gettin' round the family. And we actually started to believe the stories and some of the rumors that we were hearin'.

Some of us was even beginnin' to think that Daddy had backslid and was goin' on a rampage. That was one thing that we was kind of a little bit afraid of when we went up to the oak tree to talk to him 'cause some of the family had called around and we'd got word even before we'd went and talked to him. But as far as when we did talk to him, there was nothin', you know, happened.

Well, we was up there at Jackie's, and we was kind of talkin' about the rumors that was goin' around. And somebody called from David's lettin' us know Daddy was on his way down there. And it even had some of us scared. But Daddy come in, and he said, "You-all hear what happened?" And we got to talkin' to Daddy, wantin' to know what was goin' on. He said he don't know. He'd been asleep, and Grandma and Aunt Charlotte had come in up at his house and woke him up. He heard that Darlene was in the hospital in Birmingham, and so he wanted to take Marty and leave from there and go to Birmingham and see how she was doin'.

So him and Marty left from Jackie's right a'ter we'd talked there a few minutes. Actually, my sister Jackie, she was kind of worried about some of the rumors that was goin' around, and she called down into Birmingham ahead of him, you know, lettin' the police know that he was on his way down there. And the police stopped him inside, I think, a parkin' garage down there and about shot him over rumors, more or less, that some of the kids had heard.

Later on, me and my brother Junior—and seem like our wives went with us—we went down to Birmingham and saw Darlene down there. Seem like it was the next day that we left. And her family and them was down there with her. She was in a room by herself, and they was workin' with her. Even then when we went and talked to her, we was just trying to find out, you know, what had happened, what was goin' on. And we really couldn't get a whole lot out of her. We really didn't know what all had happened.

She kinda talked like Daddy went off the wall and caused her to put her hand in a serpent box. I can't remember what all she was sayin'—it's been so long. I think she was talkin' like he was accusin' her of things and was jealous and was on a rampage with her. I don't know what all, you know, whether he was accusin' her or whether he'd caught her or whatnot. But we couldn't get a whole lot out of her.

Even at that point of time she wasn't swelled like when Daddy'd get bit and swell up. She wasn't like 'at. I heard they later gave her an antivenom, and it made her sick and liked to kill her. Seem like she said they was goin' give it to her, but at that point of time they hadn't. And that's the only time we had went down there.

Glenn's Second Son

After Daddy got arrested down in Birmingham, I think it was my aunt Barbara and her husband that got him out. Me and my wife or me and my little boy left and went to Daddy's to talk to him. And when we got there, the detectives was there with him. And they wouldn't even let us talk to Daddy. There was some detective went into the house. And the detective had Daddy in handcuffs, and then was walkin' him around outside. That's when Daddy got arrested and put in Scottsboro.

Actually when we begin to believe Daddy's side of the story is when we got to goin' to Daddy and hearin' what he had to say about it. He's told us his side of the story, and she's told us her side of the story. And we ain't really heard all her side 'cause when she come back from Birmingham, then she went to her family. And we never have really got to go out and talk to her or nothin' like 'at, you know. I don't know whether she'd really want to talk. But we've got with Daddy and talked to Daddy, and he's told us his side of the story. And his side seems as real as what I think her side would be. And I actually believe as much of his side of the story as I do hers. But as far as knowing what happened between them two, it's just him and her and the Lord.

And as far as him making her put her hand in the snake box, I don't know if he would stoop that low to do that. I kind of figure, the way Daddy was, I figure he'd just took a gun and shot her. Myself, I really feel like he would've, rather than to use the serpents. I really feel like he would've. 'Cause Daddy was the type when he got mad—he had a real bad temper when he did get mad—and when he'd unwound, it's just like he went crazy.

I think at home Daddy and Darlene probably fussed, probably argued, and he might have slapped her. I ain't goin' say he didn't. He might have slapped her. Before he ever got in church, I seen times that he did get mad and he did slap her—'cause he was just that type of person before he got in church. But I know that the Lord changed him in a lot of ways while he was in church. And I don't really know how he was at that point of time, how far out of church he was, if he would stoop that low to slap her. I don't know.

I don't know how much they may have argued, how much they may have fussed 'cause they kept it private between them two. Daddy was always one that felt like you wadn't suppose' to leave room for your good to be evil spoken of. And I think there was a lot of things that they kept behind closed doors. They didn't let nobody know. And I think that's the way it was on that situation. But I can't say that he'd make her stick her hand in the snake box. I really can't say that he did.

Bill Summerford

Now, when we was at the oak tree, he'd talk like he was goin' get a divorce. And when they come over to the house, they was talkin' about gettin' a divorce. But he didn't become aggressive or abusive to nobody. At times she was cryin', and she was kind of takin' things hard. I think it was just real hard on both of 'em. And I can understand it bein' hard on 'em. But I don't know whether he had completely made up his mind that he was goin' get a divorce. I know he was talkin' about it, and I know he might have.

They was times when Darlene, you could see that she wadn't happy. And they was times when she wanted, maybe, go back to her old ways and do things she used to do. When Daddy was snakebit up there, we seen Darlene smokin'. From the time Darlene and Daddy got in church and they both quit smokin' up to that point of time, we never had seen Darlene smoke—which was probably seven, eight year. But when Daddy was snakebit, we seen her smokin' and flirtin' around with some of the other guys. And I kind of got the attitude in my mind that maybe she was wantin' to go back doin' things like she used to and wantin' out of the marriage. That's kind of what I got in my head. Now I really don't know. There was times in their marriage she said things that she probably didn't really mean—I know there was with Daddy.

Before her and Daddy got together, she'd lost a child, I think because of being unfit in some kind of way. She had a little girl before her and Daddy got married that was taken away from her. And she was afraid that Daddy would keep Marty if they got divorced. I believe Daddy would've, 'cause I believe Marty would rather be with Daddy. Marty always like to hunt and fish, and he'd always stay with Daddy ridin' horses and stuff like 'at. I know Marty loved his mama, but I'd really think Marty'd stay with his daddy if he had a choice. And I think Darlene realized that.

From the time Daddy got the Holy Ghost, I believe he was livin' right. Yeah, I really believe he was, really do. I figure he had to do a lot of fastin' and a lot of prayin' to read because he never had an education. The Lord's helped me in the Bible. And I figured the Lord helped him a lot too in understandin' the word and reading the word of God and really gettin' the spiritual outlook and understandin' of it.

I feel like Daddy did do a lot of fastin'. And to do the things I've seen him do in church, I know he had to do a lot of fastin' 'cause you don't just cast out devils without really fastin' and seekin' the Lord. I've seen him cast out devils like I've never seen anybody else cast out devils and bad spirits that people would have on them. He was so close to the Lord that people come in that was bound with alcohol and drugs and things, and he could pray for 'em—and spirits would break off of 'em. And they could pray through to the Holy Ghost and receive the baptism of the Holy Ghost. And I feel like he had to do a lot of fastin' and prayin', you know, to get to that point. I've done quite a bit of fastin' and quite a bit of prayin'. And I don't think I got to places that I've seen him in.

You know, I'd get in church and get out of church. And I'd go listen at him preach, and I loved to hear him preach. They couldn't nobody preach no better than he could. He could make a child understand it, you know, the way the words of the Lord come out through him. It'd be just like anybody could understand it. And the way he studied scripture and brought it out, he'd just bring it out as plain as day. And, you know, if you didn't understand it, there's maybe somethin' wrong with you. But I believe anyone could understand what he preached. And I think the doctrine he preached was real good doctrine and a real good standard. And I think if anybody listened to it, I think they'd make it into heaven. And I really believe that he lived what he preached—I do.

I don't believe a preacher could do the things he done without livin' close to the Lord like he did. Once I went in and repented and was prayin' and got in church for a short period of time. And me and my wife, we'd kind of laid out of church one Sunday and went fishin'. We was wadin'-fishin', bream fishin', catchin' bream—that time of year bream's on bed. And I got snakebit when I got out of the water to get my shoes. I got snakebit on the foot. Boy, it scared me to death. My foot swolled up real big before I even left the bank there.

And I got back in the water where my wife was and told them I'd got snakebit. And we headed to the house. When we got to the house, my foot's swelled up so big, couldn't get my shoe on. And we got back in the car. I said, "I don't know what to do, but I ain't goin' to the hospital. We done laid out of church—let's just go to church. I'll get Daddy to pray fer me."

I went into the church, and I can remember it just like it's today. I went into the church, and there was another preacher that Daddy was letting that night preach. And this was before Daddy ever started bringin' serpents into a church. He was in a bookstore up there on the square in Scottsboro, in the basement part of the building. And I went in and Brother Jimmy Long was preachin'. I went up to the preacher, and I said, "I need you-all to pray fer me. I've been snakebit."

I walked up with just a sock on my foot, my foot hurtin', scared to death, 'fraid I was goin' die. Got up there, and the preacher said, "You gonna have to sit down and wait until I get through preachin'. And then we'll pray fer you." And Daddy jumped up out of his seat, and he said, "Naw, we ain't. We're prayin' fer him right now." And he jumped up and went to prayin'. The church got to prayin'.

And the way my foot was swelled at that point of time, it just froze. It didn't swell no more. And before I could leave, the pain was leavin'. And, actually, by the time I got back to the house, I could put my shoe on. It was just amazin' how the swelling and stuff went down. It amazed me and amazed my wife. I was deathly scared. I thought I was a goner 'cause we'd laid out of church and went fishin'. I reckon the Lord's got ways of gettin' your attention.

And now that Daddy's in prison, I really feel like he's prayin' a whole lot. If he got out, I feel that he would be in church somewhere. I don't feel like he'd get out and go back to drinkin', go back to runnin' wild. I don't feel like he'd do that. I feel like he'd get right back in church and carry on with the Lord 'cause I know he's wantin' to make it to heaven. I really feel like that in my heart. I don't think he'd hunt Darlene up and bother her in any way. If she come up to him, I think he'd talk to her. But I think he'd stay away from her and go on with his life.

Daddy always looked toward Brother Aubrey a lot. I figure Daddy'd probably ease out there and see and talk to Brother Aubrey—he's been preachin for fifty-some year. That's where Daddy actually started at, Brother Aubrey Hastings' on Sand Mountain, right at the top of Section. Brother Aubrey's gettin' kind of old now. I figure Daddy might even start up another church. They's times I go down and talk to Daddy. And he said that when he gets out, he'd just like to steal away to hisself and pray and see what the Lord wants him to do. I think if he got out, he could help a lot of people. I really do. I think what time he's been in prison that he's really done a lot of studyin' and readin'. And I really think he'd probably be a better preacher when he gets out than what he was when he went in. I really do.

I know that if I put myself in the situations that he was in, things he was going through in the family, I think it would have a big toll. I think it would break down a lot of families—you know, the situation of catching his wife runnin' around on him, things like that. I think it had a big toll on him and just made him weak. But I think he's gettin' over it. I really do. I think he's fixed things up with the Lord. I think he'd go on with his life and help people. I really do.

And back whenever all this happened, they was other situations. I don't think the cops in Scottsboro done the investigation like they should have. I really don't think that the outcome of the trial should have come out like it did. I think that before Daddy got with the Lord, I think he just had a bad reputation with the police and with people there in Scottsboro. And I think that was part of the outcome of the case.

And during the time of the trial, they was incidents with the lawyer and things. Me and Junior, we'd talked to Daddy different times and tried to get him to tell his side of the story. We knowed that the people, the public, needed to hear Daddy's side of the story. And Lackey, Daddy's lawyer, wanted him to be hush-hush and be quiet about it. The lawyer kept tellin' Daddy, "Well, I'm afraid to put you on the stand, afraid of what you might cause to yourself, hurt you. And me and Junior kept trying to get Daddy to tell his side of the story. And I really believe if he'd told his side that it'd been a different outcome. I really do. I believe it'd been a different outcome of the public, of the newspaper writin's, if they could have just heard, you know, Daddy's side of the story. He never did get to tell his side.

And even durin' the trial, they was incidents where me and my brother, we wondered when Lackey was goin' use us for a witness in the case. And I think somethin' like twenty-three, twenty-four people signed up for Daddy's witnesses. And the lawyer didn't use the ones I really thought that could help Daddy. Because I think me and Junior and some of our uncles and brothers and sisters, I think we knew more of the story than what the public was hearin'.

Me and Junior and Daddy—the day we went to talk to Lackey—we went in and sat down and told Lackey our side of the story. And Lackey let on like he was goin' use us on the case, use us in the trial to tell things that we knowed. But all the way through the trial he wanted to keep Daddy off the stand. I reckon 'cause Daddy was so tore up and so hurt, you know, from the outcome of things, from what he'd suffered, that the lawyer wanted to keep him off the stand—'fraid he'd hurt hisself. I really don't know.

At times, I think Lackey kind of sold Daddy out. I really do. I don't think he was a lawyer that really gave a hundred percent in Daddy's behalf. I think, if anything, he sold him out. I really do.

Bill Summerford

J. L. and Martha Lewis
Longtime Friend and His Wife

J. L. Lewis

I started to church before Glenn, but I didn't get the Holy Ghost until after he did. He believed in the Jesus Name, but I was baptized in the Trinity: Father, Son, and Holy Ghost. We didn't knock one another. I just didn't believe the way he believed, and he didn't believe the way I did. I went to church with him probably two and a half, three years before the Lord ever showed me that there weren't but one God. Matter of fact, him and me baptized several hundred people, him on one side and me on the other. And I's baptizing 'em in the Trinity, and he was baptizing 'em in Jesus Christ. But he had enough love in his heart to hang in there with me, and just kept praying for me instead of putting me down like most people would be, till God really opened my eyes up to the situation.

For three or four years Glenn Summerford was as good a preacher and the finest child of God that I've ever been around. I know God really used him. When he was livin' for God the way he was doin', I'd rather hear him preach than anybody I've ever heard. And God really did use him. I've seen a lot of wonderful things happen at that church. I've seen a lot of demons cast out of people. I've seen people get healed of cancer. I've seen people get new hearts. One lady in particular, one night they was practically three towed her in—God healed her. She had been sent up to Birmingham for an operation and was supposed to go, I believe it was, on a Tuesday night—and which the church gave her the money. And Glenn told her to go down there, but make sure she had them to check her again. So she went down and told them how

J. L. Lewis.

much better she's feelin'. And she come back to church and testified that they'd told her she had the heart of a fifteen- or sixteen-year-old kid. I've seen cancer fall off of people up there. I've seen a lot of great miracles happen in under Glenn's ministry. My oldest brother received the Holy Ghost up there. My wife received the baptism of the Holy Ghost up there.

And then Darlene—I started seein' a whole lot of stuff out of her. My wife finally had to quit sittin' with Darlene on account of some of the things Darlene was doin'. Darlene was trying to go with several different men. I heard it first by a son of one of the brothers—he played the guitar. And I really didn't believe it when he told me. I just didn't believe what he was sayin'. A matter of fact, he told me that she had tried to go with him a year before ever I started seein' anything. But then I started seein' a lot of things happenin'.

The people that owned that buildin' where Glenn was having church up on Highway 79 told him that he had to move, that they needed the buildin' theirself. So Glenn didn't have nowhere to go there for several months. Then he found a little buildin' over in the hollow by the hospital, Woods Cove— which I had helped Glenn out with the rent and the light bill and different things from time to time.

Anyway, he called me and told me he had found a buildin', but he needed some money. Glenn really hated to ask for money and would talk around it for a long time before even asking. And instead of him coming down there at the office, he sent Darlene with Marty.

And I gave her the money. And then about a week later, they called and needed some money to turn the utilities on. They owed some other bills, and they needed like three hundred, three hundred fifty dollars. I told him to come down and get it. Again he sent Darlene and Marty down there. And they got the money.

After Glenn got the building over there in the Cove, I quit. I didn't go over there very many times at all 'cause I knew what Darlene was doin'—you could see what she was doin'. You'd invite somebody to come to the church; and right off the bat, she'd try goin' with the man—which wasn't doin' the church any good or whoever you brought either. Darlene just really turned bad to the bone. And Glenn didn't want to turn her aloose. I believe Glenn knew it from the very beginning, but he did not want to turn her aloose. As a matter of fact, I had prophesied when he was on Highway 79—and he rebuked me for it—that there was a certain man there that she was gonna go with. And she wound up goin' with him, and that man'll tell you the same thing. It was told to me later that she was meetin' him over at the cemetery, goin' with him.

Anyway, I started helpin' Brother Clyde and Sister Rachael. We was havin' some revivals at people's houses—there was twenty-seven people received the baptism of the Holy Ghost, and they started a church. But Glenn got on to me about not comin' up there workin' with him, and I didn't want to tell him why that I wadn't comin'.

Then over at Lacey's Spring, the Coon Club—a lot of people over there wanted to know about the snake handlin' and wanted him to come over there and hold a revival. They asked me if I'd get him, and I said I'd talk to him. He came over, and we had a good revival goin' on over there. Again, he got on to me for not comin' up a-he'pin' him. I still didn't tell him nothin'. I'm almost positive he knew, but he just did not want to turn that woman aloose. I believe if he had of, he'd still be in church doin' great today.

But I have heard Glenn testify probably twelve or fifteen times that he had gone back on the Lord one time, backslid—and that the Lord had spoke to him that when he did take him back, if he ever went back on him again, there was no more hope for him. He said, "If I back up on God, there'll never be no more hope for me again." He said God told him that.

But goin' back to that lights and stuff at the church—they was wantin' to have some services, so I borrowed a couple of generators from a friend of mine and took them up there where they could have utilities. And they was having church up there probably seven, eight months before he really messed up bad.

Glenn's son Junior was workin' for me, and we was working out of John Gann's buildin' on the south end of Huntsville. I went over there to John's office and had some plans and some figures on jobs that I was callin' about. And Junior, he hadn't showed up. One other man worked for me—he was there, and I sent him to do some stuff. Then Glenn and Darlene pulled up.

Glenn was about half or maybe third drunk. Their little car quit, though, when he pulled off the parkway. He raised the hood, and then he finally got it cranked and pulled it on up there to the buildin'. We raised the hood again, and we talked about forty-five minutes. I said, "You-all come on in. I gotta go in and call this man about this bid." But Glenn said, "We'll just wait out here." So I went in there and come back out and talked to him a pretty good while. That man who worked for me, he came back. Junior still hadn't showed up, and I asked him if he had seen Junior. And he said, "Naw." And I said, "Well, he supposed to been here about fifteen till seven." He said, "No, we ain't seen him." And I had propped my arms up on the hood, where it was raised up— was talking from time to time, and sit on the fender some. I tried two or three times to get Glenn to come in. I figured he'd come down there to borrow some money. That's what I thought he had on his mind. Course we talked about several different things.

Then I went back in the office again and called this man, and come back out again. And we talked about another ten minutes. Darlene at that time was sittin' in the car, and she got out. Course she hadn't sit in the car all that long, but when I came back out the last time, she was sittin' in the car. She got out on the passenger side, walked around both of us, and come over to my left.

I had give Glenn a rackin' horse. I had a quarter horse, a stud horse that I had bought, and Darlene wanted him 'cause she didn't have nothin' to ride. And both of them was poor and didn't have no money, so I just give 'em both of the horses, a horse apiece. And she said, "Brother Lewis, you know that horse you let me have?" And I said, "Yeah." She said, "I hope you don't get mad at me, but I traded him for a palomino horse." I said, "I give him to you, whatever you wanted to do." And about that time, my head got rattled with that timin' chain by Glenn. It was a truck timin' chain, and it was longer than normal, 'cause it retched from the front of my forehead to the back of my head

164

and brought blood all way cross there. He had it taped for a handhold, and he rattled my head pretty good with that chain. He come with the intention of doin' what he done. And as a matter of fact, if it hadn't been for the good Lord, he'd probably killed me.

Now, if he had confronted me and then hauled off and hit me, it'd been a different story. Any other time, to be honest—it had to be God or I would have cut his head off, just as smooth as a whistle. And if I thought he was come down there to start somethin'—there was a pistol layin' in John's drawer in there—I could have put that in my pocket. I had no idee of what Glenn was goin' to do. I said, "What in the world's wrong with you?" "You know what's wrong with me." "No," I said, "I don't know what's wrong with you. You crazy?" And Darlene said, "I told him about me and you." I said, "What are you talkin' about?" Then it dawned on me to look back, and he was fixin' to hit me again. I said, "You don't want to do that, Glenn. One time is enough. You better get in the car and leave." But Darlene had got her purse—she had it sittin' where she could get it—and when he first hit me, she grabbed her purse. It had a gun in it, and she got it out.

And Glenn got so weak till he had to hold on to the car to get back in it—onliest thing I can figure out was, it was God. It had to be God, just trying to help me, I guess. There weren't but one lick passed. Glenn was fixin' to hit me the second time when she got my attention again. I guess he had hit me so hard, it rattled my brain; and I wadn't thinkin' as fast as I should have thought. But he got in the car and did leave. And I went in the bathroom and washed my head.

What she thought was that I would kill him. That's what she really wanted me to do, was to kill him. She was goin' give him the gun. He told her what to do in order to get my attention where he could hit me—was what it boiled down to. If I'd had an idee that there'd be any problem or any trouble, number one, I wouldn't be out there with him; and if I'd been out there with him, I'd carried that gun in John's desk top drawer. She wanted me to kill him, or him to kill me, where she would have got rid of him. Darlene was trying to get rid of Glenn Summerford.

I would say she was drinkin', but not as much as he was. Glenn has already been drinkin' probably for a week. Now, this didn't happen within two or three days—this is like a week, a week and a half, because Junior had already told me about his daddy catchin' Gene Sherbert and Darlene locked up kissin' and huggin' on the back porch. See, Glenn's supposed to been squirrel huntin'.

Longtime Friend and His Wife

But anyway, Glenn called me back, cryin', apologized unto me. He called a second time, saying' he didn't want me to have him arrested. I told him I wasn't thinkin' on it, told him I forgive him for what he done. But I said, "The way you did this, Glenn . . . I can understand you bein' mad at me . . . what's she's doin', she trying to get one t'other of us killed." Anyway, I told him I forgive him, and I wasn't goin' have him arrested. I just didn't want to fool with him no more, not never come around me. Said, "You knowed me for over thirty years. You've never seen me with a woman. Me and you been out for weeks at a time. Me and you have worked together. Me and you coon hunted together, three or four nights a week. You ain't never seen—when I was in sin, you never seen me tryin' to go with a woman." And he agreed with me.

He told me that after he caught Darlene, when he was supposed to be huntin', he said, "Somethin' was tellin' me to kill 'em both, and the Lord was tellin' me not to. It had to be Satan tellin' me to kill 'em." He said, "I took the shells out of the gun, and I throwed the gun one way and the shells another way." And he said, "I went in there and fell down on my knees and cried out to God. And I got over that." And he said, "Gene Sherbert apologized to me." And then said, "She told me about goin' with one of my brothers, having sex with one of my brothers." Said, "I prayed—I got over that. She told me about another one of my brothers she went with. So I prayed and got over that one." He said, "She told me she went with two of my sons, Junior and Bill." He said, "Now, I prayed, and I got over that." And Brother Uly Lynn, he was an old man—I guess Brother Uly was eighty-seven, eighty-eight year old at the time— I know he was a real old man. But in his past, he was very mean too. And Darlene even told Glenn she went with him. She told Glenn she went with me. She told him she went with Johnny Ingram. He named off a list or a bunch of people that—and he said, he kept prayin'. And finally, he just couldn't take no more, and he got drunk. He kept prayin', but finally she broke him, or finally the devil got to him. That was his story.

The third time he called me back was two or three days later—the first two calls were the same day. And each time he'd call me, he'd ask me to forgive him. And he told me the third time he called me, he told me, "Yeah, me and you been friends for years. We went to church. We worked side by side. I know what kind of man you are, and you're the one I want to baptize me. Will you come up here and baptize me?" I said, "I'll pray and ask God. But the way I feel right now, I will not come and baptize you, Glenn. I'm goin' tell you again. It wouldn't have bothered me . . . and I forgive you for doin' it . . . I just don't want to have nothin' to do with you. And the reason I don't want to have

J. L. and Martha Lewis

nothin' to do with you is the way you did me. I've he'ped you all these many years. You knew me like the back of my hand. You knew what she was doin'. And if you'd just come up to me and whipped me, come up to me and shot me—I'd be up there and baptize you, if I was still livin'. But to sneak up on me or to have her to get my attention and you do what you done, I don't go with that." So I told him, I'd call him back. And I prayed and called him and told him no, I couldn't come.

He also wanted me and him to get together and talk. And I's supposed to met him at New Hope. And he's supposed to come alone. But when I came by down there, there was three or four with him, includin' Darlene. And he wasn't even supposed to bring her along. So I didn't even stop.

Now, Glenn, I think, has told that the reason he hit me with that timin' chain had somethin' to do with the times Marty and Darlene came to the office for money—for sending Marty for cold drinks out to the store on a road where he might get run over.

The day that Marty and Darlene came down to the office to get the money, I was in John Gann's office. When Darlene and Marty came in, they sat on the couch to the right of the desk. I asked them if they wanted somethin' to drink, and they said, "Yeah." And I said, "Well, I'd like to have one myself, too." I gave Marty change out of my pocket, not to go to the store, but just to the drink machine outside a door down at the end of a little six-foot hall. In the same building, the receptionist has got a big office by the front door—immediately to the right of that is another office, and at end of the building there's Gerald Gann's office. Gerald and the secretary both was there, with people comin' in and out all the time. When Darlene and Marty come in, they shut the door. And when Marty went to get the drinks, Darlene closed the door to talk about some things she didn't want others to hear. Marty goes and gets three drinks. He comes back to the door, and the door was locked. Darlene just reached up—she wasn't far from it, probably four or five foot, just reached up and undone the door. I don't even know how the door got locked. So Marty never went to the store.

The next time they come, the kid did go to the store. When they called, I told Glenn for *him* to come. Glenn was supposed to came himself. Glenn's son Junior was there. And they wanted—I believe it was three hundred and fifty dollars, was the money discussed the last time any money was got. Now, when they came up, Darlene said, "Somethin' is wrong with the car—it's smokin' terrible." I told her to crank the car, and the car didn't have no oil in it. And I said, "Well, you-all want to get in and I'll run down here and we'll get oil to put in the car?" And she was scared that Glenn would accuse me and her bein' together, 'cause Glenn was very jealous of Darlene. He didn't want her off with no man, period. She said, "I'll get the oil." And I said, "You shouldn't run a car nowhere without the oil."

They came back in. Her and Marty talked about thirty minutes. What I did was I opened my wallet up to give her the money, and I think I had like five hundred dollars. And I didn't have no twenties or fifties or nothin'—all I had was hundred-dollar bills. And I said, "You need to get me the fifty dollars." We walked out the door of the office, and she walked out front. When me and her and Marty walked out the office, I thought both of them went to the store to get the oil. But she didn't go. She stayed in the parkin' lot, and Marty went on down to the store. Ever'time Darlene was with me, there was at least three people around, and I never sent Marty to no store to get no cold drink. And all he had to do to go to the store for the oil was to leave the parkin' lot, walk around one building and he was in the parkin' lot where the store was—about 150 yards away.

I will say this. Darlene would have done anything at this point in time to get rid of Glenn. According to what she told my wife, Glenn hadn't slept with Darlene in over a year, as far as sex. Course Darlene could have been lying about that. Darlene was bad about lyin'.

And Glenn's lawyer was running for district attorney at that time, and he wadn't even tryin' to he'p Glenn no way. They do not want a snake-handlin' church in Scottsboro or nowhere else, as far as that part goes. Instead of gettin' in there, doin' what the lawyer was suppose' to done, he done enough to put on a little bit of show. If he would have presented what he was suppose' to have done, with the information that was give to him, Glenn wouldn't be in the penitentiary today. 'Cause he did not force that woman's hand in that snake box. She was not bit by no snake—she was bit by their pet coon. And they didn't want Glenn off—they wanted him out of Scottsboro. And Darlene wanted rid of him. If Glenn would have just told her to hit the road, got the divorce—that would have been it. But he wouldn't turn her aloose and let her go. Someway, somehow, she was fixin' to get rid of him; and she proceeded to do that. And that's what it really boiled down to. Some of the things she told was the truth.

Darlene was bad from the word go. I talked to Bill, and he told me that when him and Junior was kids, they even went with Darlene—not after they got grown, but when they was kids, both of them slept with Darlene. I knew Darlene before Glenn ever got her. And I knew about the twenty-one men in a pasture in New Market—'cause I knew seven or eight of the men. That's before

J. L. and Martha Lewis

Glenn ever got her. Darlene was a bad egg about all her life, and her sisters too. I'm not just puttin' Darlene down. Darlene straightened up, got the Holy Ghost, and was doing good for a while, but then when—this is my opinion—when the sex was cut off at home, her yearns is what started her doin' back what she was doin' from the very beginning.

Martha, my wife, can add a lot from what she knows.

Martha Lewis

Glenn was a good man before Darlene started all this, as far as I know. I got the Holy Ghost up there in that little church. I sat with Darlene every Sunday and every Wednesday night I went. And there was one man in particular that would come in with his wife and stepdaughter, and Darlene would just have a fit over him. Yeah, I knowed she wanted to go with him. But now you can tell when they start—you don't know if you've heard it right the first two or three times—but then, she'll be trustin' you a little more, and then she'll tell you. She talked about goin' with other men and stuff like that. You know, I knowed what she had on her mind. It finally got to where I moved because I didn't want to be around nothin' like that.

Martha Lewis.

And I never did hear Glenn Summerford say a word like that. And he never said nothin' out of the way to nobody that I know of—a true man of God. He wouldn't even hug a woman's neck in church—well, you got that handshake. Now, he wadn't unfriendly. He just didn't believe in it like that. But you could be thinkin' somethin', you know, in the Lord—or needin' somethin', and that man could tell you before church was over. Whatever it was, God told him. And it'd be what you needed. I seen Brother Glenn try to cast demons out of Darlene in front of the whole church. Glenn was a good man. You could tell he was close to God. I mean, it was Jesus, J. L., and Glenn—that's the way I felt about it.

She was tryin' to get Glenn killed, and she figured she had found a feller right here—J. L.—that would do it. 'Cause they used to run around before they got in church, and she was tryin' to get him killed. She told me she fed Glenn rat poison—I don't know if she did or not. But I believe with all my heart she lied on the man, very much. Put him away for ninety-nine years.

When she commenced to talk about Glenn not sleepin' with her (she said he couldn't) and when she commenced about the men and all this stuff— well, she'd get up there and handle snakes with the rest of 'em. Now, after all this talkin' to me like she done, I's sittin' here wonderin', Lord, how come they ain't eatin' her up?

I mean, Glenn was a good man of God. We can all mess up. It don't mean he can't get back right, you know—in my book. Now, if he don't own up to what he done, all that goodness is shot, 'cause he did mess up—we all can mess up. But you don't hit somebody and do stuff and still not have to repent for it.

And it just about killed me when all this happened. I didn't trust anybody anymore.

J. L. Lewis

And I will add to what my wife says: I never knew Glenn goin' with another woman, period—talkin' to 'em or nothin' until he caught Darlene and Sherbert doin' what they were doin'. After Darlene went to the hospital, that's when Glenn started goin' with that other woman. And I can't say he was having sex, but I know she stayed with him up there probably a week and a half, two weeks.

Now, I'm goin' say somethin' else. I think, probably, Glenn—knowing Glenn when he got to drinkin'—he probably slapped Darlene around. He probably give her two or three good whippin's—ain't no tellin' what he did do

J. L. and Martha Lewis

to her. But makin' her put her hand in that snake box—I'll never believe it. I really won't believe it. I think she got bit by the raccoon, and she probably done somethin' to him to get bit in order to send Glenn off.

Darlene knew how mean me and Glenn both used to be, and she figured if she could get us into it, one t'other of us would get killed. And one t'other of us probably would've been killed if it hadn't been for the good Lord. When someone wraps a timin' chain upside your head—if it ain't the good Lord keepin' you on your feet—you're gonna hit the ground. But Glenn got so weak till he had to hold on to the car to get back in it. And I believe with all my heart, it was the good Lord. And why that I didn't walk over there and just do somethin' bad to him, terrible bad, had to been the good Lord keepin' me from doin' it.

I could have went with Darlene probably the last year and a half 'bout anytime I wanted to, if I'd wanted to went with her. I did not want no portion of Darlene. I never touched her, never had sex with her. I got accused of being in bed with her, and him catchin' me, and all that stuff—that's not true.

I can say for four years, I went to church with Glenn on an average of seven times a week. I put over a hundred and fifty thousand miles on that van of mine goin' backwards and forwards to Glenn's church. And for about seven or eight months after all that happened, I like to have lost it. I just couldn't believe a friend that close could do somethin' like that. But I can assure you that Glenn didn't make Darlene put her hand in that snake box.

Willie Southard
Converted Antagonist

When Glenn shot me, it was because of a friend of his'n and supposed-to-been a friend of mine, that had lived across the road from me. This "friend" worked at the sawmill with me. He had went down at this trailer drunk, showin' out, doin' somethin' or other. And so he came back and told me some things that wasn't true. And that was back when I smoked dope and was mean as the devil. I didn't care, and they knew it. So this supposed-to-be friend said this other guy wrote a note and said for me to be over 'ere to his trailer this evening, which was on Saturday afternoon—and he'd whup me or settle it up with me. I left the sawmill and went over. This guy who worked at the sawmill with me went too, but stayed up on the road.

So I knocked on the door. Then me and the guy in the trailer was arguin'—he said that he didn't write the note. And Glenn come around the corner of the trailer. Glenn knowed the onliest way that he could ever do anything was to shoot me, and this other guy didn't have enough of guts to—he's wantin' Glenn to do it, and Glenn was waitin' on him to do it. And the first thing I did was reach in my pocket for my gun, but then I remembered that I had just sold it a day or two before. Glenn and I hadn't got into it with one another, but it was either shoot or be shot. And so when Glenn shot me, it still didn't stop me, you know. It didn't knock me down or nothin' like 'at. And even after he shot me, they still wouldn't fight me fair. And so this other guy up on the road come around, and he was so skeered, he couldn't do nothin'.

And the guy in the trailer had his old lady call the law. So the law come over 'ere, and we explained to him what had happened. And this guy who had told me this stuff, he was wantin' to bad-mouth the law and all that, so they

Willie Southard.

put him in the squad car. And I knew the law, and I promised that I would take him home. So they didn't take him to jail. They took Glenn's guns, but they never did try to take the bullet out of my leg or nothin' like 'at.

So like I say, really it was over some stupidness because this guy had lied. He was just trying to stir up trouble. And this other guy in the trailer, he wadn't brave enough to stand up for his own mouth. And he knew I didn't care. And just like I said, if I hadn't of sold my pistol a couple of nights before that, then I'd a-shot Glenn and him too. I don't have no feelin's now of shootin' nobody or nothin' like 'at. I still have shotguns and rifles and all that, but I don't have none of them thoughts no more. And I don't hold it against 'em.

So a few months later, this same guy that was in the trailer, his wife had left him. She came up to our house 'cause he had beat her up and all that. And she asked my wife Jewel if she could stay up there a few days. So her husband found out about it. And he said his brag, said he's goin' come over 'ere and he's goin' whup me, my wife, and his wife.

And when he come up 'ere, I told him, I said, "When you come on inside my gate, I'm fixin' to whup you." And when he come on inside the gate, I beat the fire out of him. He hit the ground. Then his hat spun around, and it hit the ground. Each and ever' time he'd get up, I'd kick him down, stomp or do somethin' 'r other. And it was a few days before he could eat or talk. Finally, a couple of days later, his wife left and went back to him. And I haven't seen them since.

But, you know, if that guy, right today—if I was to pass him on the road and he's out of gas, I'd stop and ask if I could he'p him. 'Cause what happened then, happened *then*. It's not what happened now. If I was to passed him up and gone on and say somethin' bad about him, the love of God wouldn't be in me, would it?

But I did whup that guy, and that's exactly what happened. And it wadn't because I'd got shot or nothin' like 'at, but it's because I's a man of my word. If I told you I's goin' bust your head, I'd bust it. And I didn't care. When you're like 'at, you really don't care when you get mad—you get mad. And I had a very, very short temper.

You know, I carried a motorcycle chain in my blue jeans for many, many years in Chicago. I's raised up with them hoodlums up in Chicago and Paint Rock Valley. Really, I was born over yonder where Food World's at in Scottsboro in '46 'fore that road and all came in here. Borned at home—later on moved to Paint Rock Valley. I started to school up there. And then we moved back down here outside Scottsboro, and then we lived up on the hill for a long time. I went up to Chicago in the '60s. Then I was drafted in '67 from up there and went to Vietnam in '68 and '69. And I come out with a honorable discharge, Army Commendation Medal, Bronze Star, and this, that, and another—but which it didn't matter. And then I got back in the service about fifteen years ago, and in the National Guard now.

I's always kind of a loner, you know. Kindly stayed by myself. And what I done, I done by myself. Then thataway I didn't have nobody to tell on me. My daddy always told me, you know, "It's better to be on the outside lookin' in, than is on the inside lookin' out." And I had to run from the law a lot. But they'd get a'ter me here, and I'd hitchhike and be in Chicago or Indiana somewhere for tomorrow night. Wouldn't have much clothes with me. But, you know, when you kindly have friends all over the world, you can, kind of, just go all over the world. Some of 'em that were my friends then, they're still friends of mine now, even though I'm on the other side of what you call the fence from 'em. And they respect me fer it. They don't cuss—and, like, if they drink, they don't drink or nothin' like 'at when I'm around.

And the guys in the service, lot of 'em respects it. We went ten months of a school down here in Huntsville, in Redstone—Patriot. They would go out at night, and I'd set and read my Bible and stay there in the barracks and all. I still don't go out on the town or nothin' like 'at. And they respect it. But you can't please everybody. I told one guy, I said, "I please everybody." He says, "How you do that?" I said, "I please some of 'em when I get there and the rest of 'em when I leave."

But until you can feel the Lord, it's hard to explain how it feels—until you know him as I've knowed him. He's healed me of sicknesses, diseases. I've not took an aspirin or nothin' like 'at in, I guess, twelve, thirteen years. Like they said, "If you's arrested for being a Christian, would you have enough proof to be found guilty?" I want to have enough proof that I'm a Christian to be found guilty.

Now, see, Glenn and I, we knew each other in the world and in God too. We used to fight and all that and have knock-down-drag-outs, but I was mean as he was. And we had that out-and-out when he shot me. But, you know, several years later when the Lord was dealin' with me, I called him and talked with him about goin' to church. He asked me to forgive him over the phone, you know. And I felt the witness of the Holy Ghost, even though I didn't know what it was. I told him what I felt. And he said that was the witness of the Holy Ghost, you know, that was a sign that people could feel when a Christian was tellin' the truth.

Ever' since then, the things that happened before was in the past. And we didn't never mention it or didn't have any sayings about it no more. We just looked towards the future. I still have some of his tapes and him preachin'. I can still feel the anointin' off of 'em—still listen to the words he's speakin' and all. And he still gives me a great joy, you know, to hear him, because I've been there when he would preach. The anointin' would get on to where he would be preachin' and he'd turn blue in the face. And he'd still keep preachin'. But like I say, we've never talked about the things before then.

And when I talked with him about comin' to church and all, he welcomed me. I went over there beside C. W.'s Pit Stop in that restaurant building—that's where he had his church at. I'd had my daughter with me. She'd went to sleep, and I had to bring her home. Me and her mama, we was separated and still are, divorced. And so I came home at the same house where I am now. I came by, and I got me a cup of coffee and a Budweiser beer. I came

Willie Southard

in, and I's sittin' on the steps. And the moon was comin' up. I drank the coffee, but the Lord was dealin' with me, so I throwed the beer back in the house—didn't even take it in there, just rolled it in there and shut the door as I went back over 'ere to church.

Some of the guys outside, they's sayin', "Hey, come on, let's stay out here and smoke a cigarette." I said, "Naw," I said, "that ain't what I come over here for." So I went back in. And it was a sister—she was a Baptist preacher—she came back 'ere where I's settin', 'bout on a Wednesday night after that. And she said the Lord had sent her back there to pray fer me. So she prayed fer me. The anointment and all—I felt somethin'. I didn't really know what it was at that time.

And Brother Billy, Glenn's cousin, and Brother Glenn helped pray me through to the Holy Ghost. And Brother Glenn baptized me. That was in the early '80s. Then it just went on from there. One night Brother Glenn said, "Who here has the faith to take up this serpent?" And nobody else would do it. And so I didn't realize what it was 'cause I just been baptized a few nights earlier. But I was sittin' over 'ere at the door on a pew, and somethin' just felt like it picked me up. I went up there, and I took the serpent out of his hand. Then as the serpent went down and it come back up, it's bumpin' my arm. But it didn't bite me or nothin' like 'at. It coiled up on my arm. And ever' since then, I realized that I could take up serpents.

One time up in Woods's Cove up 'ere, I'd been a-prayin' for the Lord to bind the serpents' mouth so we could take 'em up, you know. So as the Lord dealt with me to go into the serpent box, I went into the serpent box. And I couldn't pull my hand back out—the serpents was hittin' my hand, but they couldn't open their mouth. And then after that I asked Brother Glenn what it was. And he said, "That's the Lord showin' you that he answers your prayers and all." So ever' since then, I've been takin' up serpents, believin' it, drinkin' strychnine. I really believe in the Lord. I've seen him do many a things.

When I got bit at Brother Carl's, I didn't get bit because it was sin in my life, it was just time for me to work in my ministry. And so when I got bit, I had two serpents. One of them bit me, so I just laid 'em back on the altar up 'ere and went back where my Bible's at. And I said, "Lord, I believed you enough to take 'em up. Now I believe you enough to take care of me." And he spoke through Brother Pepper's wife and said, "Fret not, I'm wi' you." So I didn't get scared or nothin'.

Brother Carl, he said, "Come on, we'll drive you home." I said, "You don't have to drive me home." Then I stayed until a'ter service was over with. And

Converted Antagonist

Brother Carl said he was goin' drive me, and there was another brother was goin' follow us. And I said, "You don't have to do that." I said, "The Lord done said, 'Fret not,' he's wi' me. So why should I be a-skeered?" Then I loaded up my serpents, throwed 'em in the front seat of the truck, drive my fivespeed— whole arm kindly swelled up. And I drove all the way from Kingston, Georgia, to my house here in Scottsboro.

That's on a Saturday night. On Sunday, we'd started a brush arbor out at Brother J. L. Dyal's. Of course I's swelled up pretty good size—looked about like your leg—and wadn't able to drive, so I didn't get to go. About Tuesday all the swellin' was gone down. And the bottom of my arm was just as yeller as it could be. And so, when I went in there to pray—which I prayed all the time—and I got through prayin', it's just as clear as it is now—that yeller's all gone and all.

Then another occasion one time, they was some people in there didn't believe that was real strychnine we's drinkin'. So the Lord let it bloodshot my eye, just like you'd stuck your finger in it. And Brother Glenn, he told me, "Don't let no fear come on you or nothin'." He said, "It's goin' be a witness." Said, "There's people that don't believe that's real." And I said, "I'm not a-skeered because I'm hit."

That was on Saturday night, and my head was just like somebody was a-bangin' in it. So I kept prayin', and the headache went away. But my bloodshot eye didn't go away until that night after Sunday service and them people was still there. Then after Sunday service, my eyes was just cleaner as they was now.

And I got bit by a spider twice, and my toe was rotted down almost to the bone. You could see the layers of skin as it went down rott'nin'. So we was foot-washin'. And a day after we had that footwashin', it was just as well as it is now.

And I know that Brother Glenn, he really had the faith. I remember one time he and I was castin' out a devil out of a woman. She was little and skinny. I had holt of one arm, and Brother Glenn had holt of the other one. And that devil in her got mad and was slingin' me and him both all over the place. And we finally weakened it to where it got down—we's all three on the floor. And it jerked her hand back away from me. I retch and put it on the Bible, and smoke come from it. And she had circles on the back of her hand.

And then me and Brother Glenn, we's determined, you know, to cast that devil out. Now, when a spirit like that sulls up, it's like an old 'possum. Then when it begin to realize that it was goin' free her, it begin to talk. When a spirit like that, a devil, when it gets ready to start comin' out, it'd start talkin'. And so I'd heared Brother Glenn say that you can always tell when the devil's lying. And I asked him, "How?" He said, "Sometimes, just ask him if he likes to make a fool out of God's people." So that night that thought come in my mind. And I took the microphone and spoke to that spirit right there. I said, "Devil, do you like makin' a fool out of God's people?" And what do you think it said? It said, "No." So you know it was lyin', 'cause the devil ain't nothin' but a liar and the father of it.

We cast that devil out, and several other times we cast devils out. One time we's castin' a devil out of one, and it come out like a waterdog—hit the floor and went into a crack in the corner. It was long and sort of brown-black and slimey. And on other occasions we'd cast them out, they'd be spittin' up blood and ever'thing else. When that demon starts comin' out of 'em, it tears 'em. And we've worked together like 'at in several occasions.

Brother Glenn preached on faith, love, charity—brotherly love and how the church should do to grow. He'd preach about like some of Paul's words in Corinthians—you know how Paul would teach them how the church should grow and they should stick together and not be talkin' about one another and not let things come between them because of division. Brother Glenn wadn't bad to cut other denominations down. And he didn't continuously bring Mark 16 up, about handling serpents, but if someone would bring up the subject, then he would quote it to 'em.

He wadn't what you call a clothesline preacher. He didn't preach about your clothing. You know, a lot of people, if you clothes ain't just spick-and-span and all that, you ain't nothin'. He never did say anything like 'at. Like, some new people come 'ere—maybe their dress was a little short or they had on makeup or somethin' like 'at—he didn't get up there and preach on makeup, preach about this, that, and the other. You can't do that. You can't get 'em in if you run 'em off before you get 'em in, can you? Like I say, Brother Glenn, he was really sincere about the word of God, and he really believed it. He had faith with his works. I know that the man, he preached the truth, and he lived it the best he could.

And it's just no way that I believe he done what Darlene said he done, that it happened the way she said it was. One day I was prayin' as I was at work at the sawmill and askin' the Lord what happened. And he told me that Darlene was out there drinkin', tryin' to handle those serpents, and she got bit. That's what I've stood by, and that's what I'm goin' stand by, you know, 'cause I don't believe that he done that.

Now, Darlene didn't talk much to me about what happened. She'd say, "Well, you know, he stuck my hand down there." And I told her, I said, "Naw,

179

if he'd stuck your hand down in there" . . . and I've seen people bit by rattle-snakes and all before—you can't crawl from that house across that ditch and all out to the road. You can't ride around in a car and go down there to the store and all that, you know. You just can't do that because that's just not right, you know. It just don't work like 'at.

I've seen Brother Glenn when he got bit by that Mojave rattler. I was on summer camp. Then I come in and went over 'ere to see him. And he had balls of poison where they'd accumulate—see a Mojave rattler, the longer it stays in your body, the more it accumulates. They'd be like blisters. Then they drop off and all. And I've seen him bit two, three other times than that. It was always somethin' that helped him on in there. He helt on to the faith. And like I say, I don't believe that he done it.

Now, this is just speculation or hearsay, but some says that Darlene *said* she went out there to get a serpent to bring 'ere and put on the couch with him. And I don't know. I didn't hear her say it or nothin' like 'at. But she did tell him that she would get a divorce one way or the other, and so evidently she got it the other.

Like I say, I just don't believe he done it. I know he didn't have a fair trial. I know that. And the second time he came up here, they say it was for a hear-ing. Then when they found out some of the witnesses and all wadn't there, they said, "This *was* the hearing." But he will be in prison till the Lord gets ready for him to come out.

But Darlene, she just got to where she changed there, you know, very quickly. Her ways really changed. She was already slippin' around smokin', and then it got to where that you couldn't feel the Godly love, or somethin' other, around her like you used to could. On many occasions when her and Brother Glenn would come in before service would start, she'd be mad, she'd have an old mad spirit on her. And many of 'em at church heared her say, "I'm tired of bein' a preacher's wife." She'd want to wear makeup and all that, and then Brother Glenn'd tell her, "Naw, that's not right. You ain't goin' do that and make me look bad"—because he preached it and he had to stand on it. And so she just used one thing after another till he just had to slack up from preachin'. She was a-tryin' to really destroy the church and him. She knowed if she could get the church destroyed that she could destroy him. And some-time she'd be a-raisin' cane at him, "I just don't see why you just don't close this church down and all."

And she'd act strange. He'd be a-tryin' to get her to sang, to get in the service and all that. And after service she would be a-talkin' to this, that, and the other. And it wouldn' be sisters she'd be talkin' to. It appeared to me as if she was tryin' to cause division with him and his converts and all. And I believe a lot of this that Darlene has said and done was just to get Glenn to really fall and backslide, you know—caused things to happen that really shouldn't have happened. She was tryin' to use whatever she could use to destroy him.

I guess most knew the incident about Gene Sherbert and all that—which Brother Glenn, he didn't let it interfere with his ministry, in preachin' the truth, you know. He had it turned over to the Lord. All you can say about that with Gene is just the lustin' spirit. That's usually what happens is a lustin' spirit. The devil, he'll let you see things that's not really real. He'll let you hear things that you don't really hear. And onest you let that desire and all get in you, then it overtakes you. Then it didn't take much for it to happen.

I heared that Gene apologized to Brother Glenn and all, and Brother Glenn accepted it. And what she runs around and tells I don't know, you know, because I don't get out much and don't hear much. A lot of times you ask the Lord to give you a deaf ear to some of this stuff, and he does it. You don't hear it. I've never talk to Gene about it. He's been back out there at Brother Billy's several times, and we have never discussed it. A lot of times we'd be a-talkin', he'd say: "It'd be nice if old Glenn was here."

And Darlene told Brother Glenn stuff about me. And, see, all this stuff she was doin' was just trying to really make Brother Glenn mad because he was like I was, he really had a bad temper *before*. And Brother Glenn, he came over here one night and talked to me about the situation. She was in the car with him.

He was calm, and he said, "Brother Willie, I want to talk with you about somethin'." I said, "All right," I said, "come on in" 'cause I was in bed and I'd got up. And he come on in. He said, "I want to ask you somethin'. I want you to tell me the truth." I said, "I will." He said, "Have you been messin' around with my wife?" I said, "Lord no! I ain't been a-messin' around with your wife or no other body's wife and no other woman neither." And he said, "She says that you have, that you-all had sex and all that." I said, "She's a-lyin', Brother Glenn. And the Lord knows, it wadn't nothin' like that."

We was lookin' at each other. And he or I neither one didn't lose our temper because he knew I was tellin' the truth. And I could tell the expression in his face that he was glad I was tellin' him the truth. It wadn't no mean, ugly look, but it was the expression of gladness that he really knew and believed that I wadn't—which I wasn't. I had too much fear of the Lord in me to do anything like that.

Converted Antagonist

And when he got ready to leave, he stood and shook my hand. We give each other a brotherly hug and all. And he said, "I sure appreciate you for tellin' me the truth and all that." And so he went and got in the car, and he left. He's never throwed nothin' else up to me about it or nothin'.

And all the other people that she's called the name of—'cause she couldn't get him to flare-up and get into trouble by hurtin' them, you see, she had to go another way about a-gettin' away from him. Then it just got to where that one thing 'r 'nother got him, more pressure got on him. I could see where they was havin' trouble because Brother Glenn and I were real clost, and I could see that it was really interferin' with him, somethin' really botherin' him. And she realized that she was workin' in the right way, and when she got her chance, she laid it on him.

And they'll never make me believe, though, that he stuck her hand in there, that he helt a gun on her, and she got snakebit and crawled all that time, waited all that time. Naw, 'cause she'd been a-swelled so much, or she'd died one.

Like I say, I still pray that he'll get out and he'll come back. Now I believe that he will come back. It may be a little while longer, but he'll be back. And you know a lot of people may not want to accept him and all that, but those that really knew him, they will. It may not be a big congregation, but here later on, the truth is not goin' be found in the big congregations. When he gets out, I'll certainly be a-sittin' in one of the pews there.

But as for her, she knows she done him wrong. And it may be on down the road, but it'll come back to her. What goes around comes around. The Bible says, "Touch not my anointment; do my prophet no harm." A lot of us, we think it ort to happen the next day or a week or so like 'at, but it's in his time.

Willie Southard

Marty Summerford
Glenn and Darlene's Son

It was pretty scary that morning after all that stuff happened when Daddy came for me at Kenneth's. (Kenneth married my sister Jackie and later raised me.) My older brothers, Junior and Bill, were there. And they said, "If he comes up here to get you, we're just goin' kill him." They had the guns loaded, boy. They'd done heard Mama's side of the story, and they went wild or somethin'. Daddy come up and talked to them—then didn't nobody think nothin' about it. Kenneth, he give him fifty dollars to go down there to Birmingham hospital.

I'd already been comin' down to Kenneth's probably three weeks before then, every weekend. Me and Michael, we'd come down and hit the fields and go down to the creek, play around, have fun—just to get away from it all. I guess Daddy and Mama just called Kenneth to come get me that Friday—they's into it pretty heavy, and they's leavin' to go somewhere, I can't remember. They might have been goin' to get some more alcohol or to see J. L. Lewis.

It was bright and early when he come and got me. And I was practically in my long johns, but I went with him. Kinda glad I did—last time I ever went anywhere with him. He didn't talk much goin' down there—he's talkin' like he's just goin' down to see Mama. And he talked about them gettin' a divorce—I know that. He was talkin' about there weren't no need of her trying to kill herself like that . . . all they's doing is gettin' a divorce . . . she could see me whenever she wanted to . . . she wouldn't get me—we talked stuff like that, but that's about all. He really didn't care too much about talkin' to me about what was goin' on. He didn't want me to know much about it. As far as him goin' to kill somebody or somethin' when he got there—no, he didn't talk

Marty Summerford, Glenn and Darlene's son.

nothin' like that. He was calm. He wasn't worried about no law gettin' us, or nothin' like that. We's just going down there to see her.

On the way to Birmingham we stopped. Daddy got some V-8 juice, and I think he got me a chocolate milk and some Skoal Long Cut. That's when he found out that I dipped, on the way to Birmingham. I said, "You got me out of the house a little bit too early this morning." And he said, "What do you mean?" I said, "You got to stop and get me some Skoal 'cause I left mine at home." He said, "Huh?" I said, "Yeah, I needs some Skoal." "When'd you start that mess?" Shoot, I was dippin' when I was seven year old. He never knew it. And Mama, she didn't care. I made deals with her. I wouldn't tell on her for smokin' if she wouldn't tell on me for dippin'. One time, me and Michael, we skipped school. We was up there in the barn—man, it was cold that day. We slept between two hay bales. We crawled up between them, let the bus leave; and we fell asleep right there. Then we got up and went over to another barn. We sat there and watched out through the cracks at Mama sittin' down there beside the house smokin'. Daddy, I think, he left. We went down there, and Mama said: "I'm goin' to tell you-all's daddy on you-all." I said, "We're going to tell on you for smokin'." "Better not"—'cause they had like a thing goin' where they couldn't smoke, you know. I guess because they's in church and all.

Anyway, when we pulled up down there at Birmingham hospital, we thought, What's goin' on? If I hadn't had Daddy's knife, the damn law would have killed him. They told him when they arrested him down there—they told him if he had as much as a pocketknife, they's fixin' to blow his brains out. They scared me because I was sittin' there with a pistol between my legs in Mama's purse. She had a pistol permit, and it was in there with it, or should have been anyways. I looked down at the pistol, and I didn't say nothin'. I just left it alone. It was in her purse though, but I had his pocketknife in my pocket. He had a timin' chain in there too, taped up 'cause he couldn't close his hand all the way—I think that's what he hit J. L. with. It was under the seat though. But they got it, too, with the pistol in the purse—I think they got him for all that.

Shoot, they had me scared up down there. I mean, as soon as we pulled in the parkin' lot, they's about ten cop cars around us. We weren't goin' nowhere! Daddy stopped and just sat there till they told him to get out. I mean, they brought the guns out. I thought I was goin' down—like somethin' you see on TV.

They sent me on up there with Mama in the hospital room. And then when I got up there, she was like, "There you are"—she's all happy and stuff. She wasn't sick or nothin'. She was okay. She didn't look hurt. She didn't act like it neither. She faked it—that's all there is to it. It was all just a big scam, was all it was. I mean, I know my daddy well enough; if he wanted to kill her, he'd a-killed her.

I know that what she got bit by wasn't a snake that she said she got bit by. It wasn't no western diamondback—I know that. I know what they'll do. I remember her getting bit by a coon. I don't know if it's the same place that she said she got bit by a snake, but it was on the same hand. I do remember that. We had a pet coon. And we had a screen door, you know, and the other door was open. And this pet coon was hurt in its back hips, so alls it could do was to pull with its front legs—we's trying to help it get better, you know. This Walker dog run up on the porch, and it started trying to get through the screen to get that coon. And it bit her—fouled her up a little bit. And it could have been a coon bite that she said was a damn snakebite, but I don't know. But she always talked about a copperhead wouldn't hurt you if you were over a 160 pounds or something like that. If you were over so many pounds, it wouldn't hurt you—I do remember her talking about that all the time. And if she got bit by a snake, I'd say that's what she got bit by. 'Cause I know a western diamondback did a lot worse than that. It didn't even swell her up. And I seen her, like right after it happened.

Glenn and Darlene's Son

Before that night, they's fightin' all the time. I stayed outside, built me a fire down by the road there in a cut-off barrel—I'd cook on it. I didn't much care for goin' in the house. They was fightin' about her cheatin' on him all the time. But if Daddy'd want to kill her, he would have killed her the day he walked in on her and Gene Sherbert. Daddy come back from squirrel huntin'—he come in with a gun, and they's both there in the floor in front of him. If he'd wanted to kill them, he would've. And he could have got away with it like that. But he didn't want to kill her—they'd been talkin' about gettin' a divorce too much. They's wantin' to get a divorce.

Gene Sherbert, he came down from Georgia, him and his boy; and they stayed there at the house. The whole time they's there, they'd stay there at the house. They'd bring their suitcases. And stuff started happenin'. Yeah, if Daddy hadn't been tryin' to live right, then Gene, he would've probably regretted the day. It would have been bad news. Even Daddy knew then—Daddy knew if he killed them both, he could get away with it. He knew a dead man couldn't talk.

How many people's goin' go out there and do half a murder and then go in the house and go to sleep. Daddy wouldn't have done that. If he'd wanted to kill her, he'd a-killed her—nobody never would knew her side the story. And a whole bunch of her story was lies. I mean, she's always talkin' about gettin' out of there, how she's goin' do it. She always just talked about it. She'd always talk about how bad she hated him—said she'd feel ashamed. "Well, what'd you marry him for?" I'd say.

I 'member she said she was all beat up and bruised up because he beat her up and stuff. But I know what happened to her when she got beat up. 'Cause we had horses back then. Right before that, we just got a new palomino. That was the calmest horse—I ain't never seen a horse like that—shake your hand, stretch out for you to get on him. Everybody around could ride that horse. And Mama got on that horse, and that horse bucked her, threw her, and everything else. She couldn't ride him. He didn't like her, I don't guess. That horse bucked her off—looked like a rodeo. Me, her, and Daddy was ridin' that day. Yeah, she got threw. That's where she got her bruises from. That's somethin' else I can't figure out, why that horse threw her—that horse ain't never threw nobody. Either she made it do it—it's kind of hard to go in there and bang your head on the sink, make it look like someone beat you up . . . get a horse to do it for you. She could do it—it ain't hard to make one buck. That's what I kind of had the feelin' about it—I kind of figured. She had it planned out pretty good, the way I seen it.

Marty Summerford

She's cheatin' on him all the time. There was more than just Gene Sherbert—Willie Southard and another guy (I can't remember his name). She's just that way. And J. L. Lewis—me and Mama went down there to J. L.'s. We was goin' to borrow some money—Daddy was wantin' us to go down there and get some money or somethin' from him. J. L. handed me a hundred-dollar bill and sent me to the store to get it broke. I guess he knew all them convenience stores around there wasn't goin' break a hundred-dollar bill for a nine-year-old kid. After I went to about four of them, I figured it out. I went back, and the door was locked. They wouldn't let me in. So I just stood there and waited, and finally they opened the door. But I know what she'd done. Right there it is. Mama, she 'fessed up to it eventually, I'm pretty sure. I could tell the way she was lookin'—she finally told him the truth about that. But she lied to him all the time.

At the very first when she was in church, she was doin' pretty good—at the very first. But after that, I think she's just in it for the men or somethin'. I mean she'd get up there and play with them snakes just like everybody else. I don't think she was trying to do right. I think she was just using it—like the first church they had, she cheated on him at that one. I just can't remember that guy's name. He played the bass fiddle and the guitar. Once she cheated on Daddy with him, he didn't ever come back to church no more. His guitar case sat there forever. Somehow, I think, Daddy found out about that too. That was when they first started out with their own church.

I know he tapped into the phone line, listenin' to her conversations on the phone. I sat out there and watched him. He'd unhook that little box off the wall and just hook another phone up to it. And when he left the house, he just left them two wires unhooked so she couldn't call nobody. I guess he was afraid of what he might see when he come home.

And they was fightin' a little even before he got serpent bit that summer—the way she was doin', flirtin' with everybody and stuff. He probably would never have got bit if he hadn't stuck his hand in front of the snake when it was trying to bite her or somebody else. I ain't really sure. He had the serpent laying up on the altar or somethin'. And it was striking at somebody—I can't remember who. It might have been her, 'cause she was always up there beside him. But he stuck his hand in front of it, is the reason he got bit.

She cheated on him, but she was caught a bunch. And it just all got crazy there for a while. She told him about all that stuff. And by telling him about all that, she might have just wanted to get a divorce or just get out of there, make

Glenn and Darlene's Son

him drunk. She might just want to get him drunk, so she could do what she did. And they started drinking that week before I left—they both drank. They'd just fuss and argue—they'd fight like cats and dogs. But I didn't see either one hittin' up on one another.

I remember once or twice when she took a bunch of pills, and Daddy would make her drink a bunch of milk because it made her sick so she's throw them back up. I remember that a couple of times. One time he took a gun away from her, a .22 pistol. She just gets crazy like this sometimes. She used to do it all the time—she's always trying to do somethin'. And she still tries to kill herself sometimes. I'd go out there by her mother's where she lives now, and she's tried to kill herself. Didn't matter where's she at. The last couple of times I went out there—she had cut marks all the way down her arm and stuff where she'd been whacking on it a little bit. She'd get feeling sorry for herself, and she'd be tryin' to kill herself. You can look at her arms—I mean, there are big old scars across there. There's nothing to her to have a big old scar on her arm—she tried to kill herself all the time. She'll mess up one of these days and really do it.

That woman's crazy. She'd get to drinkin' and stuff—she's crazy. She don't even have to get drunk. She tried to kill herself one time 'cause me and my wife got married and didn't tell her about it. We just went to the courthouse—courthouse, you know, was quicker. We went up there and got married, and we went out there to where she lives about a week later. And she had a few more cut slashes on her arm. I mean, they was fresh—they're still laid open. She got to talkin', "Why didn't you-all invite me to your weddin'?"—"We didn't have no weddin', I'll have you know."

My uncle's out there, and they'd tell me what'd she do, how she'd do it, and why. I asked her what she's goin' do when she killed herself—just leave Megan there alone, you know, her daughter? And that made her feel bad again. I think she's probably goin' to try to do it again.

But to be honest with you, I think Mama tried to kill herself or somethin' and put it off on Daddy. 'Cause right before all that stuff happened, she told me she's goin' get me—and me and her was fixin' to move. I think she done it because she said she'd make a way we could be together.

I tell you one thing about the "suicide" letter. Daddy didn't write it, and it sounds like Mama talkin'. She talks like that, kinda in circles. I know it ain't Daddy's handwritin'. He didn't force her to write it. If he did, she made it up for herself. The way I'd get it, she had this planned. The letter was probably wrote a long time ago before this ever happened—it was probably somethin' that she had wrote, planning what's she's goin' to do and how she's goin' do it by the snakes. Probably about when she told me that me and her was goin' get out of there. See, that week—I never got any new clothes or nothin' like that. But during that week that all that was goin' on, she was tryin' to suck up to me real big and stuff, and try to get along with me a whole lot, 'cause she kept on tellin' me that me and her was fixin' to leave there. She went and bought me clothes and all this good stuff, and lot of those clothes I never seen. I think she had them packed and waitin'. I think that's when she wrote the letter. She might have wrote it 'cause I wasn't there. But she knew I wouldn't live with her, no way.

There's somethin' I didn't catch at first in the letter. She wrote the letter right before she walked out the door, probably—started goin' up to Mrs. Johnson's. Yeah, she probably got him good and mad about Junior and Bill and all them. Got him another bottle of whiskey. That's what I figure. You see, he used to be an alcoholic back a long time ago. She knew what would make him get drunk. And I bet Daddy would say he wasn't drunk. He was. He was drunk. I know he was drunk. She's perfectly right he was drunk. If he wasn't drunk, he might have killed her. If he wanted to kill her, he'd a-killed her. I know he would when he walked in on her. He didn't want to kill her. He just wanted to get rid of her, and didn't really want to do that.

Mama'd talk also about she'd rather live with her mama or somethin' like that. And Daddy, he always tried to keep her away from her family. It wasn't because he didn't want her seein' 'em. It was because he didn't want her being like them, 'cause all they are's a bunch of drunks. Her mama, she not no better than any of them. When they's young, teenagers growin' up, that's how her mama'd make her money—run her own little house thing, sort of. She'd pick their pockets, and her kids would keep 'em entertained. That's how she made her money. Fact, still do. When one of Mama's boyfriends leaves her house, he ain't got no radio—I doubt he's even got a spare tire. They rip 'em off. One old guy, I felt plumb sorry for him—I liked him—old Larry Williams. He had a lot of money till he started seein' her. Then he started goin' broke. He's a drunk, and his wife left him a long time ago. Mama messed him up. And the only time she ever calls him, if she needs somethin'. She's a crazy woman. She lies a lot.

Mama ain't much of a woman. Her whole family—all her sisters and stuff—they're all that way, just about all of them. She'll have a different boyfriend every day of the week. That's the way she's always been. I don't ever go see her, but I used to go out there a lot. I'd go out there, and she'd let me drink and get drunk and do whatever—I was fourteen year old and thought I was pretty cool.

Glenn and Darlene's Son

I knew I didn't want to move with her—she's always mean to me. When I was a kid, she'd come in there and get me up for school—which most of the time she didn't want me to go anyway—but she'd come in there and make me get out of bed about five o'clock in the mornin'. She'd come in there and grab me by the hair of the head and just yank me out of bed. She wouldn't tell me nothin' else. She'd just yank me out of bed. And her and me'd get into it all the time—she's pretty rough. She always wanted a little girl, and I wasn't goin' to be her little girl, I don't guess.

After Kenneth and Jackie come and got me, then I didn't have nothin' to do with her for a long time. I wouldn't even talk with her on the phone, hardly. She'd come down to see me and stuff. And I got to talkin' with her a little bit. Then I finally started goin' out there—I guess 'cause she had a little girl, my little sister Megan. I was goin' to see my little sister. And I'd get out there, me and my cousins—we'd jump in the car and take off.

When I got thirteen, I went to the square with my uncle and few of our friends and got drunk and went to jail. We got dog drunk down there at the courthouse square where everybody hangs up, and I walked out in front of a cop—he about run over me. And they carried us to jail. Mama, she come back down there and got me. My uncle had to stay in jail 'cause he had a fine—distributing to minors. She told me to get in his truck and drive it back out on the mountain, keep it from gettin' towed. I wasn't but thirteen year old, still about drunk. I think we got arrested about two o'clock in the mornin'. She come and got us, little bit before five. I's still about drunk, but she told me to drive the truck home. She didn't care—ain't never cared about nothin' but herself, and sometimes she don't even care about that.

The last time me and my wife went out there, the first and last time that my mama ever seen my little baby, a little girl—she's seven months old now—that's the only time she's seen her. (She's two months old then.) We was over at my grandma's. And we told Mama we wouldn't bring our kid out there around all that mess. That hurt her feelin's, I reckon. She got all mad and started cryin': "I'm just a bad parent—I'm an alcoholic." And she said, "Why didn't you-all call me?" We said, "You ain't got a phone." We'd called her mama, which is my grandma—we called her and told her that we had a little girl and to tell Mama. And she got mad 'cause we called her mama. She got mad about that and went home.

If you ever just went out there and seen—man, it's somethin' else. I tried to get my little sister from her—can't. I was trying to take her away from her. That's one reason I don't go out there any more. 'Cause, you know, if I go out there, and Megan wants to come home with me, then I'm goin' bring her home.

Marty Summerford

There's a different drunk over there ever'day. Most time, there's at least three drunks over there ever'day, a different one. My little sister doesn't need to be around all that, a bunch of perverts. If I go out there and somethin' happened, then I'll carry them to court. She might get took away from them and have to go and live in a foster home. I might not get her, but there's somebody that would care about her. And Megan, I don't think she's Daddy's girl. I think she's somebody else's. Mama, I don't think she wants to give her up for the tax write-off. I tell you, my mama, she's about the sorriest woman you'll ever know. I'll tell her that. She is. She is just that way.

I've got what?—nine brothers and sisters. And I'm the only one that graduated high school. And I wouldn't done that if it wouldn't been for Kenneth. But if all of this with Mama and Daddy hadn't of happened, I would've been in a home for a long time—I'm twenty-one now. 'Cause I was fixin' to get sent off when all that happened. See, Mama, she'd always get me up for me to go to school. Then she'd always decide, "Well, no need in you goin' to school." Then she'd always say, "Well, you're quittin' when you turn sixteen."

I hated school when I was a kid, 'cause everybody picked on me. I had to fight somebody ever'day 'cause I's poorer than them, I guess. I started beatin' up on them. I didn't really care. Which is the way, I's raised—someone start somethin', finish it. If I come home, and someone done whup me at school, and I started it—I's fixin' to get another whuppin'. I ain't never let anybody fool with me. I'd get kicked off the school bus all the time for fightin'. And wouldn't ever do my work at school. What homework I done, Mama done it— and all the answers was wrong when she done it. They still knew I didn't do it 'cause it wasn't my writin', I guess.

One day the principal brought me home, brought all my books with me—I's supposed to do a bunch of work, but I didn't. Then this woman started comin' to school to see me—I mean this woman was rough, boy. I don't remember what she was or nothin', but she's like somebody from a foster home or somethin' like that. I ain't sure. She hassled the heck out of me. She'd come to school—I'd like miss ever' Monday, at least. And the first time she come to school to see me, she asked me why I've been missin'. She'd get me out in the hall and be yellin' at me, boy. I'd tell her, "Yeah, I ate a lot of candy on Sunday and was sick on Monday—I didn't come to school" . . . "That ain't no excuse." Then I went home and made up my mind—I said, "I ain't goin' back to school. They can't catch me here."

I messed up, though. I's out there 'round the back fields. And Michael and Joe was out there ridin' a three-wheeler, and I's on it. I was just comin'

Glenn and Darlene's Son

back around the field, and I seen a car pull up in the driveway, across the little ridge like. They'd never knew I's back there if I hadn't ridden up. But I went up there, and I seen who it was. It was my principal, my teacher, and that woman. They's drivin' a old, beat-up blue car. I guess just so we wouldn't know it was them. Anyway, I slung the three-wheeler around and hauled butt back there and let Joe get on 'cause he'd done quit school or somethin'. He went around there. Then I had to go back around there. "Where's your daddy at?"—they's fixin' to send me off. And then all this happened.

And I come down to live with Kenneth. And till I was a senior, I didn't miss a day of school. Proved Mama wrong. She was at my graduation. She come in there, "I knew you could do it" . . . "Yeah, that's why you always said you's gonna make me quit when I turned sixteen, ain't it? You didn't see me quittin'." She run up like she put me through school. It bothered Kenneth a little bit, 'cause she run through everybody to come up there and hug me for graduatin'. And I just walk right by her. Went back there to Kenneth—he'd done left. I guess it kind of hurt his feelin's. I'd rather her not even been there. That's the way I felt about it. I ain't got no use for her. She ain't my mama. Mamas don't treat their kids like that.

My sister Jackie, the one that raised me, she ain't my mama neither. You see, Kenneth left. And he give me his place. He bought him a place after him and my sister split up. The reason they split up—I didn't know this till just here the other day—reason she left was 'cause of me. She told Kenneth, it was either her or me. And he said, "Well, I'll see you later." He said, "I made your daddy a promise, and I said I'd take care of him and put him through school." Said, "He ain't leavin.'" She said, "Well, I guess *you* will." I don't know if that is the real reason; but that's what she said, so I know she said it. I don't have much to do with her no more.

Mama tried to convince me what happened that night between her and Daddy, till she seen that I knew better. I knew better. I'd talk to her about it. And sometimes she'd get pissed off, but especially when I started catchin' her in lies and stuff—I'd catch her in some lies about a bunch of stuff. Eventually she told me about some of them, but I just catch her in all kind of little old lies. And she'd always tell me how bad a man Daddy was and all that. He ain't that bad a man. If you ever pissed him off or somethin', you know, he might— yeah, he might have want to fight. But not while he was in church 'cause I seen people run all over him while he was in church. I mean, he'd just say, "God bless ya" and go on. But when he wasn't in church, back before he started goin' to church, he's pretty rough.

Marty Summerford

I know they took snake handling a little too far. They did do that, I'm pretty sure. There for a while they was gettin' it for a show, look like to me—started doin' it for a show. I might be wrong. Maybe that's why a lot of this happened the way it did. They may not have realized it, but after a while that's all they talked about in church, was snake handlin'. That's all they ever preached about. And ever' night, they'd handle snakes. And back before that, it wasn't like that. They'd preach about everything, you know, in the Bible. But after that, all they'd ever preach about was snake handlin'—snake handlin', drinking the poison, or whatever. Then they started doin' that all the time. Maybe that's why they started gettin' bit—God's lettin' 'em know. Daddy, he might be gettin' punished for it, I don't know. Maybe that's why everythin' happened the way it did. I wish my daddy wasn't in prison and all that—don't get me wrong. I'd give up everything I got during the time he was in prison, except my kid and my wife—I wouldn't give that up for nothin'. But my schoolin' and all that, I'd give up just to see him out.

If I had it to do over again, I would never left. I would have stayed there at home—I'd a-found out what happened. I could have lived down there in the woods, and they'd never knew.

The way I kinda had it figured, she done it all to get me and keep her own name clean. She would get depressed over Bobby Joe, her first boy—if she hadn't been the way she was, she never would have got him took away. I know one day, she said, "Do you see that hussy right yonder?" I said, "Yeah." She said, "That's the one that got your brother took away from me." She said, "If I catch her outside, I'll kick her ass." I said, "I'll watch"—I didn't care. And to beat it all, that woman couldn't have been thirty year old. She couldn't have been the one that had it done—she wasn't old enough, or she didn't look it anyway. Yeah, Mama, she's a psychopath, to be honest with you. She is.

And they wouldn't even let none of us testify. They wouldn't let me on the stand. They wouldn't even let me go to the courthouse. I couldn't even go a hundred yards around the courthouse, anywhere. I think Gary Lackey done it. I would have told them everything they wanted to know, but they never would put me up there. I guess they may have thought I was too young to hear all that mess, but I done knew. I had to sit, and Kenneth, he had to tell me what happened after the court was over. He sat and told me. I didn't believe him for a little while—they railroaded Daddy.

And Tammy Flippo, who was a witness—that was his transportation. That's how he got places. I know what he used that for, to get places. If I was a woman, to be honest, Tammy Flippo would have went a round or two. She

Glenn and Darlene's Son

got all of Daddy's guns—I's supposed to got all of them. She said the house burnt, and they burned up in the house—liar. I got my .22—he traded a horse for me—a little bolt action. I still got it. And I had his knife for a long time.

And Gary Lackey—at the time of the trial, my mom and Marlin Smith and "Little Red" Smith, they was haulin' wood for Gary Lackey. I know that 'cause my mama done told me. My mama was goin' with Marlin at the time, and Marlin is Gary Lackey's cousin. And they's haulin' firewood for him durin' the trial. Pretty messed up—messed up little old world. They railroaded Daddy, *I* think.

Marty Summerford

A Friend of the Family

I know all those Summerfords, Mances, and Collinses. And I know those church folks too. I've seen and heard a lot of stuff. And what I know is not just talk.

Well, I guess all of this started when Glenn and Darlene were living in New Hope. At that time they weren't living right. He was drinking; she was drinking. And Darlene was still going with two or three others. One was a guy named Jackie Lee. Another guy—that she went with down there, Willie Southard—and Glenn got into a fight about her. And Glenn wound up shooting him in the leg.

But then Glenn got to livin' right, and the reason he got to livin' right was that his son married a preacher's daughter. And his son and his wife got into it, and Glenn went over to the preacher's house and said he was going to kill him. At least the preacher said he was. But he talked to the preacher, Brother Peace; and after that, Glenn started going to church. I knowed Glenn for a long time. And I knowed all his background, what he used to do and what he didn't do. But he changed and got to be a Christian.

Later on, after Glenn and Darlene moved to Scottsboro, Willie Southard, the guy he shot, comes up and starts going to Glenn's church. And they got to be good friends. And there was another guy that became friends with Glenn, a preacher, and started comin' to church. And Darlene got to goin' with him. (And she also tried to go with a few of the church members—and they brought attention to Glenn about it—which she denied.) But this preacher told Darlene how to get rid of Glenn. And they would go off to Kentucky together. He said he knew he could preach in Kentucky or Tennessee, and Glenn would never find him. And he told her what to do. He told her to get bit by a copperhead, and call and get some help. But as far as handling snakes, she would handle them just like Glenn would. She'd even been bit a couple of times before. But she'd always been bit by a copperhead. So she knew herself what snake would kill you and what wouldn't. Well, she called for help, and they sent an ambulance over there. What she was going to do was put Glenn in jail for assault. And she was going to get her antivenom shot. Then this guy, the preacher, was supposed to pick her up; and they were going to leave while Glenn was in jail.

Everything went all right. She got snakebit. The ambulance went down there. And members of the family on both sides met them at the hospital, including Darlene's mother, Emma Collins.

And it's no secret that Emma Collins and Glenn had a long background of problems. She didn't want Darlene and Glenn to get married. Well, one night about twenty years ago, she invited Darlene and Glenn over there at her house. And several of Glenn's friends were there that night. And she had three of Darlene's friends to come over to jump on Glenn. Well, they couldn't whup him. Emma Collins thought they'd whup Glenn, and Darlene would go off with them. But it didn't happen. They got into an argument, and a fight broke out. Then Darlene's mother was going to cut Glenn with a knife, and he told her: "When you get close enough to cut me, you're close enough for me to hit. Now, I ain't done nothing to you, and the best thing is to move and let Darlene and me out the door." She said, "Darlene ain't goin' nowhere with you. I'm goin' to cut you." And whenever she swung at him with a knife, he grabbed a vase off the mantle and hit her upside the head. And it took fourteen stitches. Well, they went to court, and the judge really laughed at her: "The way we look at you, you's all drunk. And you had a fight, and you got cut." He dismissed it, throwed it out of court. So Emma Collins said she would get Glenn back for that, and several has heard her make the remark after this happened, "Well, I got him back finally. It took a while, but I got him—I told him I would." But I heard that she did say that "I don't think he should have got the time he got." You know, that's a lot of years. And she done it through Darlene.

Another thing workin' against Glenn was that members of other churches around here don't like it because he handles snakes. They would have people kick him out of the building that they'd leased to him. And they evicted him out of all kind of buildings, just simply because he believed in handlin' snakes. And I guess the way the public looked at all of this stuff with Darlene was simply a way to get rid of Glenn. Then again, Chief Smith and Bolte—all the investigators that helped get him sent off—had their run-ins with Glenn a long time ago

A Friend of the Family

whenever Darlene was writing a bunch of bad checks. You see, Glenn would try to keep her hid out. So they chased them all over the place. Chief Smith run and caught him one day in a field, and Glenn took his gun away from him. And that made the chief mad, and he hated Glenn ever since.

About that preacher Darlene was planning to leave with—the way some people found out about him was the time Glenn got snakebit bad. Glenn was bit twice, but preached the rest of the night. Well, they carried him to his house and put him on the bed. He finally wound up in the floor. In about two hours he swelled up until his shirt was bustin' off him. He was the kind of Christian that he wouldn't pull his shirt off in the front of no women. And I mean he just swelled up and busted his shirt. I wouldn't give two cents for his life when he was laying in the floor. Everyone thought he was goin' to die. But they didn't take him to the hospital 'cause he didn't believe in goin' to the doctor. All the time he was snakebit, he never went. He wouldn't go. He said God would take care of him. And he'd lay on the floor; and what time he was conscious, he'd pray. And he got better—I didn't think he would—but he did.

And while Glenn was in the house laying on the floor, forty or fifty people were there all the time, church members. Well, this preacher come in, and he told Darlene, "Come show me what snake bit him." Well, she went walking out there with him to the snake house. Now, it's nothing unusual for church people to hold hands or shake hands or hug one another or whatever, Christian people. So they went out there to the building where the snakes was kept, which was just a big shed. And Darlene and this preacher kept staying out there. Well, Uly Lynn and several other people were outside, and they wanted to look at the snakes too. So they opened the door, and there Darlene and this preacher were all hugged up. And they wasn't in no church way. So they just shut the door back to. And Uly told Glenn about it later, and Glenn was the type of person that he'd pray about stuff if somethin' was botherin' him—he'd go to the woods and pray. After he prayed, Glenn told Darlene, "You don't have to go back to church if you don't want to anymore. I'm not forcing you to go to church. If you don't believe in our ways, you don't have to go." So she started back to smokin' and a whole bunch of stuff. Really, she done as she pleased, and he kept going to church. And she was wanting away from him and to run off with this preacher.

But later, when she got out of the hospital, this preacher caught Darlene with some other guys; so he quit seein' her. And then whenever court started, they tried to get him to be a witness for Glenn, but he wouldn't do it. He wouldn't do anything. But he was goin' to leave his wife, and he and Darlene was goin' to run off together. That's what Darlene and he had planned.

Now, when Glenn's family went to choose a lawyer, they got Gary Lackey. They thought Lackey would be pretty good because Lackey's father killed Darlene's brother Larry, and Gary defended Mr. Lackey. Larry was about sixteen or seventeen years old and going with Mr. Lackey's daughter. Mr. Lackey was drunk and walked up and told Larry: "If I catch you back with my daughter again, I will kill you." Well, Larry and Gary's sister got off the school bus together out there in front of the church—them and the Collinses, Lackeys and Collinses, lived in seeing distance of each other. Mr. Lackey seen them sit up there at the church at the picnic table, and he got his gun and walked up behind him and told him, "I told you, I'd kill ya if I caught you with my daughter again." And he shot him and killed him. And Gary Lackey got him off for only ten years. And Gary told Glenn, "Yeah, I'd like to pay them back for some of the shit they done to my father. My father had a right to kill him. He was going with my thirteen-year-old sister."

But whenever Glenn got Lackey for his lawyer, he didn't know it, but Gary used to go with Darlene back when they was kids when they lived there side by side. And Lackey didn't defend Glenn any at all. I could have defended him a lot better than Lackey did—anybody could have. He could have defended hisself. Glenn's boys was there at the courthouse, his sister—and Darlene's own brother was going to testify against her. And Lackey didn't call any of them out, and hardly anyone else.

I think Glenn got a raw deal. But Lackey made Glenn think that it would be easy to get him off. Glenn told me, he said, "It ain't nothin' to this. I didn't do none of this." And you know, you get a good friend off by hisself and talk to him—I mean, you say, "Hey, look, I'd like to know the truth. What happened?" And even after they sentenced him, I talked to him. And Glenn said, "Son, nothin' happened."

I known Glenn back when he drank, and he done this and done that. If he had somethin' against you, he'd come and tell you about it, or he'd come and beat the shit out of you. He was that way. But after he started goin' to church and got to be a preacher and this and that—hey, people come into church and slap his face; and he wouldn't do nothin' to them. Now if he was a violent type person, you think he'd stand and take that? I wouldn't, and I don't think anyone else would. But the whole congregation of the church has seen him threatened. Junior Blair and two or three others, they come to his church, cussed him, called him everything and slap him in the church—and him stand there and ask God to forgive 'em. And if a man can do that, in my opinion he can do a lot of stuff.

A Friend of the Family

Now, Glenn and Darlene would have fusses like everybody else. A lot of the times, I think they argued about his kids and his ex-wife—they were both around all the time. But they would argue about one thing or another. One time, Darlene held a snake up, a copperhead, and deliberately let it bite her on the titty 'cause they was in a fuss. She was bad to throw a fit, and she'd get mad and she'd do stuff. She took bunches of pills. And Glenn and Marty would walk her around, keep her goin' all night long till they'd wear off 'cause she wouldn't go to the hospital. And if you look at her arms, she's cut her wrists—there ain't no tellin' how many times. She'd do it for attention, what it amounts to.

And I asked Glenn after he was arrested, "Were you and Darlene into it about something or other?" He said, "Yeah, me and her were fussin' a little bit, and she told me all the people she went with." He said, "She told me she went with J. L. She told me she went with Willie"—and when he said "went with," he meant "went to bed with." And she named off five or six, including his own brother and sons.

What Darlene wanted was to have Glenn out of the way, to get shot or shoot someone else. Like J. L. Lewis—you see, J. L. and Glenn's always been friends. Now, J. L.'s a big heavy-set feller. And he always told Glenn and Darlene both, he said, "Hey, if me and anybody had to get into it, I'd just shoot 'em—I can't fight 'em." Well, Willie Southard, the guy Glenn shot in the leg—he made the statement, "If I ever get in a fight with Glenn again, I'll shoot him 'cause I know he's gonna shoot me." Well, those are the ones she said she went with.

And she went down at J. L.'s with Glenn and told J. L. what she'd said to Glenn. And J. L. said: "Glenn, I gave your wife a ring and this and that. And a lot of stuff happened back years ago that shouldn't have happened, and I should done confessed to you about this and about that. And since you are a Christian, and I've got to be a Christian—I think I am, but undoubtedly I'm not 'cause I haven't got forgiveness for everything I done." And Glenn didn't kill him, and J. L. didn't shoot Glenn.

So then Willie Southard, when he heard what Darlene had told Glenn, he went to Glenn and told him in front of Darlene. He said, "Hey, I didn't go with her. She tried to go with me. During church she's pinched my butt many a time, but I'd move. I didn't go with her."

She was wantin' Glenn to leave is what it amounted to. And she poisoned him one time with rat poison. And it about killed him. He got to the point where that he wouldn't hardly eat her cookin'. She's the type of person that you wouldn't believe unless you went and seen her.

And all this got started when she started messin' around, doing this and that. Well, now, she's always—before he married her—was runnin' around. She was just a wild young girl, goin' with this one and goin' with that one. Back before Glenn and her ever got married, she was going with three guys at one time. And one of them killed the other one over her. He shot him. They got in a fight out there at her house, and he shot him and killed him—the man run in the road and died. And that story about her takin' on a bunch of men in the field is true. And there's that story, after Glenn was sent off, about the bet she had to see who could have the most men in a month.

And there's all kind of stuff that goes on all the time out there where she lives. Roger Buttram got beat up out there one night—and cut up. The law had to go out there. And when they finally found him where he'd went down to the woods, he's about dead. It took over a hundred and somethin' stitches in his neck, his arms, and in his back. But she lived with him about three or four weeks, as long as he would pay her bills.

The Law's been called out there so much, they wouldn't go half the time. They call it McCordville. And anytime they call about McCordville, none of the officers want to go out there. They all say, "You know what's goin' on. Let 'em kill theirself—maybe they'll kill theirself out." And they wouldn't go out there. They sure wouldn't. The county'll get fifteen or twenty calls a month to go out there on account of the drunks always fightin'.

And Darlene just wanted to get rid of Glenn 'cause she was tired of living as a Christian and havin' to do this and havin' to do that and look good in front of the public. The whole plan was to get Glenn in jail long enough for her to get away—her and that preacher, they were goin' together.

And at the trial Glenn never had a chance to defend hisself 'cause Lackey told him to be quiet. But Darlene was going down and table-dancing for Lackey and his friends down at their barn, at their parties, all the time court was goin' on. And she'd go and entertain his buddies—he'd built a big fancy barn in Boxes Cove, and they'd have parties. And Darlene would go there and entertain them. It was goin' on while the trial was goin' on, but nobody knew nothin' about it till later. Well, she done Lackey a favor, and he done her one, I guess—the way I look at it.

200

A Friend of the Family

Bobbie Sue Lynn
Faithful Helper

knew Glenn when I was just a small girl. Glenn even tried to get me to marry him before he married Darlene, and I wouldn't do it. But while he was married to Darlene, I didn't have much contact with him because she was very jealous. I went to his church a few times, about three, before this snakebite of Darlene's was suppose' to happen. And then I went quite a bit after. That was the church out in Woods Cove Road, out past Jackson County Hospital. I went ever' service—on Friday night, Saturday night, and Sunday night. And when we would have revivals, it would be different nights. Now, all this was before Glenn got sent off to prison and me and Johnny got married.

But after Darlene left Glenn, I probably thought I was Glenn's girl-friend. And he probably thought I was just a sister in the church—that's my understanding of what I get off of people as he told. But actually, I ort to knew better than what I was doin' because Glenn wasn't divorced from Darlene. Back then, all Glenn needed was somebody he could trust and talk to. And I was young in the Lord, and I didn't know the difference.

I guess I've known Glenn forty year of my life or maybe a little bit less. And, see, he just needed somebody he could talk to and trust and depend on and somebody to he'p him. And I didn't have all that separated from maybe being his girlfriend. So I guess you could say I was his helper. I he'ped him in ever' way I could. I tried to he'p in anything he asked me to he'p in. Like I'd go down there, and I'd make sure the church was kept up and kept clean. Things that's needed in the church, I made sure it was there. I'd even keep it mowed, and whenever he would need somebody to he'p him work in the altar and stuff, I'd he'p him do that. And also I'd go to his house and keep his laundry

Bobbie Sue Lynn.

done up and he'p get his house cleaned up and straightened up—I just he'ped him in just about ever' way I could.

I would treat it different now because I know more than what I knowed back then. I was just a young child in the Lord. And probably if this would have happened now instead of then, Glenn wouldn't be in the shape he's in because I would have knowed more about how to he'p him.

I was born March 27, 1955—I was thirty-six years old back then. But I hadn't been a child of the Lord all that long. But yet, back prior to that in the past, I would live right awhile and not live right awhile. Whenever I was in that stage, I wadn't close to nobody in the churches because I didn't stay in enough to get close to 'em. But, see, whether I was in church or not, I was close to Glenn 'cause I've just known him all my life. His mama married my cousin F. A. Gilliam and stayed married to him for a long time. But, see, I still knowed them before then. After my mama died, my brother lived in my mama's house; and that's where Glenn started preachin' at, in house meetin's up there at her house. And then he started from there—course he was goin' to Albert York's church then—and he started gettin' him a church of his own. But I wadn't stable then. I wadn't as stable then as I was when I thought I was Glenn's girlfriend.

It got romantic—I guess that's a lot of what led me on. I'm not saying I was in this by myself either. I'm saying I was there in the time of Glenn's sorrow. And it just went from there—a-pettin' and a-huggin' and a-pattin' and tryin' to encourage him, tryin' to keep him goin', and tryin' to keep things from gettin' as bad as they did.

He got involved with Tammy Flippo at the same time. I'd think she considered herself as a girlfriend—most certainly. If she didn't, I did. That's a lot of what made me back off. I went over there to Barbee Lane one day; and I walked right out that little old road there in the weeds to see if Glenn was out there, 'cause he didn't answer the door. And that was the time we was all supposed to met down there at the square 'cause he was goin' in there to talk to Gary Lackey about his boy Marty. So I kinda walked out past there in the woods to maybe see if he was out in there, and I spotted this car. And it was Tammy's car, hid back in there. And Glenn was down at the courthouse. So I went down to the courthouse and rode around in front of the lawyer, and I seen Marty. And I said, "Tell Glenn that I spotted that car he had hid in the weeds." So I went back up my sister's house, Dorothy Nape up in Hollywood, and about an hour, hour and a half, the phone rung and it was Glenn. And he told me to come to his house, so I came down there. He was askin' me what I was talkin' about a car. And I went out there to show him where that car was at, and it was gone. Course Tammy was gone too. I knew she was in the house when I went down there 'cause I heard a racket whenever I stepped up on the porch and knocked on the door. At the time, I thought it was that little old raccoon thing in there—they had a little old raccoon they kept in the house. And I figured it might have knocked somethin' off—until I walked around there and spotted that car. And I really didn't recognize the car until I got to church that Friday night, and there sat the car. And when Glenn saw that I recognized the car, he made some kind of sign to Tammy. Then she went out there and got in the car and left.

According to the word of God, Glenn backslid. But back whenever I's caught up in all that stuff, I didn't think so. But now, see, I've recognized enough about the word of God that I can see clear—back then I's lookin' out of foggy eyes. Now I can see clear. Yeah, he was backslid. If he'd died or got killed or somethin', he'd went to hell, just straight to hell.

And Glenn must have considered himself bein' backslid after Darlene supposedly got snakebit—and I'm goin' to say "supposedly" 'cause I still don't believe she got bit—because he had Carl Porter to come over here and rebaptize him. He repented and got rebaptized. Now, I do remember that. And that is before even this stuff started between me and Tammy Flippo and him.

And later, on his court day, Glenn tried to get me to park his stinkin' car on one side of the courthouse—that thing would fly; it was worser than greased lighting. Then when they let him come out in that witness room, he would go down, and him and me would run off to Mexico and then to the Philippines. And that's when he tried also to get me go get wine—Mad Dog 20/20—and bring it up there in a cup during breaks at the trial and let him drink it.

And, see, like I say, I didn't know then what I know now. And I'm not laying this all on Glenn either. Some of it's my ignorance. But Glenn ort to knew better than to get me to do stuff like that. I figure if he'd been where he was supposed to be with the Lord and with hisself, he wouldn't have put my soul to that jeopardy. So that's how I know he didn't care for me like I thought he did. 'Cause when you care for somebody, you're not goin' put them up to ignorant stuff. I can see him puttin' me up to somethin' contrary to man, but not contrary to God.

I didn't get him the wine up at the courthouse, but at his house I got some Mad Dog 20/20—I went right out here at Five Points and bought it at that store on the left, right there. I went in and bought a thing of wine for communion, and I felt like a sneakin' dog buyin' that. He used some of it for communion. And then after the communion, I say, "Are we not goin' to bury that?" 'Cause, see, I thought they buried the bread that was left over and the wine that was left over because that's supposed to represent Jesus' flesh and his blood. And after you have the Passover and stuff, I thought they's supposed to bury it. I think he let 'em bury that bread, but he didn't let 'em bury that wine. 'Cause I went over to his house the next day, and I liked to never got him to the door. And he looked like death warmed over. And then I went to the store and come back, and he was laying in the floor, moanin' and a-groanin' with that old shotgun beside of him. And I couldn't get him to the door or nothin'. So I just left. He was drunk as Cooter Brown. And next time he tells me he wadn't drunk, I'll tell him he's lying.

I didn't park that car outside the courthouse neither, like he asked. To get him away from the courthouse, I'd had to be in a jet and throwed a big magnet and sucked him up. I have thought about that and thought about that and thought about that, and I have made myself sick. That about worried me to death.

And then Uncle J. B.—course he's dead and gone, that's Glenn's mama's brother—come up to Dorothy Faye's, my sister, and got me and carried me over at Glenn's 'cause he's trying to get me to see that Glenn was havin' an affair with Tammy Flippo. And Glenn was a smooth operator. Now, son, I

Bobbie Sue Lynn

mean he was so stinkin' smooth, he'd cut your head off and it wouldn't bleed. Uncle J. B. carried me over there, and Glenn was out in the woods on the edge of the river on those old benches—right there is where they stayed, Tammy and Glenn. And when Uncle J. B. carried me down there, Glenn got mad and made J. B. carry me back out of there. And Glenn got rid of his little woman and called me. Ever' time he'd get rid of her, ever' time I'd catch him, he'd call me. So I just quit foolin' with him—other than goin' to jail visitin' him, sendin' him money, and makin' sure he got his allergy pills, and tryin' to he'p him. 'Cause by then I'd done woke up. I mean, I was a young child in the Lord, but I still in flesh wasn't an idiot.

There ain't no way Glenn can get out of his drinkin' 'cause I tried to find loopholes to get him out of it. Although at the same time, I had this thought in my mind, he's guilty of drinkin'. But yet, I was so caught up in him that I was huntin' him loopholes to get out of them sayin' he was drinkin' and stuff. But before Glenn and Darlene got messed up, I don't think Glenn was unfair. And up until that point of Glenn's ministry, personal life, and all—I'd say Glenn was all right with the Lord.

Before I even knew any trouble was in the church, what let me know that somethin' was boilin' is that I walked in and Darlene had on a blouse—I'm talkin' about at church—she had on a blouse that you could see through. You could see her bra through it. Glenn wouldn't let her get up there and sang 'cause she had on that thin blouse. Course after all this happened, I went in with a thin blouse on. And he said somethin' to me about wearing thin blouses in there—"Just don't wear no thin blouses." He wanted you to be dressed right. And Darlene, as his wife, he wouldn't let her get up there and lead the singin' and stuff and her dressed like that. So that right there is what let me knew somethin' was goin' on between Darlene and Glenn.

But the first I heard of all this mess was when I was over there at work at the old Holiday Inn on 72. I was in one of those rooms, makin' up the bed; and I'm bad to turn the TVs on when I go into the rooms to listen to the news or gospel sangin' or whatever's on while I'm in that room. And it flashed acrosst the TV screen that Glenn had made Darlene stick her hand in a snake box. It might have been on a Sunday when I heard that, and I's at work. And— they was no church that night—I was setting up at my sister's, and Glenn called to talk with me Sunday evenin'. I know when he called me, he told he had been in jail. And Glenn was drunk then when he called me.

He didn't tell me what happened then. But he always told me—and I know Glenn was telling me the truth when it comes to this . . . down deep in my heart, I know Glenn Summerford right now when it comes to this. He'd say, "Bobbie Sue, if I wanted to kill Darlene, I would not kill her with no snakebite. I would fix her up with this"—and he'd shake that strychnine at me. And he said, "There would be no trace of this." And I know if Glenn wanted to kill Darlene, she'd been a dead duck. And they wouldn't have caught him at that so quick either. And if he'd wanted to hurt her with his fists or if he'd wanted to done anything to her at all, she wouldn't have been able to crawl to no road. And Glenn is the type of person that he wouldn't have done it at the house.

So that's why I'm telling you, they got Glenn all figured out wrong. That's why I'm telling you, they're running off of somebody else's story—and not what really happened to Glenn. It ain't all come out yet. And when it all comes out, everybody goin' really, really see.

When I tell you Glenn drunk, I don't tell you Glenn drunk to criticize Glenn because I know, that devil can sneak a quickie on anybody. He can cause me to take a drink of somethin' and not know what's in it, just that quick—to get his little ups, ups on me. Now, I'm talking about the devil—I'm not talkin' about Glenn—get his ups and ups on you. And then he'll take that story, and he'll raveled it and twist it, screw a little screw in it over here—just like he done Glenn. When the truth is just settin' right there for somebody to tell it. I'm like Preacher Larry Gilliam: "The devil will tell a lie on you and be a mile down the road before the Truth can get up and put its shoes on." And that's what's happened in Glenn's case. Glenn's not that bad of a person. Glenn's ashamed of drinkin'. Glenn is ashamed of what he's done toward the Lord's sake. And really, to be truthful, Glenn was merciful to Darlene—to what Darlene done to him. Just like God's merciful to Glenn, Glenn was merciful to Darlene. Or, honey, her tail wouldn't hold shucks.

If Glenn has repented of this and all these men down there in that prison is praying under Glenn's ministry, Glenn is there for a reason. And that is to minister to these people because the word has got to go out into all the world. Maybe it took Glenn gettin' drunk and gettin' trapped by the devil to get down there where God wants him. And nobody really knows why Glenn's down there. 'Cause he sure ain't down there for makin' Darlene stick her hand in no snake box. And if Glenn has repented from drinkin' that whiskey and that beer and that wine, smokin' them cigarettes, and what have you, then we better leave that alone. 'Cause whatever we reach up under that blood and get and pull out, it goin' be applied to us. But I'm not kissing Glenn's feet about him tellin' lies, either. He needs to say, "Yes, I drank and I repented to the Lord for it—and God's who I got to repent of." If he don't want to own up to drinkin' 'cause he don't want everybody to know it, he needs to say, "Yes, I did drink, but I do not want everybody to know it." And that's what he needs to do.

I happened to have kissed him, and I knowed what he done. I could taste it, and I could smell it. But nevertheless, I'm not Glenn's judge. Not only did I kiss him, he laid on my shoulder for I don't know how long and cried. And I was his calculator—I was his ever'thin', 'cause I'd set down when Darlene come up pregnant with this last baby that she's got. I went from the last time that Glenn said him and her had any dealings with each other, and I counted back. That's how he knew—and he said he *knew*—this baby wasn't his. Glenn said that other than one time, it was two years between their relationships. Not only did Glenn say that, Darlene said it to someone I checked it out with. So that's how I knew Glenn wasn't lying right there. Course if you know Glenn, you can tell when he's telling you the truth and when he's telling you a lie anyway.

I think Glenn was set up from the word "kit-kat." And Glenn is sorry that he drank and he done this and he done that because Glenn was a *true, true, true* man of God. Glenn was gun-barrel straight till the devil put a burr up under his saddle. And I think one particular preacher, that we all know, was a major burr, and of course there are others who were burrs. And Glenn was so stinkin' straight till he couldn't see it—until it destroyed him.

But, like I say, there was this one particular preacher—now this is strictly from Glenn whenever I was settin' over there while Glenn was wallerin' out all of his tears, 'cause everybody else left Glenn but me. And if he didn't call me ever' other day or ever' two days, I'd go over there to make sure he was eatin', and this, that, and another. Well, he said he had his shotgun with him 'cause he went coon huntin'. He let on like he was goin' coon huntin' 'cause he seen Darlene and this preacher whisperin'. Glenn walked on down there and he heard this car comin' in, and he come back to the house. And it was this preacher. And Glenn said he walked in and Darlene and him was havin' sex, right in his own bed. And Glenn said he retched up over 'em and put his gun back on that gun-holder thing mounted on the wall. And he said that preacher begged him to cut his arm off—said he went out in that little pasture thing where they kept the horses and asked him to cut his arm off, as a brother in the Lord.

So, why would Glenn let on like he's goin' coon huntin'?—which that right there was untrue and unfair to start with. If I didn't trust her, I'd a-told her right off the bat: "Get your little ditty bag and get out of here. You done slept with too many men." 'Cause, see, they're claimin' that Glenn wanted to kill her where he could get him a younger woman. And they say, according to the religion, that the only way Glenn could marry would be, kill her. If she was havin' sex with men, that released him, right there. And Glenn just told that preacher, "Just go on and get out of here." Glenn said he didn't do nothin' hisself but cry and pray. If he hadn't been prayed up, he would not just slapped her around, but that preacher too. Now, that's the type of man Glenn is. He would put your stinkin' runnin' lights out in a minute. But, no, he didn't. Glenn forgave him and Darlene, 'cause he said he did. You just got to know Glenn. You just *got* to know Glenn—how he really is. 'Cause if he hadn't been straight, they'd been two dead tails. One of them would have been that preacher, and the other one'd been Darlene. And, honey, he'd a-shot 'em right there, Johnny-on-the-spot—if he hadn't been livin' right.

Now, Darlene's always been knowed as a cat. Darlene's whole family's always been knowed as a cat. And that's why I couldn't believe my eyes when Glenn married Darlene. Course that was two captains, right there. Glenn and Darlene was just alike—that's before Glenn started preachin' and livin' right. And if Glenn'd a-been at hisself, he'd never married her—I don't guess he would've. Maybe that's what it took to calm him down. Ooh, lordy, poor Glenn.

But Darlene was supposed to got up one night and confess to the church, and ask the church people to forgive her for the life that she had lived at home and other places and get down there in church and do like she has done—I was there that night. Why this happened is because Glenn caught Darlene in a bunch of her mess and stuff, and this, that, and another. Now, Glenn was straight up until then, 'cause he had pressed so hard for her to get up to confess to the church what she had been doin' and repent and go be rebaptized. And he was goin' stay right on and live with her through all of that and carry right on with his ministry. And Darlene wouldn't do it. And Glenn said in his letter to me that the reason Darlene wouldn't get up and tell before the church what she had been doing—and the reason that she hung him—was to keep herself out of jail. And that's where he brought it in about her having sexual relationship with his two sons, and that he could have hung her and took Marty from her. And, see, Darlene had a kid prior before that—that she never got to see and she never knowed where he went.

Glenn was framed. Let me tell you somethin' else I know personal. Right before all this happened, they had a regular church service and a birthday dinner and ever'thing for Glenn down at the city park. As I said, I worked up here at Holiday Inn in Scottsboro, and they told me to take off from my dinner break and come and eat down there with Glenn and Darlene. I did. And me and Annie, which is Glenn's mama, was setting on back of a car listenin' to two people—I could give you their names. They were telling Darlene how to get rid of Glenn. They said they wouldn't have to kill him to get rid of him, but they could set him up for life. And me and Annie set there and heard that on back of that car—how to get Darlene out away from Glenn. It was all regarding settin' Glenn up because Darlene claimed she was scared of Glenn.

Now, look at the people who will have to give account—and Glenn's goin' give account for his people, too. Their blood is probably clear up to his elbows on his hands. The Bible says: "Little known, little required; lot known, lot required." And they was a lot required of Glenn. And until Glenn really, really, really does what he's supposed to do to the Lord and all these people that he has crushed, even to me—Glenn's crushed me—God's gonna keep on whuppin' his tail like a red-headed stepchild.

And, see, I had to come in on the tail end of it because the junk was done started when I got there. And it didn't take me but a few times to go down there to Glenn's to know somethin' was wrong—and them up there handlin' them stinkin' snakes. I'd tell Glenn, "I'm comin' down there, but you better keep your snakes in your box, better keep 'em out of my face." I handle 'em now when Lord lets me. But when I first startin' goin' over to Glenn's, like when we'd go from church and Glenn would handle them snakes in the house, he would always tell me to stand back. And then whenever I first started handlin' them snakes, try to handle them at his house, he would let me get around behind him. And he'd put his hand right up there at its head and one back there at its tail, and he'd let me just feel of it in the middle. He wouldn't let me nowhere near where it could bite me.

Now, sometimes I'm as guilty as the next one. But sometimes I could set down in a bed of snakes and know they won't hurt me. Sometimes handlers sicken me out with snakes—they have "snake" services instead of "Jesus" services. And they handle them stinkin' snakes whether God's in it or not, and that's when I call it a "snake" service instead of "God" service. And that's when somebody has to pay. And that's when I stay out of it. I know when it's *me* doin' and *God* doin'. When it's God doin', if them things bite you, they can't hurt you. I know them snakes is somethin' else. I know I've handled 'em by faith, and I know I've handled 'em with anointin', and then I've handled by—I don't know what I handled 'em by. But I know when the faith's there, and I know when the anointin's there.

And Gene Sherbert learnt me a lesson. I used to handle ever' snake Billy Summerford would handle, whether the anointin' was there or whether it wadn't. He'd just get it out of the box, and I'd just reach and get it. And I'd run across one in the road—I'd get it. I wouldn't care—I'd get it. Gene Sherbert said, "You're gonna get eat up." He said, "You better leave them snakes alone

Faithful Helper

till you know what you know. And you know the difference." And he said, "I'm leavin' it there." He said, "You know the difference."

Wadn't long after that, Melinda Brown come up bit and died. Punkin Brown died right in my face, I mean right in my face. I'm probably the last one he spoke a word to. 'Cause I asked him, "Punkin, if you can hear me at all"—they were slappin' that man so hard it sound like fire crackers popin'. I said, "Don't slap him another lick." I said, "If he ain't goin' die, you-all goin' to give him a concussion or bust one of his ear drums." I said, "Don't hit him another lick." I said, "If he ain't in shock, you-all goin' to throw him in shock." And I walked up there, and I bent down. And I said, "Punkin," I said, "if you can hear me at all," I said, "please, open your eyes." And he barely cracked his eyes, and it looked like his eyes was bleedin'. That's how red they was. And I already knew then he had a heart attack. I knew that his heart busted when I seen the whites of his eyes—even the blue or brown part. They look like they were bleedin'. And I said, "Punkin," I said, "do you want me to call 911, or do you want me to let them call 911?" He shook his head no, and pointed up like he was goin' home. And I sat down and begin to clap my hands and praise the Lord. The tip of his nose turned almost purple. His ear and his chin turned that color. And his fingernails was as black as sut. And when I got down there and begin to do CPR on him, I could feel my blowin', bubblin' plumb down in his chest. It wadn't doin' a bit of good—it was goin' straight past his lungs—shaaaah—right down into his belly. 'Cause his heart was all busted, and the air couldn't get out into his lungs. And every time I'd blow and hear that bubble, I seen Gene Sherbert and heard "You know the difference."

It was a long time I wouldn't even look at a snake box. And then I felt that anointin' cover me one day; and I knew, I knew the difference. And when I retch and got that old serpent, it same as died in my hands. I could have just tied it and twisted it and tied it and twisted it, tied it in knots and tied it in knots and tied it in knots. And from now on I wait on *that*. 'Cause when you're covered by *that,* a car could hit you, truck could hit you—you could be in a building and it burn up, and I believe you'd still be standin'. Some of those handlin' them snakes are anointed; and some of them, I feel, they're takin' them up because they don't want you to think they're not livin' right.

And if Glenn would had only stayed prayed up like Glenn was to start with—there is no better preacher on the face of the earth than Glenn Summerford. And Glenn has a mighty power with God, a mighty power. Like one time Darlene was in the kitchen cuttin' some—might have been chicken that she was cuttin'—and the knife slipped. And Glenn just run and throwed his hand on her. And right then, that cut, it mounted right back up. Now, this is before all that junk started happen' between him and Darlene. And Darlene would wanna wear them real tight dresses and get up there before the church and shake her tail. And Glenn wouldn't put up with that. But all this stuff was a setup to get Glenn where he's at now.

And after this junk happened, Glenn called me up at my sister's house and told me he didn't know how he was going to live without Darlene. You see, me and Darlene was always pretty close. Darlene's sister, Debbie, has got a child by my brother. And, see, that's the way I kept in contact with that child, was through Darlene. She would bring me pictures; she'd tell me how he was doin', and this, that, and another. And, see, Glenn knew that me and Darlene was always pretty tight. Course when Glenn and Darlene was courtin', I run with him and Darlene. And Glenn wanted me to see if I could talk to her. So I come to his house and called Birmingham, UAB Hospital, where she was at. And Glenn was on the other phone. I told her, "Darlene, why don't you come and give Glenn one more chance?" And I said, "I'll tell you what I'll do." I said, "If you'll come home to Glenn when you get out of the hospital"—and I even told her, I said, "Let him come down there and see you." I said, "I'll come with him to see you." And I said, "When you get out of the hospital, you come home." And I said, "If you're afraid of Glenn," I said, "I'll come and stay with you and Glenn." She said, "Well, no, you'll have to go out to go to work." I said, "When I go out to go to work, I'll take you out with me. When I come in, I'll bring you back in with me." I said, "If I go to the store, I'll take you with me. If I go to the bathroom, I'll take you with me." I said, "Just don't give up on Glenn and ruin you-all's ministry." She said she'd rather die and go to *hell* than ever to live with Glenn Summerford again. But she didn't tell me what happened that night. She didn't tell me much of nothin', except for, I would "find Glenn out."

But just like I told him, "Glenn, if you lay drunk for the rest of your life, I can see why. Your life is so stinkin' screwed up till you don't even know who you are." I said, "You fell from mighty to nothing." And I've scraped my pan dry, trying to he'p him get a court appeal. I've about went bankrupt on account of it. And when he was up there in the county jail—he stayed up there for about two year of his time—every visitin' day, I was there with money. And he took these Benadryls because he had allergies and stuff—his face would swell unreal. And I'd take them up there, and they'd give his medication to him.

But why Glenn snapped, I believe, was that stuff between J. L. Lewis and Darlene. That's when he snapped. That's when the cat jumped out of the bag. Just as soon as Glenn caught on to it—and Glenn didn't know a lot of this was

Faithful Helper

goin' on until after all this happened. And we would sit and watch TV while he would be cryin' and talkin' to me and tellin' me about all the hell he lived in with Darlene—her sleepin' with his kids and other stuff with his "brotheren," as he'd call it, who would come through his church. I'd point stuff out to him on them VCR tapes—things goin' on behind his back—and then he seen a lot of it.

They're just unfair to Glenn. And a lot of this goes back into Darlene's mama, back before Darlene and Glenn married. You see, Glenn broke Darlene's mama's jaw. Kenneth Smith came in over to Darlene's mama's house, and I was over there, and Darlene was over there, and I don't know where Glenn was at. But there was two men laid way and was goin' kill Glenn when he come in down there. Couldn't none of us come out and couldn't none of us come in. There we was, waiting on Glenn to come in to get killed. All right, Kenneth Smith went out, and he told Glenn that them men was over there and was goin' kill him. Well, Glenn come right on in o'er there. And everything was goin' on—now this was back before we started livin' right. The lights and everything was on, and *pow*—just like that—the lights went out. It was like a bunch of old cats in there—errrrr, errrrr, errrrr—and when the lights come on, there wadn't nobody standing but me, Glenn, and Darlene. And honey, Glenn put mercy on 'em. It's just like Glenn knew right where ever'thing was at. And, son, he hit everybody in there but me and Darlene. Glenn slapped the lights out. And whenever he pulled the plug, he pulled their plugs too. And he broke Darlene's mama's jaw. And they've had a grudge on him ever' since then.

Darlene knows Glenn as good as I know him. And she knows if he's backslid, her tail won't hold shucks. He didn't harm that hussy. But he's down there in the stinkin' penitentiary, and now she's done been out here with Tom, Dick, and Harry. And if he wanted her dead, she'd be dead even till now—even till now. And she knows that.

And didn't nobody have a chance to bring nothin' in to no trial. It's just "wham, bam, thank you, ma'am"—and it's over with. They done had that man convicted before they put him on the stand. And they didn't try him, no way, on stickin' her old hand in no snake box. They tried him on what he'd done back yonder years ago.

That's the truth. And I'll tell the truth, whether it's on me, whether it's on Glenn, whether it's on whoever. If I'm asked, I'll tell the truth. Because with one lie standing up here by itself—you have to go over here and tell one to block it, over here to tell one to block it, and over here to tell one to block it, and over here to tell one to block it. And that's five lies, that you've had to tell, when one time telling the truth'll do it.

Bobbie Sue Lynn

Junior Blair, Josie Blair, Ruby Berry, Carl Porter

First One, Then 'Nother

Junior Blair

I understand that Darlene is scared of Glenn 'cause in the past he was a pretty rough boy. And since Glenn's been in prison, I've been in jail with him—when Glenn come back for a trial, I was up there in the county jail doing sixty days. He's not mad at Darlene. He don't say nothin' bad about her at all. And all these years—I've talked with him several times—I never heard him say nothin' bad about Darlene. He won't talk about her. When he went to trial, he didn't talk about her, said nothin' bad.

Now, this justice system here in Scottsboro is bad. They're bad about settin' you up. This girl called and told me, she wanted me to sell her some pills. I wouldn't sell 'em to her. Well, I was over at the store and met this boy. He was in a truck with some people, and I give him a Lorcet Plus—a pill, pain pill for your back, a prescription. I got it from the drugstore. And that girl who phoned me was a narc, and she set me up. They had the police there, undercover. They told me I was goin' get fourteen years for just bein' there.

They told three different lies, and told me to prove what was the truth. You can't prove what's true and what's not true—which, what they got me for at that time, I's guilty. But not the way they said it. They said I was sellin' dope, but I wadn't. I give it to that boy. And it didn't happen the way they said it, or nothin'. So the justice system here in Scottsboro ain't right.

That narc told me she was goin' put me in jail, and she did. She put me and that boy both in jail. I had to serve around thirty-some days. But I didn't regret goin'. I had a good jail ministry while I was there. I was doin' more in jail—one of 'em prisoners—than I was doin' out here. I should have kept it up when I got out, but I didn't.

And when I got out of jail, I seen that narc at Wal-Mart, shook hands with her, talked to her. My wife said, "How can you talk to her after her puttin' you in jail?" "Well," I said, "I've got to forgive her." That Saturday night—I seen her, like, on a Friday night—Saturday night she got killed in a car wreck.

Now, all through this, see, I've been with Glenn—from the time they took the first warrant out with him. I got his bond signed and all. And from the start with, I haven't heard him say nothin' bad about Darlene, not one word. All he said, he messed up. I imagine I'd have some hurt feelin's or somethin' at the start with. But he wadn't, he just went right on. Glenn has nothin' to say about Darlene or nobody else, really. Glenn's a good person, and I believe if Glenn ever gets out, he'd still be a good person 'cause he's doin' good in jail. And I don't think he would bother Darlene if he got out because if he was gonna bother her, he'd be bitter at her. And I'd follow Glenn if he did get out and started preaching again. Yeah, I would 'cause if he can go down there and not say nothin' bad about Darlene, he's got to be a good man.

One time when Glenn was preachin', I seen him take a snake that was coiled up like a spring on the pulpit, and the anointin' so strong on that snake, he couldn't even get out of that coil. It sit up about a foot high, and his head just shakin', trying to get down. And it couldn't get down 'cause the anointin' was on it so strong—he couldn't move.

There's a lot more Glenn done in church, but I don't remember right now. Main reason though that I don't remember stuff is 'cause I haven't been goin' to church in a while. It's been about three years. Things just don't come to you when you ain't goin' to church. You try to block it out and try not to think about it. You try to put that in the past because if you go to thinkin' about it, things go to bother you.

But while I was in church, I handled serpents onest or twice. The first one I handled was a big rattlesnake. My wife's daddy'd been in the hospital for a while. And while he's in the hospital, I was prayin' and fastin'. I told the Lord, "Now it's got to be in the music"—'cause you've seen on TV and all where they charm them snakes with music. Well, that's got to be the music playin', to make them snakes not bite. And I walked to church that night, come in from the hospital, and didn't say nothin' to nobody.

And I was standin' in the door. And Glenn said, "Hold it. Somebody here said it's got to be in the music." Said, "It's not in the music." And he

Junior Blair, Josie Blair, Ruby Berry, Carl Porter

stopped all the music and all the sangin'. And the Lord spoke to me and told me to get it. And I walked up there and got it. And it was a big rattler—I handled it. And the anointin' was so strong on it, it killed the snake. I dropped it on the floor, and it just rolled over on its belly and died. I was the last one that handled it.

A lot of people comes against handlin' serpents, but when that anointin' is there, it's real. When you get bit is when you do it without under the anointin'. One day I was down there, and the Lord told me to get it—"but don't take it from Glenn." That was 'cause I had more faith in Glenn than I did in the Lord—I wouldn't pick it up without takin' it out of Glenn's hand.

So I made Glenn lay it down in the chair, and then I picked it up. See, if I'd reached and got it out of his hand, I'd got bit. And that's how people gets bit. And I know I'd got bit if I'd reached and got it out of his hand like the Lord told me not to. When I was in church, the Lord talked to me just like talkin' to another person. If I'd do what he told me to do, I was all right. If you don't, then you get in trouble, just like I am now.

But, I went to church with Glenn before he started Woods Cove. I'm the one that found the buildin'. It was an old store house—used to have gas pumps, and they'd tuk 'em out. Right before he got the buildin', they had a little old this-and-that store. It's been a junkyard and ever'thing else. And they've tried to have church since Glenn, but it just don't work.

What makes a good preacher is the anointin' he's got. It ain't the words he speaks. It's just bein' a good life and lettin' the anointin' move on you—bein' led by the Holy Ghost. 'Cause without the Holy Ghost, you can't preach. They's a lot of 'em tryin', but it don't work. If Glenn got out right now, if he'd want to be a pastor, I'd find him a buildin' tomorrow. I'd set it up for him, time he got home.

But it ain't what Glenn done, they stucked him for. They railroad' him because of his past and because the law didn't like him. The trial wadn't right. Where him and Darlene lived was a mud hole, and to come out, you have to cross a creek. And things that was said in the trial ain't right. And all they done at the trial was just to show snakes on TV—that's all. There wadn't *nothin'* proved, wadn't nothin' *not* proved.

Josie Blair (Junior Blair's Wife)

When we'd go to church, sometimes me and Darlene'd sit together. And two or three months back before all this mess happened, she'd say things, you know, make remarks about the men, different men. She'd point 'em out, and she'd say,

"Why, ain't he good lookin'?" or "He can kiss good" or "I went with him" or "I'd like to have him" or either "I've *had* him." Stuff like that—and *went* and *had* is being with 'em, not like sister and brother in the Lord—it's like you go with a person, like, to bed with 'em or somethin'. I mean, that's what she'd say. She'd just say things that a Christian woman wadn't suppose' to say if she's married. And she'd say it with her husband there.

And I've seen Darlene kiss J. L. Lewis after church down here at Woods Cove. We're talkin' not about a holy kiss, but a kiss-kiss. A holy kiss, you don't kiss somebody in the mouth and stay there a few minutes. Darlene was standing outside of the church—some van out there with the door open—and I seen her reach over and kiss him.

She'd told me she went with that Willie Southard—which I don't know, now. That's just what she told me. But the only thing I ever seen her do was kiss J. L. Now, I seen that with my own eyes.

And, well, there'd be several other men I wouldn't even know there at church, you know. She'd just point 'em out to me. And I seen her play around with Gene Sherbert, but I ain't never seen her go with him. I have heard she went with him. And she's told me that she's kissed him. She didn't say she done anything else.

And then I was there one night when Darlene got mad at Glendel. You can tell when somebody's into it, you know. Then she just jumped up and got in the snake box and handled snakes and went back and sat down. She's mad at him while she's doin' it. I don't know how she done that, but she done it. I guess God just had his hands over her, 'cause she'd be mad, and she'd go up there and reach in there and get the snakes.

And when she got bit, I don't think Glendel put her hand in the box. I think her hand was put in a box, but I believe she done it herself. She knowed what she was doin'. She had it all planned out, I believe, when that happened. She knowed exactly what she's doin'. She meant to send Glendel off. She meant to do that. She made it look like Glendel done it to her. I mean, I think they might have had trouble—every couple has trouble. And he got up at church and told everybody he needed 'em to pray for him, that he's havin' some family problems, just pray that God would move in it. But I believe that she had it planned, she knowed what she was doin'. I don't think Glendel put her hand in that snake box. She knowed what it would take to put him away, and she done it. I believe she knowed exactly what she's doin'.

But I don't think all the reason that Glendel is in jail has got to do with all this mess about Darlene. I think Jackson County had it against him to start

216

with. I think they just got him on the snakes, and that was it. They'd been wantin' to get him.

And I think Darlene was kindly a-skeered of Glendel. Before he started church, he was a pretty rough boy. But I know that after Glendel started church, he wadn't the same Glendel I knowed, you know, years ago. I believe he was livin' right before all this started happenin'—I believe he was. But after she got all that started, she had to keep it up, you know.

I don't think Glendel should be where he's at now. I think *if* he should be where he's at, she should be in there with him.

Ruby Berry

Darlene would tell me at church, "I'm tired of being married to a preacher. I'm tired of being a preacher's wife." And she fooled around on Glenn because she fooled around with my brother Floyd. This was way on back. It was probably about three years before all this other stuff happened. She'd call down at our mother's house, and Floyd'd answer the phone, and he'd go in the bedroom, and they'd talk on the phone and stuff.

She was messin' with Floyd because I took him over 'ere to meet her at her own house, myself. I wanted to see if it was really goin' on, and I seen it with my own eyes. He had went and bought her a outfit for her birthday. And he wanted me to carry him over there to give it to her. Glenn had got snakebit at church about a week before, and he was in the bed, still pretty bad off.

And when we got over there, Darlene came outside. She hugged Floyd, and he kissed her. And she told Floyd to be quiet because Glenn was in there asleep on the couch, and she didn't want Glenn to come out and catch her. And Floyd gave her the outfit, and he asked her, "You still goin' leave with me?" She said, "If I can get away, and get Marty to go with me." But I don't reckon she could find a way to slip out, leave, or do somethin'. And I don't think Marty would ever go with his mama then.

But Darlene and Floyd fooled around with each other for about six months or longer. Sure did. She was goin' leave with Floyd, but she couldn't get away. I don't know if they went to bed or not, but I do know they had slipped around. They would hug and kiss each other even in church—it was right up here by C. W.'s then, the church was. Glenn would be preachin', and she would go in the ladies' bathroom. Floyd would wait a few minutes, and he'd go to the men's bathroom. Then they'd meet in the hall, and they would kiss—and it wadn't no holy kiss.

I don't think Glenn knows 'bout that 'cause Darlene kept it a big secret. She would ask us not to say anything—which I didn't want to say nothin' because I didn't want to hurt Glenn. And I didn't want to cause any trouble between Glenn and my brother. I should have went to Glenn, but I didn't. Darlene done Glenn wrong—she really done him wrong. She sure did.

And she'd talk about other men at church. She'd point at a certain person who would be up there on the platform. She said, "That man right yonder, don't you think he's pretty?" Or "He looks real good." She'd wink at 'em, flirt with 'em. Then she'd say, "I'm so tired of being married to a preacher." I think she wanted away from Glenn 'cause she wanted to be free.

She's told me about another one at church besides my brother. I can't think of the boy's name . . . I think he was from Sand Mountain. But, now, Darlene had told me that she had been seeing him, you know, and she'd quit seein' him.

Willie Southard, that's my ex-brother-in-law. He was married to my sister Jewel. Darlene had a real bad crush on him. But whether they met . . . I heard they did, but I didn't see it. But, now, I have had people tell me they have seen 'em out together. And after Glenn was sent to prison, Willie would go to the mountain and spend time with Darlene up there.

I know she would flirt with my husband when we'd go to church. And he told me, "Well, when she shakes my hand, she'll just hold on to my hand, just rub my hand." He says, "I don't like 'at." And she'd rub him on the back of his neck, or rub his head—tell him, "Well, you sure do look good tonight." And you don't tell another man that, you know, especially if you're in church. She's just seeing which one would have anything to do with her. Everybody knows that. And you know how at church they pray and fall out in the Spirit? She'd fall on men and get 'em to catch her.

Now, I do remember one time—when the church was down here at Woods Cove Road—we was at church, and it was her birthday. And I noticed her smilin' at Brother Gene the whole time he was up there, you know. And he'd look back there at her, and he'd smile. And when church was over with, people come out and shakin' hands, you know. Well, Brother Glenn was talking to other people, and Gene Sherbert come out, and he took Darlene's hand. But he didn't just get one hand, you know, he just took both hands. And he helt her hand and just shook it and cut up with her. And she closed her hand, and I was curious. I said, "What did he put in your hand?" And she said, "Shush, don't let nobody know it, but he gave me twenty dollars for my birthday." And it kindly made me wonder after that, you know, but I never did see them together.

Junior Blair, Josie Blair, Ruby Berry, Carl Porter

And the night Brother Glenn got snakebit, they took him up to his mother's house in the new project. And he was layin' on the couch. I asked Darlene, I said, "Do you think he's goin' make it?" And she said, "Yeah, he's goin' make it 'cause I couldn't be that lucky." That's what she said. That's the exact words she said in her mother-in-law's kitchen. My mother's dead and gone, but me and my mother and them was standin' there heard it. And my mother said, "Lord, Darlene, don't say that."

Now, Brother Glenn, he stood for what he preached. What he preached, he stood on it. My daughter, she was about to bleed to death. If the Lord hadn't moved for her when he did, I don't know . . . Brother Glenn prayed for her. And when Brother Glenn laid hands on her, blood just stopped right there. And her nose never bled no more.

I loved Brother Glenn, but it is just more like a family love. My husband used to be real wild, and Brother Glenn really helped him a lot. And my husband thought the world of him. But the reason my husband quit goin' to church down there was on account of the way Darlene was doin'. He said, "I just don't feel comfortable with her doin' me like 'at."

And my mother had a lot of confidence in Glenn. Course she knowed him ever since he was a little boy. My mother would call for him to come pray for her. But he never would come by hisself to my house or Mama's house without bringin' Darlene. He didn't want to be around another woman without Darlene was with him.

I've never seen Glenn with another woman—I've never seen Glenn Summerford with another woman. I don't think he would have messed around on Darlene because he was too much into his Christianity. He believed it real strong. 'Cause he has told me, you know, a lot of times, "Now, little sister, your husband loves you. You need to stay with your husband." Glenn's helped us, and I don't ever believe he would ever mess with another woman around on Darlene. I sure don't. But I know she wanted away from him. She was tired of being with him.

I've knowed Glenn ever since I was a little-bitty kid, you know. And Glenn always respected people, been good to people. And I cannot believe, and I won't believe, that Brother Glenn done what Darlene accused him of doin'. I just don't see Brother Glenn doin' it. And I don't think she was afraid. I really don't. She wadn't as 'fraid as she let on like she was. She sure wadn't. If Glenn was threatenin' her life, she had—I don't know how many—chances to get away from him. Like, when they went to the video store, I'd went in there, and I would have turned around and locked the door behind me and told that

First One, Then 'Nother

lady to call the law—"I need the law." Or when they went to the convenience store. I can't see it.

They wouldn't let me testify in court. They said the reason I couldn't be a witness was 'cause I had set in the courtroom and listen to what was goin' on. Told me I couldn't 'cause I done heard too much of the trial. But there was a girl that set in there, and halfway through the trial—right at the end—they called her out of the courtroom. She was settin' in front of me on the bench. And she got up there and was a witness agin Glenn.

And the DA, they done had Glenn convicted 'fore they ever had the trial to start with. They didn't listen. You could be out in the hall while the court was goin' on or durin' recess, or somethin'—and you could hear 'em all, even the DA and the county law, makin' jokes about Glenn, remarks about him, you know. And it just wadn't right. They didn't give him a chance. And I was there from the time the trial started to the time the trial ended. And if they would have set and listened—as many times as she had a chance to get away from him—if she wanted away, she could have went. But she didn't want to.

Carl Porter.

Junior Blair, Josie Blair, Ruby Berry, Carl Porter

And it wadn't long after he went to prison, Darlene started goin' out here and clubbin' and gettin' drunk—dressin' in little-bitty mini skirts so everybody can see everything she's got. Well, everybody you talk to, they say Darlene turned out to be real bad.

Carl Porter (Former Pastor, Church of the Lord Jesus Christ, Kingston, Georgia)

I was at the trial in the witness room, but Glenn told me that his lawyer told him it was best that I not testify. So I didn't. But I can tell you the statement I signed for his lawyer the day before the trial started.

I wrote that I called Darlene when she was in the hospital with the snakebite. And she told me that she prayed that Friday night and handled the snake and it did not bite her. And she said she prayed that Saturday night and handled the snake and it bit her. But she went on and said that Glenn had a gun and made her do it. And she told me that she was going to see that he went to jail. Also, I told her, "Why don't you just divorce him?" And she said that she was going to see that he went to prison.

It was right after that I rebaptized Glenn.

Summerford AIS 098070

In Prison

It was already daylight Monday when I got back to Scottsboro from Birmingham jail. It took us, like, all night to come back. So as soon as I got back home, I called the police department down there. I wanted to get that take care of pretty quick, you know. I told them, "I'm tryin' to find out about my son. I want to know where he's at." They didn't know anything about that. But Kenny and Jackie had come straight on down there and got him at the hospital. Marty stayed up there with his mama at the hospital until they picked him up.

I went down to the sheriff's department, and the sheriff told me, "Glenn, I ain't got nothin' on you, nowhere." He said, "I seen what's been run on TV and all—you need to get it took care of, whatever it is." And I said, "It's just my old lady acted crazy, I reckon. I don't know what it is either. But who do I need to talk to?" He said, "We ain't got anything to do with it. You might talk to the city." And he said, "Wait a minute." Said, "This might be him on the phone." So he answered the phone, but it wadn't him. "Hold on a minute," and he called the city. He talked to Clarence Bolte. And Bolte said, "Yeah, I want to talk with him. I'm already up here in town." Said, "I'll come around by there and talk to him."

So when he come around 'ere, I asked him, "You got a warrant fer me?" And he said, "Naw, I seen it on TV." Said, "I want to talk to you. You don't mind ridin' down to the office to talk to me?" I said, "I don't mind, but I got all these people who came down with me." He said, "Come on, you can ride with me. You can sit in the front seat." So I told my folks, "You-all follow me on down there, see what's goin' on." And they followed me down to the city police.

223

Glenn Summerford in Limestone Correctional Facility.

We got down there and went in a room where the chief of police was. And him and Bolte, the investigator, was the only two in there. Bolte said, "Well, Glenn, you want to give us a statement of what happened, what's goin' on?" And I said, "Naw, I don't want to give you no statement. I come down here to see if you had a warrant fer me." I said, "If you want to arrest me for anything, I didn't want you-all havin' to hunt me up. I come down here to get it took care of. And I got the people to sign my bond if you got a warrant. I seen on the TV that I tried to kill my old lady." Said, "I figured somebody had a warrant on me or it wouldn't be on TV."

And he said, "Well, we ain't got a warrant." So I said, "Well, have you talked with Darlene?" Said, "Naw, where she at?" And I say, "Well, she's in the hospital, fer as I know." "Well, we haven't talked with her, but you can give us a statement." Said, "Can you tell us anything about what happened?" I said, "I sure can't." Really I couldn't. I said, "Naw, I can't tell you what happened."

And I got up and said, "If you-all need me, you-all know where I'm at." And Clarence Bolte said, "Wait a minute, Glenn. I am goin' ahead and arrest you." I said, "What you goin' arrest me fer?" He said, "Well, I'm arrest you fer first-degree assault." So he set there and wrote the warrant out. A'ter he arrested

224

me, he handcuffed me. Then he said, "We goin' go out to your house with you. You don't care for us goin' out there and lookin' at them snakes in your house, do you?" And I said, "There ain't no snakes in my house." And he said, "You don't care for us to look, do you?" "Naw, I don't care for you lookin'. There ain't no snakes in my house."

And we went out. And the people that was outside, they said, "What's goin' on, Glenn?" And I said, "Well, he decided that he'd go ahead and arrest me for first-degree assault." And Bolte said, "He's not allowed to talk to nobody from this point on." Then he said to me, "If you try to run, you will be shot." And I said, "Try to run? I come down here on my own."

So they carried me on to the house. My son, little Bill, he come up. And they wouldn't even let him come on up to the house. Bolte went in and tore my house up. He had me standin' on the porch so he could see me. When he looked all in the living room, he told me to come on in. So I went in. He goes in the bedroom, and he pulls the mattress about halfway off the bed. And he's lookin' under the bed, and he's lookin' through the bookshelf. He's throwin' books and stuff in the floor, and first one thing and 'nother.

And I said, "You ain't got to tear my house up. There ain't no snakes in none of that stuff. We don't never keep no snakes in the house." And he said, "Well, you just be quiet. I know what I'm lookin' fer." So he went in Marty's room and moved some stuff around in there, throwed some clothes around, first one thing and 'nother. And he said, "Come on," and I had to walk through there with him. And he went on in the kitchen. And when he went in the kitchen, I heared somethin' break. I thought the coon had got a'ter him.

He took me back out on the porch, and he got out there in the yard. The other officer said, "What's in that shed?" And I said, "That buildin' there's the one we keep snakes in." I said, "It's some more stuff in there—my tools." He said, "Who's got the key?" I said, "I got it in my pocket, one of 'em. One or two of the brothers's got keys." And I said, "My old lady's got a key." And he said, "Well, come out here and open it." So I went out there and opened it fer 'em.

And they got their snake catchers and started gettin' all the snakes. So they got, I think they's about forty, forty-somethin' snakes, in glass tanks and all. They got 'em all. We had small glass tanks for the smaller snakes and big ones for the bigger snakes, you know. One was a wood cage about ten feet long with a glass front, and three feet high, and wooden lids with locks. One was about three feet square, and it had glass front. All of them had thermostats in them—if the temperature would drop, lights in the boxes would come on and heat them up. They keep the same temperature in that building all the time.

Glenn Summerford in Limestone Correctional Facility.

The shed's about twenty foot square. I had a gas heater, but the building was insulated and stayed the same temperature. A lot of times, when anybody come, we'd get out there and go to prayin' and go to handlin' the serpents. They was enough room in there—we've handled 'em in there a lot of times.

226

So a'ter I give 'em the key to open that buildin', Bolte, he told me, "Don't go in there." And I said, "Okay." So I just stood back out of the way, and he motioned fer another one that had a camera. I thought he was a newsman. And Bolte said to him, "You can go in the house now and check it and see what you think about it." The cameraman said, "There ain't no snakes in there, are they?" And Bolte said, "I didn't see any." So he started in with the big camera. And I said, "Hey, wait a minute! You go in my house, I'm goin' sue you." I said, "I might not do nothin' about you filmin' them snakes. I ain't caring about that. But if you go in my house, I'm goin' sue you." And he just give one of those old dirty-lookin' grins and went on in. So I thought he was a newsman, you know, all those years until I went into the Rule 32 hearin' and found out that it was a cameraman for the city police.

And then they made me sit in the car. They said they was goin' put a stop to this snake handlin' and all this kind of stuff, but they's usin' pretty bad words. Then they take me back to city jail down there, and they want to interrogate me for real. I ain't had nothin' to say to them, anyway. So they put me in the cell and kept me all night and all the next day—that's Monday night and Tuesday. Then they transferred me the next day 'bout four o'clock when Clarence Bolte come back 'ere where I's at.

And I says, "They signed my bond yet?" He said, "We've been investigatin' somethin' else." Said, "Come on and go with me" and unlocked the cell. He handcuffed me again and carried me up to the county. When I got up to county, why, he told 'em he was transportin' his prisoner from city to county. So they put me in the county jail. And I made a phone call. That's the first phone call I got. I didn't get no phone call at the city, but I knew my people was out there waitin' on me anyway.

I called home and Mama said, "Well, we've been waitin' on 'em to bring you up here, to set your bond. People all over town's waiting to sign your bond." Said, "All we got to do is let 'em know you're up 'ere." The trustee come back there and said, "Hey, Glenn, I tell you what—they's so many people out there to sign your bond, the courthouse's full of people. All around the courthouse, they lined up to sign your bond." And I said, "What's takin' so long?" He said, "I don't know." So they made a lot of people sign my bond, but it wadn't but $20,000.

When I's out on bond, I got a lawyer, Gary Lackey. A'ter I talked with him the first time, he would, like, avoid me whenever I went to see him—'cause I asked him, I said, "Mr. Lackey, are you the Lackey that knows my wife and her family?" I said, "Are you the one that growed up with 'em?" See, my

In Prison

old lady used to go with him, you know. And he said, "Naw, Mr. Summerford, I don't know your wife, and I don't desire to know her." He said, "I'm goin' win this case fer you." I said, "Okay, I'm sorry I asked you because there are some more Lackeys, you know."

When I would go to talk with Lackey after that, why, he would just talk to me for a minute. He said he had things to do, but he had ever'thin' under control. I went to talk with him about four or five different time, but he either wadn't there or he was leavin'. And then on the Sunday before the trial, he called me at home and told me, said, "Glenn, I want you to come my office." But when I got there, he had to go to a funeral or somethin'. And that's the way it was ever'time I tried to talk to him. He seen me once *before* that Sunday and then *on* that Sunday and at the trial on Monday—we never did get to discuss nothin'.

The longest that I stayed with him and talked to him, he was trying to get me to let *Dateline* or one of those big programs to come and interview me. That's the longest I even got to talk to him. He didn't take a deposition. He made me believe he'd already got the information from somebody else. And I was wonderin' how he got information from somebody else. As far as talkin' to Lackey about the case, I talked to him before that Sunday three or four times, ten or fifteen minute each. And that's all. But I was up there a lot more.

And when Lackey called me to come up there that Sunday, he said, "I'm goin' have quite a few of your witnesses 'ere too, and I need you-all to be on time." So whenever we got up there to his office, why, he told me he wanted to talk with me. Then him and me went back in his office. And he said, "How many of these witnesses that knows anything?" And I said, "I don't really know, Gary. I know I don't even know much myself—I don't know how much they know." And he said, "Can you have them to write it down what they know?" And I said, "Well, I don't even know who's goin' testify." And he told me the names of the ones that was goin' testify. So I said, "Why, you might ort take care of all that." And he said, "Well, I got to go to a funeral. One of the police officers died." And he come out and talked for a minute, and then he left.

He never did work no testimony out of me except when we went to the preliminary hearin'. He told me that evenin', he said, "I can beat this first-degree case. That ain't goin' be no problem at all." Said, "You heared her testimony, and you know pretty well what you got to answer to." And I still didn't know nothin' much.

And he straight out lied about me a-testifin' at the big trial. When I went to court—it started Monday morning—I kept on tellin' him, "Look here, I got to testify. She's tellin' all this, and I ain't gettin' to say nothin'." He kept tellin'

Summerford AIS 098070

me, "Boy, you better be quiet. I'm trying to keep you out of prison." And that's all he ever would say. He made me think that they wadn't goin' let me testify because that I'd had a prior felony—that's what he told me to start with, but then he changed that.

One time he even got the judge to recess for a minute so he could talk to me and carry me back 'ere in back. And me and him got in an argument about it. I said, "Look here, they ain't no way that I can see that I can win this if you don't let me testify." I said, "She's up there tellin' lies, just straight-out lies." And I said, "I'm the only one that can say she's lyin'. Me and her was the only one there." And he said, "You goin' have to sit quiet and let me hear what's goin' on so I know how to double question." But all he done was to talk to 'em about handlin' snakes and this, that, and 'nother, you know. He'd get so fer questionin', and he'd quit.

Then he told me that he wadn't goin' to put me on the stand because I was too nervous. And I told him, "Look here, I ain't as nervous as you think I am. I need to testify on my behalf, and I want to testify." And he said, "We'll play it by ear as we go through it." Said, "I'll let you know then." And I said, "Well, why can't I testify?" He said, "They goin' give you ninety-nine year or life if they find you guilty, 'cause you was a ex-felon." And I said, "That don't matter if they find me guilty—they's goin' give it to me anyway, I guess." And I said, "She's sayin' ever'thin' that the DA's wantin' her to say. And he's just leadin' her, you know." And I said, "I want to testify." So he said, "We'll just have to wait and see."

Lackey didn't even let all the people testify that was there wantin' to testify. Then he got up and closed it out and said, "That's all we got, your honor." When he said that, why, I thought we goin' recess again and come back tomorrow 'cause the other people hadn't testified.

So the judge talked about an hour, and he let the DA talk about an hour and then the lawyer talk about an hour. Then the judge let the jury go deliberate. And when they went to deliberate, they stayed hung up for six hours, somethin' like 'at. And finally, part of 'em come out of the deliberation and went around there in Judge's chambers, talkin' to him 'bout what the difference was between first-degree assault and attempted murder. So when he told 'em whatever he told 'em, they went back in there and found me guilty. And they locked me up that day.

They was only two people that testified fer me, and they both testified that Darlene was tryin' to kill me. One of 'em was Brother Peace's son. He said that she was wantin' me killed, you know, wantin' to get rid of me. But, see these things I didn't know until a'ter it happened.

And the other one that testified was a girl, Tammy Flippo—Darlene and her was good friends. I know that girl risked her life to testify fer me, and I didn't even know she was goin' to testify. That lawyer never told me nothin'. She didn't have to do that, but I know she risked her life 'cause she had a mean husband. If I'd even knowed what she was goin' to testify, I'd told that lawyer not let her testify.

But there was all kind of talk got started 'cause that girl testified in trial fer me. It's a bunch that started 'cause that girl and her husband had had problems. So a whole lot got started about that. And it wadn't true. I don't know about all their problems or nothin', but they's just a bunch of stuff that wadn't right. She was one of the church sisters, and I never had went with her—I never went with no woman the whole time me and Darlene was together. All it was, like ever'thing else, it just got blowed out of proportion. So I'll just leave it like it is.

Besides, all the time I was on bond, either Uncle J. B. was with me all the time or Brother Uly. Bobbie Sue, she come over several times. My sister and them come over several times, you know. But I can prove where I was at all the time because they was somebody with me. And all the people knows that them two men was with me all the time 'cause I was afraid that Darlene was goin' tell somethin' else.

Now, the reason they sentenced me to ninety-nine year is they enhanced me fer two prior convictions. I had gone to prison once, twenty years before, for second-degree burglary. And there was never nothin' to a grand-larceny case. The charge was 'bout a boat and a motor way back around '65 that belonged to this guy Lawson Miller. Anyway, he's just an old friend of ours. He was a commercial fisherman. He left his boat there all the time, and he drank. We's just young boys, and we was fishin' over there. He was drinkin', but we's using his boat—'course he was with us. We went to the bank, and he went and run his lines. When he come back—he's so drunk, instead of pullin' in where we was, he pulled way on down and locked it up to a tree. He come staggerin' up and got in his old car and left. Then next day, they got a warrant for me or somethin' for stealin' his boat, when his boat was still locked to a tree. Course they dropped it. It didn't amount to nothin', and I never went to court on all that.

But they couldn't enhance me on just one conviction, so they used two. They shuffled a bunch of papers up some way or 'nother and made it look like there was burglary and grand larceny all together. I'd only pled guilty to a second-degree burglary. And they was a plea-bargain deal made on that, but

230

they won't come up with them records. They say they ain't got it. I tried to fight 'em in court. I filed it ever' which way, but I couldn't do nothin' with it. There wadn't nothin' I could do 'cause it was so old. They's a two-year statute of limitation, is what they say. But I never been to prison but one time, and it was for second-degree burglary—Central Records in Montgomery got the record of that.

Whenever all that stuff came about, my family on Mama's side lived in Florida. As I've already said, me and the guy that was runnin' around with me—he's dead now—we went to this house up here in Jackson County. I was drivin' the car, and we pulled up in the yard and got out and walked around. I never did even go in. He went up on the porch, knocked, and the door was open. He walked in, and it's just an empty house. Best I remember, they wadn't nothin' there.

At that time I was married to Doris, my first wife, and we went to court two or three different times. The people never even appeared agin us. But the court just put it off and put it off and put it off. And first time we was in court, the lawyer made 'em work the bill fer me. They told me, if I'd plead guilty, they'd give me probation and that'd be the end of it. They had the probation man there; his last name was Jones. I paid the pro-man, and they put me on eighteen months probation right then. And I was seeing him. Course all them years ago—the parole man died, and they ain't no record.

And the sentence was already up when they picked me up. I had got the case and pled guilty in '67. They didn't deny the probation till '69—they didn't break my probation, they denied it. I come in from work one night, and they was there to get me. Said they had a fugitive warrant on me, and they locked me up. I didn't never go before a judge or nothin'. They sent me straight to Old Kilby and then to Draper and Fort Payne Road Camp. So I went ahead and did my time like a man, and didn't do nothin' about it. I figured, well, they just messed up their record or somethin'. I acted right and got out and stayed out of trouble.

But see, I'm doing time on that, like, three times. I did it on probation, I did it in prison, I'm doin' it again now. But these records that they cooked up to enhance me is not the same record. They added all that later.

But since I've been in prison, I sued the city for the way they threatened me and all—and the way they took all them snakes out of the shed. They was under lock and key. And they's supposed to get the one that bit her, but they confiscated all of 'em—all the glass tanks and all that. It costs a pretty good bit for all of it. 'Sides that, I heard they sold the snakes and everything. I filed on it to try to make 'em give the snakes back to the other brothers 'cause all them snakes wadn't mine and Darlene's. Part of them belong to different ones of the brothers.

I also filed that they violated my rights because they arrested me October the first 1991 fer first-degree assault. And it was a false arrest, what it really was. After I filed it, they made affidavits and swore their statement of how they arrested me. They said that they went to the hospital and talked to Darlene, and Darlene wanted to prosecute me—and they went to the DA of Scottsboro and obtained warrants for me for attempted murder on October the first. And that's their sworn affidavits. And, see, all that had to go through the same court. So why would they lie like that when we've got the records?—'cause they knew that I's fixin' to beat the case.

You see who was sendin' me to prison—it wadn't the county or the state, it was the city. It's plain to see—it's gettin' me out of that town. I know one thing: when God gets ready, they'll have to let me go.

But I ain't goin' to sue any more. I'm through with it. I'm sick of it. All these years made me sick of it. I don't even like to talk about it. I try to stay prayed up all the time, and the more I have to talk about it, why, it makes it hard spiritually when I go to prayin', seekin' God. Just like resurrectin' somethin'

Glenn Summerford in Limestone Correctional Facility with Captain Eddie Carter.

Summerford AIS 098070

that should be just left buried, you know. So I ain't goin' fool with it no more, or I ain't plannin' on it.

Anyway, after the big trial and my conviction, I was put in jail in Jackson County for a while. Then I went to Kilby for about two week, where they processed me, and from Kilby to West Jefferson. They's supposed to sent me up here to Limestone Correctional, but they didn't. They sent me to West Jefferson—that's a maximum security prison—and I stayed there four year. At West Jefferson they raised my custody up to a level six. You got a ten-year setup on a life sentence, and when you get within three year of that ten-year setup, you're eligible for custody. They's supposed to put you in fer it, and Montgomery suppose' to deny you or grant it. But I haven't got custody.

When the parole comes up in ten years, they ain't no guarantee you make it. The warden told me that I wadn't likely to make parole when I come up. He didn't give me no reason why. But if I had custody, I could go to a honor camp. And there I could see my children and grandchildren all at one time. Here I can only see four grownups come at a time. And you can only change your visitors list ever' six months.

Why, I got ten kids, you know, and all them's got little ones. Some I've never seen or nothin'. I think there's twenty-seven hundred people here at Limestone. And they jam so many visitors in here—my boys come, and we've stood up the whole time they've been here, you know. And that's one reason I didn't want them to bring my little grandbabies and all, 'cause it's so crowded.

When I went to West Jefferson Prison, why, it was kind of slow to start with. Then God got to dealin' with people. And they start comin' to me, and I ministered to the whole prison there, just about it, at some time or 'nother. And I handled two serpents while I was there, the only ones I've handled in prison.

The first serpent was when they called me up front. See, at West Jefferson I worked up front, cleaning up and ever'thing. They had a room close to the warden's office. And the officers up there called me on the loud speaker and told me to come up there ASAP. So I'm just draggin' around figurin' what's goin' on. And they kept callin' me, and finally an officer come and met me. He said, "Come on. You gotta go with me." I said, "What is it?" "It's urgent. Just come on. Ask no questions." So, I got up there, and he said, "Go on, they waitin' on you out there." And I said, "Who waitin' on me?" "Go on, man." He couldn't come no further and had to go back 'cause he was workin' yard out there.

So, I go on up there to the gate. And it's like a room where you go through—it's electric doors, you know. And there's a cube there with this woman in it, and they always shake me down when I go in there, you know.

So she pops the door, says, "Go on, go on, go on." I said, "Naw, I ain't goin'" until they shake me down." She said, "Go! They waitin' on you. Step in that room." So I figure, well, I'm goin' step in there, and they goin' shake me down. So I stepped in there. And that door closes, and she opens the other door.

And I see a whole bunch of officers out there with sticks—they got broom handles and ever'thing. So she said, "Go on, Mr. Summerford, go on, go on." She's got that door open and holding the button, and it's a-buzzin', you know. They look like they fixin' to club somebody out. I ain't goin' out there— they's about thirty-five, forty of 'em. "Go on! Go on!"

Finally they seen me, and they run over 'ere where I was. "Come on, Mr. Summerford, come on." Boy, I figure I'm in trouble now, you know. So I step out there where they at. And they take me to a room back 'ere where they stored stuff, and it had these platforms where stuff set on it, you know. And they had two more inmates up there that worked in that part. And they was trying to get this big rattlesnake out—he was up in under there. They'd been punchin' at him with them sticks and handles and all—and they had him mad. He was mad mad.

And I said, "Why you-all call me?" And they said, "Well, you can get that out. We got to get that out before the warden gets here." And I said, "Looks like you done got it beat to death, probably." They told me, "Naw, you can hear it under there. You got to get it out." I said, "If you get back with them sticks, I'll try it." So I knelt down there and asked the Lord let me get it out, you know, and not let it bite me.

I didn't hardly have room to get my hand up under there, but I did. When I felt him, I just asked the Lord to let him move around so I could feel which way it was goin' and I'd know which way his head was. Then I moved it around with my finger a little bit and got aholt of it. I pulled it out and stood up with it in my arms. And they all lookin' at me and got them sticks drawed back. One of 'em hit at it. And when he hit it, I dropped it. They was a-hittin' at it and ever'thing, and it run real fast back up in under there. So I run out of that room.

They couldn't get it, and they's callin' me, "Come on back in here and get it." I said, "I ain't goin' do it and you-all hittin' at it with 'em sticks." I said, "I don't know if I can do it anymore or not." Then I said, "If you just get out of this room, I will." So when I got down there on my hands and knees that time, it was really mad, worser than it was other time, I believe. It was wild.

Finally, I felt it and took it out. I had it up in my arms again, and I see 'em wantin' to hit it. So I hold it close to me so they won't go to hittin' it. And I walked out, and all them officers just followed me, a whole crowd of 'em. I

234

take it out front where's a flower bed out there, and I lay it down. I stepped back, and when I did, it's like a army went off—all them sticks and handles and ever'thing a-hittin' that thing. Boy, they knocked the hide off it. From then on, anywhere I went in the prison, they didn't never shake me down. They never did put their hands on me no more.

The other serpent I handled was out on the pavement. One of the guys had found a serpent out there and had it in a hobby-craft box. I handled it, but it was just a copperhead—it wadn't a rattler. But it helped them to believe what God could do. It made several believers, you know, out of 'em.

And I'd preach to 'em at West Jefferson. I'd teach 'em the Scriptures and how to get right and help 'em pray through to the Holy Ghost. I don't know how many got right with God 'cause I never kept up with it. And God give several miracles—He healed a lot at West Jefferson. One man, he had his leg cut off 'cause he had sugar—diabetes. Then he got sugar in his other leg, and they said they's goin' have to take it off. And it was swelled up. It was humongous, swelled out, and done turned blue and red—blood-shot lookin'. And me and the other brothers prayed fer him that day. And the leg went down right then. God healed it instant. So he didn't lose his other leg. They was just several different miracles and things.

Sign at the entrance to Limestone Correctional Facility.

Limestone Correctional Facility.

I guess I got pretty popular there, so that's why they transferred me up here to Limestone. But this is a evil place, right here, real evil. It's sort of like Sodom and Gomorrah. You know how that was. God just showed me to leave 'em alone—just stay by myself all the time.

I got a cell partner—it's a two-man cell. We're locked down most of the time. They only let us out so many hours a day. They let us out to eat dinner and supper and breakfast, but they lock us back at each time. Sometimes I get out walking—that's 'bout all. I don't do nothin'—ain't nothin' to do. I don't never work out on weights. They got basketball, and I don't play basketball. So I don't do nothin', but just walk.

I'm a "level four"—that's what this camp is, a level-four camp. Some of 'em here are lower. They got custody and all. See, like I said, I'm eligible for my custody, but they won't put me in fer none. I've been locked up goin' on nine years. And I ain't had a disciplinary or a citation in all these years, and they won't put me in for no custody. And all I've got is *attempted* murder. And the guy who works in the warden's office, he's the one that got tried and convicted for a murder the same day I got *attempted* murder—at the same county and same courthouse. And he's got custody and works outside.

I'm not given work detail 'cause I got a "medical class three" when I was workin' in the kitchen at West Jefferson and got my neck broke. They told me

236

I's goin' be paralyzed, but God's took care of me. I believe in God's goin' take care of me as long as I can hold on to him.

But I don't preach none up here. I believe in preachin' whatever God gives you to preach, you know. But you can't preach a baptism or nothin' here 'cause God can't confirm it through you—you can't baptize anyone. They won't let you, not in here.

See, a man of God's suppose' to be on fire fer God. If he's got some fire, you know, then you can get kindled up by it—have that fire. But if he's just speakin' and not believin' and not got the Holy Ghost fire, you know, it wouldn't do no good to get baptized by him. John said that they's just one goin' come, and he's goin' to baptize 'em with the Holy Ghost and with fire. Most people's missin' the fire. So I believe if anybody gets baptized, it's got to be the Bible-right way. The prison system, they got their own way of doin' things. They not goin' let nobody that's on fire for God to come in and baptize people. They just got certain people to do that. So I hope and pray these guys get out and go get baptized—most of 'em is gettin' out . . . one went home yesterday. When they get out, I tell 'em where to go to find somebody who'll baptize 'em the right way.

At this prison we just have prayer meetin' and seek the Lord. We have prayer different times. Most the time we pray to ourself and read our Bible. And then sometime we'll get together, you know, just set in the cell—when they let us set in the cell—and read our Bibles. But, see, the brothers don't get together that much. They got so many different dorms, and part of us is in different dorms. Brother Ray, now, he's in the same dorm I'm in. They's about four or five in there, you know, and we get together and pray and read our Bible. If they find it out, they split us up. We kind of do it under secret, you know.

They's been—I don't know—quite a many that's got the Holy Ghost since I've been here. They just come to the cell and want to pray, and I pray with 'em. I tell 'em about the Lord and the way the Scriptures says, you know, and help 'em pray through to the Holy Ghost. They get the Holy Ghost—pray through to the Holy Ghost—but they can't get baptized here.

As I said, this is an evil place. But I know God turned, like, a cursin' into a blessin' fer me, 'cause besides the people that has got the Holy Ghost since I've been here in prison, there's been a lot of miracles took place too. One man just got healed a couple months ago. He was deaf in one ear for twenty-five years—had a car wreck, and it did somethin' to that side of his head, a brain hemorrhage. And they said he wouldn't never hear out of it. And God healed him. He started hearin'—I had my finger in his other ear—and he said,

"Sound like I hear somethin' away off." Then he said, "I do hear somethin' away off—it's gettin' closer." Then he went to hollerin', "I can hear! I can hear!" And he'd go around listenin' to ever'thing anybody says. He said it feel funny hearin' out of an ear that'd been just like it wadn't there, you know.

I've seen a lot of miracle. My cellmate, the one that's in with me now, he'll be going home before too long. The warden knows that that boy was into ever'thing till he put him in the cell with me. He was on escape when they caught him, and he come back. And they put him in there with me, and he'd been bad on dope and all—just in and out of lockup for disciplinary. And all this time that he's been back and stayin' with me, he ain't got into nothin'. God's been good to him.

He didn't never know God before, you know. But I'd been prayin' and readin' the Bible, and one day he come in where I was at. He said, "I need to get you to prayin' fer me." Said, "I'm dying." I said, "What is it?" He said, "I've been trying to go the hospital and get somethin' done fer my head, and I can't." Said, "That guy that's been prayin' with you over here, he told me I need come over and let you pray fer me. I wouldn't come—I stayed on that bed three or four days—but I'm dyin'." Said, "You got to help me."

And I said, "Well, sit down here on the bed, and we'll let the Lord see if he'll move fer you." And he was crying too, boy. His head was bustin'. He couldn't get nothin' fer it 'cause you have to sign up to see a doctor. It'll take three or four days to see one a'ter you sign up. And he'd done signed up two or three times. But the Lord showed me he had some kind of infection in his head, and his ears were infected. So whenever we prayed fer him, why, God healed him right then. He repented, and he stayed repented.

He wasn't my cell partner then—my cell partner I had at that time went home. Ever' cell partner I get, just about it, they'll either do right and get out and go home, or get transferred to work release or somethin'. I've had one or two cell partners that was just like the devil, you know—they got their mind made up that they ain't never goin' do right. But they didn't stay in the cell with me long. The Lord's been good to me—they can't stay in there long if they don't want to pray and seek God. In a few minutes they'll be wantin' to get out of there.

When I first got up here at Limestone, they was so many preachers—or supposed to be preachers—walkin' around preachin', you know. They's trying to make a show, trying to get out of prison like 'at, I believe. And one did get out that way. He's in for rape, robbery, and all that. And he come in and started actin' like a Christian. And the chaplain help get him out, got him a place to

238

stay. Then he went and done the same thing to the family that he was staying with, and they sent him right back. Stuff like 'at makes it hard on people that's really trying to do right to get out.

And, you know, if I get out, I'm not goin' go out there and hurt somebody and kill somebody or nothin'. I'm goin' stay away from people—and fast and pray and seek God and get back in church. And that's goin' be it.

A Law Clerk
The Litigation

On October 7, 1991, Glenn Summerford was arrested and subsequently indicted for two counts of assault with the intent to cause serious physical injury to Darlene Summerford by means of a deadly weapon or dangerous instrument, specifically, by means of a rattlesnake. The following December, the Jackson County Grand Jury issued an indictment charging Summerford with attempted murder, namely, with the intent to commit murder by forcing his wife to place her hands in a cage containing live rattlesnakes where she was bitten on the hand.

After a three-day jury trial, Summerford was found guilty of attempted murder February 12, 1992. Summerford's two prior felony convictions qualified him to be sentenced as an habitual offender, and he received a ninety-nine-year sentence. (Conviction of attempted murder is a Class A felony, and under the Habitual Offender Act a Class A felony is punishable by imprisonment for ninety-nine years to life.)

Summary of Prior Convictions Used for Enhancement of Sentence

On April 22, 1967, the Jackson County Court issued a warrant for the arrest of Glendon Buford Summerford on a charge of second-degree burglary. The supporting affidavit states that Summerford broke into and entered a dwelling with the intent to steal. In July the Jackson County Grand Jury issued an indictment charging Summerford and three other men with one count of feloniously taking and carrying away a homemade, plywood boat valued at $50.00.

Withdrawing his previously-entered pleas of not guilty, Summerford pled guilty on September 19, 1967, to charges of second-degree burglary and grand larceny. He was sentenced to eighteen months imprisonment for the burglary offense and to a concurrent eighteen-month term for the grand larceny. He applied for probation, and his sentencing was delayed pending a decision on his application. On February 21, 1969, probation was denied, and Summerford was subsequently committed to the custody of the Alabama correctional authorities for execution of his sentences.

Motion for New Trial

Following his sentencing on March 3, 1992, for attempted murder, Summerford moved for a new trial. The motion was denied, and Summerford filed a notice of appeal alleging four grounds for appeal.

He first claimed that the prosecutor suppressed exculpatory evidence, i.e., evidence that was favorable to Summerford or that could have been used to impeach the testimony of prosecution witnesses. More specifically, he asserted that the prosecutor failed to disclose to the defense a previous statement given by Summerford's wife that was inconsistent with her testimony at trial. For example, in her trial testimony, she related that Summerford had held a gun to her head forcing her to put her hand into a cage containing rattlesnakes, whereas she indicated in her statement that Summerford had had the gun in his waistband. At trial, she testified that she was beaten by Summerford, but the beating was not mentioned in her statement. At trial, she testified that Summerford had kicked her in the side, but indicated in her statement that he was kicking her feet. She further testified at trial that Summerford had urinated in her face and hair, and forced her to write two suicide notes; but these salient details were omitted from her statement. Summerford also asserted that the prosecution had only disclosed the statement during the hearing on the motion for a new trial, but that the trial court had refused to allow defense counsel to examine witnesses regarding the statement or even to see it, although the court ordered it to be made a part of the record. (The appeal brief noted that Summerford presented evidence at trial to show that his wife was known to have handled snakes voluntarily on many previous occasions and that she had been bitten while voluntarily handling snakes. Summerford also offered evidence to show that she had intended to murder him by putting a rattlesnake on him and causing him to be bitten.)

Secondly, Summerford claimed that he was denied a fair trial because his jury was not impartial. He asserted that a juror, who later was selected foreman, had failed to disclose during voir dire, i.e. the preliminary examination of prospective jurors, that he (the juror) was acquainted with Summerford's wife and her family, having known them for more than twenty years. Summerford also asserted that, during the trial, the juror had watched news broadcasts each night on a Huntsville television station which had covered the trial.

Thirdly, Summerford asserted that the jury was allowed to separate without being instructed not to reach a verdict prematurely. He also maintained that a line of questioning directed to determine if the jury foreman arrived at a premature verdict was obstructed by the trial judge and the prosecutor.

As his last ground for appeal, he alleged that he was improperly sentenced as an habitual felony offender. As support for this claim, he argued that the two prior convictions used to enhance his sentence to ninety-nine years as an habitual offender were not shown on the face of record to have been obtained according to guilty pleas made voluntarily and knowingly. (The United States Supreme Court has held that a guilty plea that is not made voluntarily, understandingly, and knowingly is constitutionally invalid.) Summerford also pointed out that the trial judge had not signed or initialed the judgments of conviction which were used as proof of Summerford's prior convictions.

The Alabama Court of Criminal Appeals found Summerford's claims to be baseless and affirmed the conviction February 12, 1993. The Alabama Supreme Court refused to hear Summerford's appeal.

Petitions for a Writ of Habeas Corpus

Summerford filed a petition for a writ of habeas corpus alleging that his confinement was illegal because his constitutional rights were violated during his trial. The United States District Court for the Northern District of Alabama denied the petition July 9, 1993. Summerford filed a second petition March 31, 1995, and this petition was dismissed as an abuse of the writ June 1997. (An abuse of the writ occurs when a petitioner files a second or subsequent petition, raising claims that were raised and decided in a previous petition, or alleges claims that could have been presented in a previous petition but were not.)

Rule 32 Petitions for Post-Conviction Relief

In July 1993 Summerford filed a petition for post-conviction relief in the Jackson County Circuit Court, claiming as his sole ground for relief that he received ineffective assistance of counsel in violation of his right under the Sixth Amendment. As examples of counsel's ineffectiveness, he asserted that counsel

1. Denied him the right to testify in his own defense
2. Failed to call witnesses, including the physician who treated the victim's snakebite wounds, to testify on Summerford's behalf
3. Failed to object to the composition of the grand jury on the basis that it did not represent a fair cross-section of the community and failed to object to the prosecutor's use of a race-based peremptory challenge
4. Had a conflict of interest
5. Failed to challenge Summerford's prior convictions used to find him an habitual offender for sentence enhancement purposes
6. Failed to object to the admission into evidence of Summerford's unsigned statement
7. Failed to move for a change of venue
8. Failed to move the trial court to instruct the jury on "serious physical injury"
9. Failed to raise an issue regarding the testimony of a state's rebuttal witness

An evidentiary hearing on the petition was held before W. Loy Campbell, Jackson County Circuit Court Judge, who had also presided at Summerford's trial. The parties presented proof with regard to the alleged errors. For instance, to support his allegation that counsel refused his request to testify, Summerford called various witnesses who stated that they had heard Summerford ask his counsel to testify. Summerford's trial counsel, however, when questioned at the hearing stated that Summerford had decided not to testify. And when further questioned about the issue of failure to call witnesses, counsel said he had concluded that the witnesses had no knowledge of the facts of the case. Summerford refused to testify at the hearing. Judge Campbell denied Summerford's petition with respect to all issues.

The appellate court affirmed the lower court's decision. It accepted that Summerford himself had made the decision not to testify, which was based on accrediting the testimony of Summerford's attorney over the testimony of Summerford's witnesses. (The credibility determination of a trial court judge, who is able to listen to the testimony of witnesses and observe their demeanor on the stand, is accorded great deference on appeal.)

Accepting that the witnesses who appeared on Summerford's behalf at the evidentiary hearing had testified to matters only marginally related to the issues at trial, and pointing to the testimony of Summerford's counsel that those witnesses lacked knowledge of the facts of the case, the appeals court found that the issue involving counsel's failure to present witnesses had no merit. The appeals court determined that the issue involving counsel's failure to present the wife's physician as a witness was also groundless in that ample evidence of snakebite presented at trial rendered unnecessary any testimony by the physician who treated Summerford's wife.

Reviewing the lower court's ruling on Summerford's claim that his attorney did not object to the composition of the grand jury on the basis that it did not represent a fair cross-section of the community, the appellate court held that Summerford had failed to meet the test for showing a violation of the fair cross-section requirement. It further found that Summerford had failed to establish his claim that the prosecutor unconstitutionally excluded a juror based on the juror's race because the state had proffered a race-neutral reason for challenging the juror and because Summerford had failed to show that he was denied a fair trial as a result of the exclusion of the juror.

The court concluded that the lower court had correctly determined that Summerford's attorney had not had a conflict of interest relative to a prosecution witness's paying or delivering part of his fees. The court found that evidence which countered Summerford's allegation was more credible than his claim.

The issue regarding counsel's failure to challenge the prior convictions was dismissed because it had been raised and previously determined on direct appeal. Moreover, the appeals court noted that the prosecution furnished (to both defense counsel and the court) copies of the court clerk's entries of these two prior convictions. Finally, the intermediate state court found that the claim had not been raised in the trial court.

Finding that the claim concerning the admission of the unsigned statement was not presented in the post-conviction petition, the appeals court refused to address it, observing that it reviews only those issues ruled upon by the trial court.

Summerford was found not to be entitled to relief on his claim concerning trial counsel's failure to file a motion for a change of venue. To prevail on this type of claim, Summerford would have had to show that pretrial publicity was such as to have a probable effect on potential jurors or that there was a connection between the publicity and actual jury prejudice. The appeals court determined that Summerford had not made either showing.

Summerford's claim that his counsel had failed to move for an instruction on "serious physical injury" was found to be groundless by the appeals court because serious physical injury is not an element of attempted murder.

The appeals court also gave no credence to the claim that Summerford's counsel should have raised an issue regarding the violation of "the rule" by a witness who testified for the state although the witness had sat in the courtroom during prior testimony. The court's judgment was based on the facts that the witness was called as a rebuttal witness, and also that allowing such a witness to testify is a matter of the trial court's discretion.

Before the appellate court had affirmed in January 1995 the lower's court's ruling on Summerford's first Rule 32 petition, Summerford filed two other Rule 32 petitions for post-conviction relief, which were denied September 22, 1994. The first petition, relating to the prior convictions used for enhancement, was held to be barred by the statute of limitations applicable to Rule 32 petitions; and the second, relating to illegal arrest, was denied because Summerford had filed a previous petition which had been denied for lack of supporting evidence and for failure to state a claim for relief.

Summerford has apparently filed no subsequent petitions for a writ of habeas corpus or for post-conviction relief since 1995. It may be that he has simply given up, feeling that he has exhausted in effect all legal possibilities open to him. And if he were interested in filing more petitions, new restrictions have made it more difficult for him to do so. For example, the Antiterrorism and Effective Death Penalty Act (AEDPA), enacted into law in 1996, imposes additional restrictions on the right of state prisoners to file habeas corpus petitions. Now, in order to file a second petition, a prisoner must obtain authorization from the United States Circuit Court of Appeals authorizing a district court to entertain the petition. Furthermore, the guidelines for authorization are restricted. Congress also passed in 1996 the Prison Litigation Reform Act (PLRA), which places additional restrictions, including monetary ones, on filing civil petitions.

Other Litigation

1. *Glenn Summerford v. Keith Smith, Clarence Bolte, Chuck Phillips*
   (Smith was chief of the Scottsboro Police Department, Bolte was

chief detective of the Scottsboro Police Department, and Phillips was chief investigator of the Jackson County Sheriff's Department.)

2. *Glenn Summerford v. Gary Lackey* (Lackey was Summerford's defense counsel.)
3. *Glenn Summerford v. W. Loy Campbell, Dwight Duke, and Clarence Bolte* (Campbell was Summerford's trial judge, and Duke was the prosecuting attorney.)
4. *Glenn Summerford v. Sam Long* (Long was the foreman of the grand jury that returned an indictment against Summerford on the felony charge of attempted murder.)
5. *Glenn Summerford v. William Haralson* (Haralson was the circuit court judge who ruled on Summerford's suit against Gary Lackey.)

The preceding synopsis of litigation illustrates that Summerford has been persistent and extensive in a judiciary pursuit to free himself. Whereas there may be multiple explanations for the extent of Summerford's litigious actions, it appears that they are attempts of a strong-minded person desperately seeking to reverse what he feels to be his unjust imprisonment.

Addendum

Glenn Summerford was eligible for a parole hearing February 2002, but because of a backlog of petitions, he did not receive a hearing until May 2003. In March 2003 Summerford was charged with the offense of second-degree escape, a Class C felony, and denied parole May 19, 2003. His next parole hearing is scheduled for May 2006.

Scott Pratt

A Criminal Lawyer on the Potential of the Witness Pool

During a post-conviction hearing, testimony was given by fourteen individuals whom the defense had not called to testify at the trial of *State of Alabama v. Glenn Summerford*. These individuals were part of a larger pool of witnesses who had expected to testify for the defense in that trial. All of these fourteen witnesses are potentially favorable to Summerford, and a few of them are potentially damaging. The question, I suppose, is "Why would any trial lawyer worth his salt fail to put up this number of witnesses?"

It would be easy to simply say that the lawyer was lousy . . . that he must have been lazy . . . that he didn't prepare because Summerford didn't pay him enough money. Unfortunately, all of those things are possible. But if one takes a close look at the witnesses—their motivation, their testimony as it relates to the facts and the opposing theories of the case, and to the effect that existing law would have had on their testimony—it becomes clearer why a trial lawyer either would not want them on the stand or would be forbidden from calling them at all. That aside, I believe that putting at least some of these witnesses on the stand would have been beneficial to Glenn Summerford and may have even turned the tide of what had to be a close trial.

I'll begin with Charlotte Colón, who described herself as Glenn Summerford's half sister. She testified during the post-conviction hearing that she was one of the first people to observe Darlene Summerford when Darlene was taken from the ambulance at the hospital. Ms. Colón says Darlene looked "pretty normal," that she was alert, her speech was clear and she was clean.

Those are all things that Ms. Colón could have testified to, because they were firsthand observations and impressions, and would have been admissible

Scott Pratt. Photograph courtesy of Scott Pratt.

as such. They could have been used to contradict Ms. Summerford's testimony that she had crawled through mud and a creek in order to escape from the house. It does not have anything to do with whether or not Glenn Summerford forced Darlene Summerford to put her hand inside a snake-filled cage, but the testimony could have been used in closing argument to ask the jury: "If she lied about crawling away through the mud, or even if she exaggerated about that, what else did she lie about?"

The testimony that Ms. Colón offered regarding things that Ms. Summerford had told her—e.g., "She had told me previously on different occasions that she would like to get rid of Glenn," and that she wanted to leave him but would not because of her son—is inadmissible. These are classic hearsay statements that are not admissible in any trial. *Hearsay* is defined as an "out of court statement offered to prove the truth of the matter asserted." I realize that the definition is lawyer speak, but it means that you cannot walk into a courtroom as a witness and repeat what someone else said, and offer it as substantive evidence in a trial. Judges and juries would rather hear statements straight from the proverbial horse's mouth. There are many exceptions to the hearsay rule—so many that it would be both confusing and fruitless to go into them here. But in this case, in this trial, in this context those statements are hearsay and would have been excluded by the trial judge.

In order for those statements (or at least the implications to be drawn from those statements) to come into evidence, the defense lawyer would have had to bring them up on cross-examination of Ms. Summerford. During cross-examination, the lawyer could have, and should have, asked Ms. Summerford, "Isn't it true that on such-and-such a date you told Charlotte Colón that you wanted to get rid of your husband?" The lawyer is stuck with the answer—which in all likelihood would have been "No"—but the jury has heard the allegation. The defense lawyer would then continue, "Isn't it true that you told Ms. Colón that you wanted to leave your husband?" etc., etc. The jury then has the opportunity to gauge the witness's response to the question and decide whether or not they believe her. The defense lawyer can then bring it all back up during the closing argument.

Gene Coots and Brenda Campbell would have testified that Darlene told them, at different times, that she was "going to get rid of Glenn." Also, Cecil Esslinger (Glenn's brother-in-law) and Doris Summerford (Glenn's first wife) would have testified that they separately heard Darlene say while Glenn was sick from a snakebite that she wished he would die. Unfortunately for Glenn, the hearsay rule would have prohibited such testimony. There is nothing, however, that would have stopped the defense lawyer from asking Ms. Summerford about it on cross-examination right after asking about similar statements she made to Charlotte Colón.

José Colón's testimony was much the same as his wife's. He said he saw Ms. Summerford at the hospital and that she seemed "normal." He testified that she was clean. He could have testified that he had seen Ms. Summerford handle snakes outside of church and that she was not afraid. His testimony would have contradicted that of Ms. Summerford, and the jury would have had to weigh his testimony in deciding whom to believe. Reasonable doubt is built, piece by piece, using witnesses who discredit testimony given by victims.

Once again, however, we have a witness who is related to the accused. The prosecutor would undoubtedly have pointed that out during closing.

J. L. Dyal, Ruby Berry, and Donna Parton present an interesting dilemma for a defense attorney. On the one hand, the testimony that Ms. Summerford "came on" to and flirted with Dyal and other men at the church, kissed and dated Ms. Berry and Ms. Parton's brother portray Darlene Summerford as dishonest, untruthful, and untrustworthy. Unfortunately, it also helps to bolster the prosecution's theory that Glenn Summerford was in a jealous rage the night he allegedly forced his wife to put her hand in the cage. Even worse, Mr. Dyal would have testified that he told Glenn Summerford about Darlene's attempts of infidelity. As a prosecutor, I certainly would welcome a witness who provided motive, especially a witness who was put on by the defense.

I would not have put Willie Southard on the stand under any circumstances. His testimony that Darlene flirted with him would have been of limited benefit. But the admission of a confrontation about Southard's having sex with Darlene would only have served to bolster the state's theory that jealousy motivated Glenn Summerford. I would have made sure that Willie Southard wasn't within fifty miles of the courthouse on the day of trial.

Glenn Summerford Jr. and Bill Summerford provide probably the most fertile ground for cross-examination as far as showing a jury Darlene Summerford's desperation. Neither could testify to any of the things that Darlene said, but it would be wonderful cross-examination material if Darlene really did try to get them to tell their daddy that she had been sleeping with them. Can you imagine having Darlene on the stand, and the boys in the front row, and asking her whether she had ever slept with her stepsons? If she says "No," you would simply look at the boys and say, "Then why did you tell their daddy that you did?" If she said "Yes," I suppose you would just look at the jury and roll your eyes.

There are only two people in this world who know what really happened that weekend. We will never know for sure. But this case is one that, based upon the facts as they have been presented to me, should not have resulted in a guilty verdict by a jury. Nobody saw anything. The victim was untrustworthy, she admitted to handling snakes in the past, and she and her husband were having serious marital problems. All of those things add up to reasonable doubt.

The fact that Mr. Summerford was convicted can be attributed to many things. First of all, juries are becoming more and more inclined to convict criminal clients and to believe that all defense attorneys are nothing more than snake-oil salesmen. It is terribly difficult to turn the tide.

Secondly, the quickest way to get convicted in a criminal trial is to stay away from the witness stand. Mr. Lackey said during this post-conviction hearing that Mr. Summerford did not want to take the stand. There was, however, hearsay testimony to the contrary by five other witnesses, namely, Charlotte Colón, José Colón, Barbara Lee, Glenn Summerford Jr., and Bill Summerford. The decision to testify is the client's to make and his alone. A lawyer can advise, but the ultimate decision as to taking or not taking the witness stand is strictly up to the client. Mr. Summerford certainly should have been urged strongly to testify in his own defense.

As for the cumulative effect of the pool of witnesses who did not testify, all I can say is that I would not want to be the lawyer who failed to call that many witnesses on behalf of my client after a jury found him guilty of a serious felony. Hindsight may be twenty-twenty, but thorough preparation cures so many ills. I suspect that a thoroughly prepared trial lawyer would have achieved a different result in this case. Glenn Summerford probably feels the same way.

The Spirit

A religious serpent handler in West Virginia invited me one hot summer day to hunt serpents with him. We climbed to the crest of a ridge and proceeded to lift up large flat rocks like oversized manhole covers, looking for any snakes beneath them. I was warned to keep my fingers close to the edge of the rocks as I lifted them. And sure enough, under one of the rocks I pulled up was a large black timber rattlesnake coiled and ready to strike.

In the process of presenting Glenn Summerford's story, I have turned up many rocks. And under a number of them I have found some rather venomous serpents. I have also received by men and women alike in both polite and crude language a wide spectrum of responses to my inquiries: they said they would not talk; they would talk only off the record; they would talk but later changed their minds; they would talk freely and openly about anything they knew or felt to be true. Most people with whom I talked, particularly kith and kin, were helpful, but I was disappointed that some of the principals in the story refused to be interviewed.

One individual told me that the incident I was asking him about had been a foolish mistake on his part for which he had paid with a jail sentence and which he desired to forget. He requested that he be unidentified in order to maintain the reputation he had since established. I have complied with his request—why remove unnecessarily a scab from an old wound? Another person said he would sue me if I even mentioned his name. Later he said I could print whatever I wanted. But what I wanted was a personal account of his involvement, which would confront the negative criticism toward him. He

Church of the Lord Jesus Christ on Woods Cove Road. Photograph by Donna Rizzo.

declined, however, and his own explanation goes untold. Understandably, he wanted to let sleeping dogs lie, but sleeping dogs sometimes permit unguarded lies to run like fire through a grain field.

I am aware that there are many ethical problems in repeating what people say and in exposing shadowy behavior to the light. Certainly people have a right to express their opinions about others, especially about individuals in the public eye. Yet I don't believe in spreading irresponsible gossip or sensational matter for its own sake. Neither do I believe that simply because something exists justifies its being spread abroad. Some things should not be repeated. Some people need to be protected, even from themselves, and some children, from the sins of their fathers and mothers. But how paternalistic should one be?

Although there are statements that I am reluctant to print, I am constantly aware that Glenn Summerford is serving a sentence in an Alabama correctional facility while many details that have been primarily imprisoned in the minds of a number of people involved in his story might provide at least some insight into the justice of whether or not he should be there. But any thoughts unlocked by my work are not repeated to whitewash, smear, distort, slant, or obscure Glenn Summerford's story. Rather, the objective of all comments, whether made by Glenn or someone else, is to provide shape and perspective. As one might expect, we hear conflicting perceptions of people and events even in a single narrative—and certainly between different ones. On the other hand, we hear throughout the monologues significant recurrence of certain motifs, images, subjects, people, events, and details. And some of these when uncovered coil ominously and raise their ugly heads. As serpent handlers themselves are wont to say, paraphrasing a verse in the Book of Ecclesiastes, "When the hedge is broken, the serpent will bite."

Glenn Summerford's story is a complex one. His life and the lives of those who complement his are individually and collectively convoluted. There is pervasive inconsistency, antithesis, and paradox—and always, the inextricable knot of Spirit and serpent.

But this complex story has gone for the most part untold. And even in the telling, we find that different people suggest entirely different scenarios. Which one would you choose? The one presented by the prosecution: an intoxicated, revengeful husband attempts to murder his wife rather than divorce her in order to provide a means of remarriage that is acceptable to his religious communion and, furthermore, attempts to cover his crime by a forced alibi note?

Or would you select another story line, perhaps one or a combination of the following?

A sincere Holiness preacher is victimized, perhaps even life-threatened, by the manipulation of a fallen, unstable woman who lives uprightly as his helpmeet for a while but who wishes to be rid of him and return to her old ways.

A redeemed hard man finally cracks under too much domestic pressure and, Othello-like, in a jealous passion, seeks a confession and/or divine and personal retribution for his wife's infidelity.

A previous felon, who had had minor offenses and repeated run-ins with local law enforcement twenty years earlier but had been converted to an aberrant serpent-handling religious sect, is accused of unseemly physical abuse and mental torture by his pregnant wife, who is of questionable moral character, and is brought precipitously to a short but sensational trial with minimal defense where he is railroaded into a conviction as a habitual criminal.

Wooden handicraft Bible made by a prison inmate and inscribed with the image of Glenn Summerford handling a serpent, and verses from Mark 16:15–20, including "They shall take up serpents; and if they drink any deadly thing, it shall not hurt them." Gift of Rev. Glenn Summerford to the author and photographed by Anna Lee Gibson.

A flawed man, perhaps under the influence of alcohol, who wants more than anything else to continue a life dedicated to God and shows complete control in confronting his wife's supposed lovers (with the exception of his best friend, to whom he was deeply repentant) is accused unjustly not simply of a violent act but of an attempted murder for which there is no witness other than the incestuous and adulterous serpent-handling wife, who offers no proof other than her snakebit hand.

A man who is unjustly or even justly convicted of attempted murder, which was questionably verified, and who has since served a lengthy incarceration for it, deserves an opportunity to resume his attempt to live a meaningful life of choice.

Any selection is complicated. As for my own perspective, from the time I started working on Glenn Summerford's story, I sought—as Robert Browning felt he accomplished in *The Ring and the Book*—to uncover the facts of a criminal case and through creative imagination reveal the truth. As Browning knew, and as it became increasingly evident to me, truth is elusive as well as relative to the perceiver. At first I thought the fact of what took place at Barbee Lane on that fateful Friday and Saturday in 1991 was the truth I would reveal. But I came to see that the truth revealed moved upon the face of darkness and a depth of the human condition far beyond the facts of those events. No doubt you will perceive your own truth through *The Serpent and the Spirit.*

Index

The Serpent and the Spirit was designed and typeset on a Macintosh computer system using QuarkXPress software. The body text is set in 10.5/14 Minion with display type set in Helvetica Neue. This book was designed and typeset by Cheryl Carrington and manufactured by Thomson-Shore, Inc.